JOB SEARCH

SUCCESSFULLY PREPARE FOR JOB
INTERVIEWS AND LAND THE JOB (CAREER
HUNTING SECRETS)

By: Bradley Banks

Table of Contents

INTRODUCTION

Are you looking for your next big opportunity and want to land the job of your dreams? Have you recently graduated from high school or college and are looking to get a job in your field? Do you have a strong resume but don't know how to enhance your interview repertoire?

If you said yes to any of those questions, then this is the perfect book for you. You may be going through a transition and have decided to change your field of interest, or perhaps you have held a job for several years and you need to brush up on your interview skills so you can land another interview and get the job that you've worked hard for. In any of these cases, it is important to develop strong skills for interviewing.

These days, more people are moving from job to job within a short span of time. Sometimes, people are changing jobs every one to two years; others may stay in the same position for at least three years. The truth of the matter is that most people will move to another job at least a few times throughout their careers. Gone are the days when you could be loyal to a company and guaranteed job security for life. This is no longer the case, and a majority of the time with millennials, who currently are the generation that is developing in the workforce, people are moving on to different jobs at least once every three years.

The reasons for this can include gaining better working conditions, an increased salary, a better work-life balance, or better compatibility with the values of the person. Millennials, in particular, want to make a difference in the world, and they see their job as a platform to change society. This is something that is unique from previous generations, though it is something that most generations have been working towards, as well.

With people changing jobs over short periods, they need to develop their interview skills. It is not easy to interview, but it is an important life skill. Just because you have landed a good job and see yourself staying there for a while doesn't mean you should become complacent and forget about the basics of interviewing. You may think that just because you have a connection with someone in the company, you are automatically in and can get whatever job you want; that certainly is not the case. You have to work hard at preparing for interviews and in developing your skills so you can get a job easily.

That takes time and dedication which will need commitment. Many times, job interview preparation can become its own full-time job, especially in today's competitive work environment, where there are fewer jobs for highly skilled workers who are well-educated and have experience. Many people don't tell you this, but many workers are out of work and looking for work in their field but who are spending months or even upwards of a year or two trying to get a job. This is one of the sad realities of today's world, and it is not an easy thing to deal with. This is why it is necessary to know how to prepare for an interview.

CHAPTER 1: EXCELLENT JOB SEARCH

STRATEGIES

Whether you are only just beginning your career or are trying to find a new job in an experienced field, when trying to find a new job, we all ask ourselves what we want. "What do I want to do with my life?" "What am I good at?" "Will this make me happy?"

These questions we ask ourselves are just the tip of the iceberg. Many of us have numerous possibilities when it comes to getting a job. While our possibilities may at first appear limited, when we really sit down and look at the options on the table, we see how vast our options are. Of course, of these options, there will be many that we are not well suited to. For instance, you might have the math skills to become an accountant, but the demands of the job might cause you undue stress.

On the other hand, you might find that a position as a receptionist doesn't pay as well, but leaves you feeling fulfilled and capitalizes on your strength of communication.
You may even decide between two jobs at nearby grocery stores, as you can work part-time and still attend college classes. We all have many choices, though, the scale of pros and cons will vary from job to job for each individual.

In this chapter, you will learn how to decide what career and position you are best suited for. You can discover this by a series of introspective questions, which help you to learn your strengths, weaknesses, needs, and desires. After you know what you are best suited for, you can tackle the best ways to find a job, whether online, through agencies, or even in the newspaper.

Finally, you will learn how to narrow your choices once you have found prospective job opportunities. Once you weigh the pros and cons of each job position, you can dedicate yourself to getting the job that you are best suited for and will leave you satisfied with your needs fulfilled. When we first realize the number of possibilities we have in our career, it can become overwhelming.

Yes, having options is wonderful, but by knowing that we can reach for the sky, we can struggle to know what to decide on. Furthermore, knowing that this decision will greatly impact and alter a person's life can make anyone anxious and stressed.
We begin to fear that we will make the wrong decision, and that once we do the doors of opportunity will be closed to us. Overcome by this anxiety, we struggle to make a decision, as we want to keep all of our possibilities open.

But the truth is that sometimes we simply have to take a leap of faith. This may mean committing yourself to complete a college degree for your chosen field or choosing one job out of multiple offers. Either way, we must eventually settle on a decision. Remember, that while you may be trying to decide on what career you want to do for the rest of your life, you don't have to box yourself in. If you, later on, decide that you want to reinvent yourself and begin a new career, that is perfectly possible and accessible!

By making a choice, you aren't tying yourself down or limiting your future, but rather making a choice that will benefit you no matter where life may take you.

Once you decide on a career and job you are opening yourself to possibilities, therefore, there is nothing to fear!

After all, even if you decide to change careers or jobs in the future, you can always use your current career to build your savings and funds, increase your strengths while learning to compensate for your weaknesses, and build your resume.
When you begin to question which field to go into, don't start by asking yourself what you want to do for the rest of your life. Instead, ask yourself what you don't want to do. Although, don't just think it.

Actively write down what you don't want to do with your life and why, which will help you better analyze your thoughts and think more clearly. By framing the question in this way, you can help narrow down your choices and prevent yourself from becoming overwhelmed. You can also better understand what will make you unhappy in the long run, and make a better choice for your lifestyle and well-being.
Deciding on a job or a career is a big decision. Yet, by taking yourself through a series of questions, you can greatly increase your chance of finding the right fit.

Deciding on a career or new job requires a great deal of self-evaluation. This means that you need to have a good understanding of yourself, your needs, strengths, and weaknesses. For many of us, we can see all too plainly our weaknesses but have a difficult time seeing our strengths. Others may have the opposite problem, where they can understand their strengths but not their weaknesses. Both of these views are unbalanced, and we must seek to balance them so that we can see ourselves clearly and truthfully.

If you are unable to see either your strengths or weaknesses clearly, despite inner evaluation, try asking those closest to you their opinion. Someone who sees you regularly might be able to help you see that you are in fact, wonderful at dealing with people and resolving conflict. Or, they might help you understand that you have a weakness of being overly blunt, which can make those you're talking with uncomfortable. While you are evaluating yourself try to consider the following:

Strengths
Try to pinpoint detailed skills that you believe yourself to be proficient in or give you an edge over the competition. These can be skills that you have learned through training and education or that you have developed on your own over time. For instance, strengths can include proficiency in Photoshop, Microsoft Word, or WordPress for detailed programs. But they can also include previous experience in both jobs, volunteering, and everyday life, such as experience in advertisement, social media, using a cash register, or serving customers.

Lastly, it may include character traits that you have developed over time, such as patience, communication, creativity, dedication, honesty, and enthusiasm. Analyze your strengths in your trained skills, experience, and developed traits, writing these out into a list. Once you have this list, you can better know which jobs you are best suited for.

Weaknesses
Analyzing our weaknesses can be hard, either because we are overly aware and critical of these weaknesses, or because we have our sights set solely on our strengths.
But it is vital to understand our weaknesses, and because of this, you are even likely to be asked about your weaknesses in a job interviewer. After all, a prospective employer wants to ensure that their potential employee has a clear view of themselves.

These weaknesses will allow you to find a job that is the best fit, as you will be able to either find one that your weaknesses are insignificant for, or you will be able to find ways in which to grow and compensate. Remember, these weaknesses are not something to feel down about or criticize yourself for. We all have strengths and weaknesses, and what is important is how we deal with them.

Some possible weaknesses you may want to consider include being overly critical of yourself or others, procrastination tendencies, overly perfectionistic, harsh and blunt honesty, a tendency to run late, over sensitivity, difficulty with public speaking, poor spelling, inability to handle spontaneity, or an unfamiliarity with various computer programs needed in the field of your choosing.

Interests
Knowing what you are passionate about and fulfills you is vital if you want to find a job that you can truly enjoy. Sure, a job will always be work and there will

be difficult days, but if you find a job that matches your interests, you will find it more enjoyable and easier to get through any rough patches. Plus, employers love hiring people who are excited and passionate about their careers, as this passion will show through in your work.

Are you passionate about working with food, pleasing customers, writing programming, creating art, or helping animals? Write out as many of these passions and interests as you can think of, as you never know which one might provide you with a job. As an example, maybe you are passionate about Japanese animation and are familiar with a wide variety of anime and manga. While most people may consider this only a hobby, there are a vast number of jobs in this field, even in America.

You might get the opportunity to work on the social media page of an American dubbing studio, become the receptionist of one of these studies, or several other positions.

Values
Understanding what you want out of your job and life is vital to picking out the right career and job. In fact, many people theorize that if you want to truly find a fulfilling career that satisfies you, then you must first consider what you value. Once you understand what you place the most value on, then you can analyze whether or not a potential career or job opportunity lines up with these values.

Do you value financial security, flexible hours, independence, creativity, personal interactions, adventure, a fun work environment, location, positive impact on the world around you, status quo daily tasks, change from one day to the next, teamwork, or a stress-free environment?

Ambitions
Most people have ambitions for their career or life in general. Maybe you want a family and to settle down with kids, a dog, and own your own home. To some people, this may not seem like a big deal, but to Millennials and the younger generation, this dream may be difficult to attain.
Yet, if you understand these ambitions, you can best find a career and job that will help you make the dreams a reality.

Other examples of ambitions include owning your own business; peer recognition; mastering a skill or field; or specific positions such as CEO, executive editor, or head of your department.

Constraints
Knowing your constraints will help you to automatically know which job and career opportunities won't work for you, therefore, allowing you to better spend your time productively. These constraints might be geographical location, financial limitations, family responsibilities, education or qualifications that don't meet your list of strengths or disabilities. Think hard about your situation and what might prevent you from saying "yes" to a job, even if it was otherwise perfect. By having a list of these constraints, you will better know which jobs you shouldn't apply for or accept.

Needs

Make a list of what needs a job must fulfill. To do this, you need to know your minimum required income, how far you are willing to drive, what you can physically handle, the maximum number of hours you are willing to work, how stiff or flexible your schedule needs to be, and whether the job will take too much of a mental and emotional toll on you. While it is commonly touted that if you do a job you love, then you will never work a day in your life, this is certainly not true.

Firstly, whether you love your job or not, it is still work. You will still get worn out, requiring rest and breaks. You will still struggle with difficulties, whether that is dealing with customers or struggling to come up with a new creative concept. The truth is that whether we love our jobs or not, we will all struggle with them from time to time. However, if you find a job that you are passionate about you can get excited about new projects, you can feel satisfied in your effort, and you can feel happy in knowing that your work makes a difference.

Yet, even if you choose a job that you are not passionate about at this time, many people develop this passion later on. After all, many people are completely new to their careers, with no prior experience. While in the beginning, they might not have known what was to love about their chosen career path, later on after they discover the satisfaction, they receive from their job they can develop this passion.

Therefore, even if you are not passionate about a job, if you find that it matches well with your answers for your strengths, weaknesses, personality, values, ambitions, and needs then you can become satisfied and content with your work. Don't slack off in writing out answers to the questions above, as these answers will guide you to a job that is truly the right fit.

While we all want a fulfilling and satisfying job, all too often, people fail to examine themselves and what would be a truly good fit. While all jobs may have their drawbacks, if we know ourselves, then we can find one with relatively few drawbacks and many positives. But you have to be willing to put in the work up front by creating a clear view of yourself and writing this down into a list of answers. Don't slack off in this task, as by taking time to answer these questions to can benefit yourself for years to come.

If you are not new to having a career but hope to change your career direction, then spend some time writing out a list of things you both like and dislike about your current job, along with the skills you have learned that may be transferred to another career.

Some people may be discouraged when changing careers, especially if their previous career choice didn't turn out to be all that they had hoped. But this is only something to be excited about, not discouraged! After all, you now have a better understanding of yourself, needs, strengths, weaknesses, values, ambitions, and constraints. When beginning a career young in life, many people don't know the answers to these questions, and they don't bother to examine themselves to learn.

Yet, when you change careers later in life, you have learned some of the answers to these questions through your day-to-day work. Not only do you have a better view of yourself when you change careers, but you have also had the opportunity to learn more skills. While certain skills aren't transferable from one career to another, there are many more that you can use in many circumstances. For instance, perhaps you worked in a grocery store.

During your time working there, you might have learned customer service, teamwork, communication, organization, and much more. These are all skills that can be used in several jobs, and which will strengthen your resume and interview.

Once you narrow down on a career field, it is time to dig deeper into research on the field. It would cost too much time to do this research on a large number of careers, but if you have a list of top three or five career opportunities, then you can easily research them all.

At this point, you most likely have a general idea of the field, but you want to have a more solid knowledge base. This knowledge will help you better understand the field and if it truly does meet your expectations. It will also help you find the best jobs in the field and increase your capability of appealing to a prospective employer during the interview process.

In order to learn more about a potential career field you can follow other people in the field on social media, read blog posts and articles, find YouTube videos detailing various jobs in the field, talk to people you might know who have knowledge of the field, and find books online or at your local library.

You might even choose to reach out to potential companies and ask them more about their job and career opportunities. Just remember that when you do this, the company is more biased than the research you find online and in books.

The company is trying to make a good impression, whereas many people talk about both the pros and cons of a given field, giving you a more balanced point of view.

To learn about a prospective career, try:
- Reading articles and blog posts
- Watching YouTube Videos
- Asking Questions on Reddit or Quora
- Watch interviews with influencers
- Follow individuals in the field on social media
- Reach out to industry influencers and leaders on social media, asking if they would be willing to answer some of your questions
- Read a book on the field
- Have coffee with or call a friend/acquaintance in the field to ask questions (be upfront about why you want to talk)
- Search Google for "day in the life of [chosen profession]"
- Talk to your school counselor
- Attend industry and meetups
- Arrange to shadow someone on the job
- Apply for internships

Once you have completed this research, you should be able to determine which career is best for you, or which you are most interested in.

However, sometimes, it may still be difficult for people to decide. If you run into this problem, try to create a pro/con list for each of the careers you are debating between. After seeing the pros and cons in plain black and white, you should be able to more easily make a decision.

After you have finalized your career decision, it is time to begin job hunting.

This can be a stressful process for people, as you may apply to many applications without ever hearing back. But it is by all means worth it to find the job with the right fit. Whether you apply to applications posted online or in the newspaper, reach out to companies directly asking for job openings, or use an agency, there are many ways to go about getting your next job.

Firstly, no matter the method you choose to use to search for a job, try to create a wish list of companies you most would like to work with. For instance, if you are in the animation industry, you may want to work with DreamWorks Studio or Disney.

While you may previously have been unaware of various companies in the industry, after researching your career, you should have an idea of the top companies, as well as those that are up and coming. If you don't have an idea, then do a Google search on the various companies in the field. Then, create a list of which companies you would most like to work for and why. This list will help you, as even if you don't end up working with one of these companies, you might be able to find one that shares similarities.

When searching for a job, attempt to keep the following in mind:

- **Create an Online Professional Brand**You want to build up your professional profile on LinkedIn and other professional networking websites. Many employers use these sites when looking for potential employees, and you want to make sure that your profile is filled out well. It is also a good idea to clean up your regular social media so that you don't have anything posted that might ward off potential employers.

- **Connect Online**
Don't just create profiles on professional networking websites, but also connect on them. You want to add anyone you know as a friend, as this will help more potential employers discover your profile. You might also try reaching out, messaging, and sending a friend request to people who have jobs in your desired field.

- **Relevant Search Results**When searching job applications, try to be as detailed in your search criteria as possible, as this will help you find more relevant opportunities. After all, you don't want to wade through application after application that doesn't apply to your situation. Therefore, try to use helpful job keywords as well as locations to find the results that best fit your needs.

- **Look Up Local Resources**You can often find local resources to help you find a job. This includes your library, local Chamber of Commerce, and even Craigslist. These are especially helpful for people who know what they want to work locally, without needing to move.

- **Don't Hesitate to Ask**
  If you are unsure if a company has an opening don't hesitate to ask. Most companies will be happy to transfer you to their HR department, where you can ask about openings and any other questions you may have. With many companies, you will need to call and ask. However, with companies open to the public (such as stores), you can walk right in and ask to speak to the hiring manager. In this case, many of the managers will be happy to help you fill out an application form if they have any openings.

If you choose to job search online, which many people in today's modern society do, then it is important to not limit yourself. Some people may job search on only one or two websites, but by doing this, you are likely to miss many opportunities. Instead, try out as many of these websites as you can, as you will be increasing your chances for success.

Some of the best job listing websites include:
- **LinkedIn.com**One of the biggest and most well-known websites for job listings is LinkedIn. This is because it is not only for listing and applying to jobs, but it is also a professional social network. Although, what you can do with a free version of LinkedIn is limited, and the paid version is rather expensive for what it provides. You may choose to stick with a free version, or you may want to simply purchase a paid subscription for the duration of your job

hunt, which you can then drop after you get hired.

- **Indeed.com**
  One of the leading job listing websites Indeed has applications for thousands of companies and websites. This includes job postings from across the web, job boards, career sites, associations, and newspaper classified ads. Indeed helps to centralize many sources of applications into one single website. However, you don't only want to use this website, as it is still possible to miss possible opportunities, which is why you should use Indeed along with other websites.

- **Monster.com**You have most likely heard of Monster, at least in passing. After all, this website is one of the original online job boards. Now, it not only includes job postings but other resources as well. With this website, you can find career advice, salary information, post your resume, review companies, and apply to job openings.

- **Idealist.com**
  With Idealist, you can easily find non-profit opportunities, such as internships and volunteer opportunities. While some people may not be able to afford to spend their time in a non-profit position, if you can afford it, then it can be a great opportunity. With these opportunities, you can hone your skills, create connections, get an in with the company, lengthen your resume, and decide whether or

not you would like to apply for a paid position with the company.

- **LinkUp.com**

  LinkUp is a great place to find only the current job listings without duplicates or scams. This is because LinkUp only takes listings from the websites of companies, which means that they are all current and verified as being authentic. This takes the pressure off of you from having to determine whether or not a given opportunity is real or not.

- **GlassDoor.com**

  With GlassDoor, a career community, you can find recent job listings and view user-generated content on many companies. This includes ratings, reviews, questions and answers, salary reports, and more.

- **CareerBuilder.com**

  One of the largest websites for job listings, CareerBuilder also allows you to share your resume, find career advice, and other resources for finding a job. You can know that their job listings are accurate, as they get them directly from companies and newspaper classifieds.

- **Dice.com**

  If you are interested in working in the field of tech, then Dice is one of the most valuable tools you can use when hunting for a job. This website allows you to search by location, keyword, job title, employment type, and company. When you register for the website, you can upload your resume and cover letter, track jobs, and get salary information on a given job opportunity. You can also discover career advice directly targeting the tech industry.

- **Us.Jobs**
  With Us.Jobs you can access over a million verified and unique job listings from companies nationwide. This website was created to help directly connect people with prospective employers and improve the job market and was created in a joint effort between the National Association of State Workforce Agencies and the Direct Employers Association. You can view job listings, upload your resume, and save your favorite job listings.

Along with searching online, you may also choose to search for a job in the employment section of your local newspaper. This may seem unnecessary when there are so many resources online, but believe me, there are many jobs to be found in the local paper.

This is because while many companies have begun to use their company websites as well as listing websites, not all companies have made the switch.

This is especially true of start-up companies, small older companies, and companies within smaller towns. For instance, while you may be able to find many opportunities online in Los Angeles, if you don't live in one of the larger cities, it is almost certain that you will find opportunities in your paper that aren't listed online.

Even if there is only a small chance of discovering a possible job opportunity in the paper, you don't want to risk giving up the perfect fit by not looking. Plus, it is easy to find and inexpensive to buy your local newspaper, making it accessible to most people. You might even be able to find opportunities on the website for your local newspaper.

Lastly, you can use an employment agency to help you find a position. While some people believe that these agencies only help people find temporary jobs at entry-level positions, this is simply not true. In fact, these agencies can greatly help a person find long-term employment at any level. You can find jobs from any position, be that entry-level or CEO. They can also help you to find permanent jobs in nearly a large number of industries.

These agencies are free to use as a job seeker, as the prospective employers pay the agencies. You can then use the agency to either apply to a specific job or search for a job in general whether or not you have an idea of what you want.
If you are hired through the staffing agency, then you will work for the company while the agency pays you on their behalf.

CHAPTER 2: JOB INTERVIEW PREPARATION

Sufficient planning and preparation lend an interviewee the confidence that he/she needs to succeed in the interview. Reflect on How You Perceive Yourself, what do you think you look like through the eyes of your future employer? What are your key abilities? How do you display them? How did you make use of them at your previous job?

Do you possess any transferable skills? More importantly, will the employer be able to recognize these skills through the information that you've given him? Transferrable skills refer to flexible skills that you can use in a variety of jobs as opposed to skills that are exclusive to a specific job position. Such skills are relevant to numerous areas of life and not just to one's professional life. Examples of transferrable skills include leadership skills, communication skills, numeracy skills, and problem-solving skills. Now, just about everyone you know may claim to possess such skills. That said, the trick lies in showing your future employer how your transferrable skill set can be useful for his business.

Be Calm

If this is your first interview, chances are good that you are extremely nervous about it. Don't worry, it gets easier. The interviewer understands that you will be nervous, especially at the beginning of the interview, but you have to try to be as calm as possible. This may seem easier said than done, but the best way to do this is through practice and, of course, preparation. The section on interviewing yourself will give you more details about this. Below is one of my favorite mottos by the famous United States Navy SEALS and it can relate to anything in life, especially interviews.

Be Confident

All companies want someone who is confident. Self-confidence, confidence in their ability to do the job, and the confidence to handle any scenario thrown at them once the job begins. Remember to say "I WILL get this job." Of course, don't say this out loud during the interview, but you need to show this during the interview. The best way to do this is through preparation. By preparing, you are giving yourself the ability and confidence you need to succeed during the interview. You will have what it takes to succeed and you MUST convey this. Be confident in yourself and in your ability to crush the interview.

Believe you are Qualified

This is one of the biggest problems most applicants have going into interviews. They think they are under-qualified for the position. You MUST believe that you are qualified. If you believe this, you will show it during the interview. Forget the idea that you don't have enough leadership experience, work experience, or the right credentials. The company has seen your skills on paper (via your resume) and it was good enough you get you in the door, but now the rest is up to you. You know what, say these ten times too: I AM qualified…

Being Caught Unaware

Now that we have cleared most of the mental blocks going into interviews, we need to speak about one other thing. I like to call it "Being caught with your pants down." In other words, this is the moment when the interviewer asks you a question and you stutter or are at a loss for an answer. Basically, it's the moment where they have you speechless. They have asked you something and you have no response for them. Well, you've just been caught with your pants down! We will constantly be referring to this phrase throughout the guide and how to avoid this awfully embarrassing scene.

The Resume-Knowing It
You should know your resume like the back of your hand. This may seem like a simple tip, but plenty of people list skills and experiences that are either exaggerated or total fabrications. If you list a trait on a resume, you MUST be prepared to discuss it. The overwhelming majority of the time, the interviewer will go line by line through your resume with you. They will ask you detailed questions, which you should be prepared to discuss comfortably.

Once your resume is in tip-top shape, I recommend spending at least 3-5 hours going through each line and making sure you fully understand what you have listed. Write notes all over your resume, explaining what each line means to you and how you intend to explain it. You should memorize your entire resume so that you don't even have to glance at it.

You should be able to go through your resume, explaining every single position, line by line, and feel 100% confident in your explanation. If you feel there are any points that you would feel uncomfortable explaining, NOW IS THE TIME TO TAKE CARE OF THIS, not during the interview. Rule of thumb: If you can't explain it, then don't list it!

Gaps in Your Resume

There may be gaps in your resume. Try not to avoid these, because they WILL come up during the interview. If you cannot explain or account for them, the interviewer will think there is something that you aren't revealing, which is certainly not a good thing. Spin the gaps in your resume into something positive or be completely honest. Maybe someone died in your family, someone got sick and needed full-time care, or you got sick and could not work.

If something traumatic happened in your life, explain this situation. Interviewers will understand, and it's much better than leaving it up in the air. If you were really not doing much, spin it into something positive. Maybe you spent just a day or two out of months doing something productive, but as far as the interviewer is concerned, you did this every single day. Let's take a look at some examples.

Good Examples of Gaps:

1. I took the time off to learn the skills I needed for this industry since I know it is what I want to be in. This time off allowed me to focus entirely on my dream and I've learned X, Y, and Z from this experience.

2. As you know, the economy has been incredibly tough. I've been looking for a job these past XYZ months. I've been cold calling and cold emailing a dozen people every day, but no one is hiring. Besides job hunting, I spent a considerable amount of time reading books about the industry and am now a self-proclaimed expert in X.

Bad Examples of Gaps:

1. I have been looking for a job, but I really can't find one. It's really tough out there.

2. I really wasn't sure what I wanted to do, so I have been just kind of soul-searching for the past couple of months.

In the good examples, we are addressing the fact that we have had gaps and giving legitimate reasons for them. We are proving that we were still productive and motivated during our gap periods. In the bad examples, we are not saying much. We basically state that we did nothing during this time. If you don't explain it, the interviewer will assume you did nothing, or worse, that there is something hidden during that period.

Getting Fired

This can be one of the trickiest topics to discuss appropriately. You were fired from the last or one of your last jobs. The interviewer will ask you about this, so be prepared to have a good response. Keep in mind that your past employer can't reveal what happened, but they can let them know that you left the company and when. You'll want to discuss this topic positively, then steer the conversation into another direction. Let's take a look at some good and bad examples of how to handle this type of situation.

Good Examples:

1. My past employer and I parted ways after several long discussions. The departure really allowed me to explore a career path that I am passionate about. I have always known that

XYZ industry is what I want to do with my life. I've been interested in it ever since I had exposure during my first internship. I have been devouring books left and right, attending industry conferences, and talking with industry experts. I can really be an asset to this company. What do you see as the most important function of this position?

2. The job was a learning experience for me. It allowed me to understand what I am passionate about. My boss and I are still on good terms and it was never a result of my performance. Do employees maintain close contact with their superiors here?

Bad Examples:
1. I really hated it at that place. The pay was too low and you hardly got any vacation time

2. I was just really bored. I found it hard to stay motivated for the job.

In the good examples, we are being honest and upfront about what happened, but we are taking a forward-looking approach. Yes, we didn't like what we did, so we are done with it and are now striving for our passionate job (this position), then moving on with the conversation. In the bad examples, we are showing more of a sign of our character. How does the interviewer know that you won't hate this place or be really bored here? You need to give a legitimate reason why it wasn't for you and how you are moving forward.

Other "Glitches" In Your Resume

We went over two of the biggest fears that people face with explaining their resumes, but there are literally thousands of different situations that can cause some doubts. They are individual to you and every single one can't be explained.

The important thing is to review your resume thoroughly and look for ANYTHING that may seem questionable. Once you've done this, review it again, bottom to top. Markdown anything that may cause the interviewer to doubt you. You'll then want to have someone else review your resume and see if they find anything that sets off an alarm since we are prone to missing obvious things after looking at them for a while.

Once you have the list of "glitches" compiled, go through each one and determine why they became a part of that particular list. You'll want to look for the positives in each instance and be able to explain them fully, with a positive spin in your favor. This helps ensure that we aren't caught with our pants down.

STAR Technique (Situation, Task, Action, and Result)

Jennifer Aaker, professor of marketing at the Stanford Graduate School of Business, explains in a Stanford University blog post that stories are up to 22 times more memorable than facts alone. She demonstrates the importance of stories in shaping how others see you and as a tool of persuasion. By using success stories during your interview, the interviewer will remember your stories before facts, figures, or data. It also gives them an easy way to describe you to others in the organization. Let's take a look at an easy way to write your success stories using the STAR technique. Let's review this acronym:

- **SITUATION:** Describe the problem or opportunity you faced, just like a reporter who would ask the questions: who, what, where, when, why and how. This helps the interviewer understand the background. Let me use an example to explain this a little better. Say I am applying for a supervisory position and am asked: how have you handled an employee whose people skills were lacking? Here is how I would provide the situation background: Jane is an employee that I have supervised for three years and all of a sudden, I started getting complaints from her colleagues that she was being verbally abusive. It was affecting the team's productivity and morale.

- **TASK:** Explain what you had to do and the challenges you encountered such as a tight deadline, a sick employee, an inadequate budget, etc. Using our example about the employee with a lack of people skills, I would go into the task part of STAR like this: I knew immediately that my task would be to speak with Jane behind closed doors to ascertain why there was an abrupt change in behavior.

- **ACTION:** Explain what you did to solve the problem or how you met a performance objective by describing the process, steps, talent and strengths you used. This is where you start promoting yourself—modestly, of course. Now, back to our verbal abuse employee. During my private conversation with Jane, I asked her how things were going. She did not seem to want to talk and looked uncomfortable. So, I was direct with her and mentioned that the team wasn't functioning well and questioned if she knew why that was. Jane burst into tears. She said that she felt that she was in over her head, and everyone on the team was telling her what to do and she didn't like it.

I thanked her for being honest and we continued the dialogue around her fears and lack of confidence and how we could get her up to speed with some tasks with which she was not comfortable. We also discussed how that could be frustrating to her colleagues. She actually admitted she had been the team grouch. So, with my coaching, communication and compassion skills, I was able to get the real story out of Jane and help her come up with a way to deal with her underlying problem—which was a skill problem—and then address her feelings of being criticized by the others.

- **RESULTS**: What was the outcome or bottom-line result? How did your action make a difference? If you have metrics, please use them. Also, if you learned something through the experience, please share that, too. Back to our example. To tout my results, I would say: Jane took to learning some new skills quickly, which raised her confidence, and she stopped yelling at her teammates. The bottom line is that I took a dysfunctional team and turned it back into a high-performing one, so that projects could be delivered on time and efficiently.

I encourage you to use this step-by-step STAR technique: Situation, Task, Action, and Result to craft your success stories.

CHAPTER 3: QUESTIONS TO EXPECT AND PASS

WITH EASE

Question #1: Tell Me About Yourself

Interviewers love to start the conversation with: "Tell me a little about yourself." It isn't really a question and it could mislead you to think that this is just small talk. Heads up... your two-minute response often determines if the interviewer wants to continue the dialogue. This statement is the #1 interview question. This question could also be disguised as: "Tell me about your background." So, be prepared for either question. You will answer it the same way.

ANSWER TIPS

I realize that it can be intimidating to talk about yourself immediately. But it is also a great opportunity for you to begin strong and shine. This response should be a quick two-minute summary. Here is the formula to use to get this two-minute opener prepared:

I want you to think in four distinct chunks: Who, What, Why, and then end with a Question.

1. **WHO**: Who you are which can encompass all your experience—a one to two sentence summary?

2. **WHAT**: Here you are going to showcase your expertise. Look at the skills you have that match the skills they are looking for. Go back to your previous exercise notes on what you believe you offer. Begin with those skills, your

knowledge, and your talent. Think in terms of how the company will benefit from them.

3. **WHY**: Explain why you are interviewing with this company.

4. **QUESTION**: Finally, ask the interviewer a question that sets them up to tell you what they want to hear from you and gives you time to breathe! Otherwise, there could be an awkward pause between the two of you.

Question #2: Why Are You Looking for a Job?
Even though you already stated why you are interested in joining their company, they may ask you again: "Why are you looking for a job or leaving your current job?" They are fishing to see if you have performance problems or issues with your boss or co-workers. You might have been fired or downsized. How you handle the question says a lot about you as a person.

Are you a complainer, a whiner, a gossip, or someone on an upward trajectory? Obviously, you want to grow and advance in your career. Be careful not to sound too cocky. Take the high road and answer the question honestly. Only you know the reason you want to leave. Avoid bad-mouthing your boss or co-workers. This will be a real red flag to them, thinking that you could repeat this behavior at their company.

Let's face it, you never know who may know your boss or co-workers, and if it got back to them, you would be burning your bridges. If you were downsized, be positive and let them know it was strictly a business decision and that you were one of several or one of many. We will devote a separate chapter on how to explain "I was fired." Also, it is not a good idea to talk about wanting to earn more money. This is a very bad reason because research shows that job satisfaction has less to do with money and more to do with challenges and continuous learning. Let's face it—the interviewer knows you want to earn more!

ANSWER TIPS

The best answers I have heard in all my years of interviewing candidates have to do with the following reasons, all very legitimate and understandable.

- Too much travel or my commute is too long.
- I am looking for more career challenges.
- My spouse or partner is being relocated to this city/town.
- I have topped out for promotion at my current company.
- My company is unstable and going under. Do not mention this if it is not already public news. Don't disclose anything confidential.
- I just graduated from college or am returning to the workforce.

Question #3: Tell Me About Any Previous Issues with a Boss

Watch this question. It is a double-edged sword because you never want to say negative things about a previous boss or a company. Keep in mind that any bad-mouthing will lead the interviewer to believe that someday you could be talking about them or their company in an inflammatory way.

If you are interviewing in your hometown, news gets around fast and this interviewer might even know your prior boss. If you are bitter about a company or a boss, this is not the time to go on a diatribe. Interviewers want to see how you are going to discuss the situation and how you grew professionally from the conflict, disagreement or clash in values.

ANSWER TIPS
Saying you have never had any problems with a boss is unrealistic. We have all worked for jerks, but we learn from the bad bosses too. Your answer to issues with a prior boss needs to be honest, respectful and positive. The emphasis should be on how you tried to improve the relationship. This is at the heart of resolving all conflict—seeing it from the other person's perspective, coming to an agreement, and staying on task. This would be an excellent time to use the STAR model to answer the question.

Question #4: How Do You Deal with Pressure or Stressful Situations?
Companies want someone who is not going to shrink or freak out from stressful situations. The big question is: can you handle the pressure, including the pressure of the interview? Companies want people who can be like the quote you see everywhere—keep calm and carry on. They want to see how you manage stress and whether your great skills such as problem-solving, time and people management and decision-making may be affected negatively when you are put to the pressure test.

ANSWER TIPS
You can't just give a short answer of yes, I handle stress well or I thrive under the pressure. It is too

generic. Describe ways that you cope with stress. Think about the techniques you use to calm yourself. For me, I take some deep breaths while I close my eyes and try to clear my mind—my quick way of doing meditation. For some, it could be your strength of adaptability. For others, it could be taking a walk, exercising, or meditation. Give some thought to a recent stressful situation and think about how you coped and use the STAR story format.

Question #5: How Would Your Manager or Co-Workers Describe You?

This question is about your ability to see how others view you. Sometimes, feedback from others can be enlightening, and at other times it confirms what you know about yourself. This question can also applaud you for how well you get along with your manager and co-workers. I know it is uncomfortable to talk about yourself, but you've got to toot your own horn here.

ANSWER TIPS

Here are several ways to jog your memory of how others describe you:

1. Take out your personal branding sheet to see if any of the words remind you of a quick story that demonstrates a passion, personal attribute, strength or differentiator, or a combination of 1-3 that you have heard others describe you as exhibiting.

2. You can also take a look at a recent performance appraisal from your boss or upward evaluation report. What were the strong positive comments?

3. Tell one of your success stories where you received positive feedback as your RESULT.

4. Bring letters of recommendation and/or LinkedIn endorsements.

Question #15: What Do You Expect to be Doing in Five Years?

This is a question about ambition and motivation to determine whether they want to invest in you. Do you know enough about their career paths to discuss where you want to be? We know that careers zig and zag, but for this question, assume you are staying with this company. You will definitely exhibit loyalty by talking about being there in five years.

ANSWER TIPS

It would be ideal if in your research you discovered the different levels and positions in the company. This would help you understand the typical career progression and where five years should lead you. The inside track could come from someone who is working there now who could elaborate. If not, you should have a general understanding of the career path progression that you have chosen. The interviewer will want to know that you have a plan and how their company fits into that plan.

For example, if you are in marketing you start out as an assistant brand manager, then become a brand manager, move to marketing director and then the top spot as VP of Marketing. If you are currently an assistant brand manager, you know that in the next five years you want to be a brand manager. I can tell you from my experience as an interviewer, many job seekers are just applying for everything that is out there. But, if you are serious about a company, you will know exactly where you are headed in your career.

The focus of your answer should be on personal development. Talk about the skills you will be using or learning on the job and the responsibilities you would like to take on. Your response can't be too general which sounds canned; then again it can't be too specific because if they don't have the position you describe, you are out of the running.

Question #7: What Are Your Weaknesses and Strengths?

This is the flip side of the "what are your strengths" question. Believe me; we all have weaknesses, so you can't just answer, "I don't have any weaknesses." You must be prepared to answer this question and not look like a deer in the headlights when it is asked. Some interviewers ask the question just to trip you up—not nice, but it happens. In this instance, and with the pressure on, it is critical to have a well thought out answer.

The interviewer will be looking to see if you have any self-awareness—do you recognize a weakness in yourself? Can you articulate how you learned from it or overcame it? This kind of self-reflection has to be done in advance so that you are prepared to answer the weakness question often disguised as, "If you could change one thing about yourself, what would it be?" They are fishing for weakness here, too.

ANSWER TIPS

Honesty is always the best policy with the weakness question. Your response must strengthen your chance of getting the job as opposed to weakening it.

Here are a few tips for you:
- Be sure NOT to talk about a weakness that is a requirement for the job. Instead...
- Talk about a weakness that you have overcome or are actively working to change.
- Offer a weakness that is not important to the job.

Start your answer with a short description of the weakness and then discuss what you did or currently do to neutralize it. Almost every interviewer will ask, "What are your strengths?" They want to know if the strengths you possess will align with the talent, skills, and knowledge they need for the job. Are you competent?

This is not a time to be shy and reserved. You must be able to focus on the strengths that are most relevant to the job which you are applying for. You may also have strengths that are not a requirement of the new job, but make a point of focusing on the relevant ones. You must be articulate and confident as you answer the strengths question.

Question #8: Tell Me About a Recent Accomplishment

Finally, the opportunity to talk about your greatness again! But, keep it focused on your professional experience. Even though your greatest accomplishment may be getting your 18-year-old to be self-sufficient or that you won the state track when you were in high school, this is not the time to talk about personal things.

This question could be asked multiple times because it is truly what the interviewer wants to zero in on. Be prepared with at least three accomplishment stories from the last 18 months.

ANSWER TIPS
Great opportunity again for the STAR answer format. You can use examples from what you have listed on your resume—just expand upon them. This time you want three stories you are proud to tell.

Here are a few tips to help you generate these stories:

1. Focus on an accomplishment that is transferable to the job you are applying for. This makes you seem more qualified—a better fit. Things like process improvement, understanding of people issues, innovation or creativity, brainpower, or the ability to be strategic.

2. Mention your work awards if you have any— employee of the month, salesperson of the year, etc.

Talk about teamwork and your ability to be a team player or team leader. One caution, if you are a leader of a team, be sure to toot your own horn as opposed to giving all the credit to the team.

I recently had a client who came to me after she did not get a job at a large U.S. utility company. We discussed how she spoke about being the team leader. She gave all the accolades to her team and the interviewer actually stopped her to criticize that she, as the leader, did not seem to take responsibility for the team wins.

Question #9: Tell Me About a Time When You Had to Work with a Difficult Person

There seems to be an epidemic of difficult people these days. You just want everyone to chill. But that would be a utopia. The workplace does hand us, people who yell, are abusive, difficult, backbiting, immature, arrogant, unappreciative, uncooperative, very demanding, and downright unprofessional.

This creates conflict at work and often leads to a toxic work environment. I know you will have a great story for this question. However, it is how you describe the situation and how you handled it that is key. The interviewer will be looking to see how you deal with these kinds of people—do you get emotional and create more turmoil, or do you find the diplomatic way of dealing with them? Or worse, do you put your head in the sand because you are not skilled at handling conflict?

ANSWER TIPS

Take the time before you go into your story to describe your philosophy of how to handle 'difficult' people in general. Things like truly listening to them often help to diffuse the situation. Asking the person how they would solve the problem empowers them to come up with their own solutions.

Also, be sure to state that you do not tiptoe around the person. Taking charge and talking with the person immediately, in private of course, is the right thing to do. The conversation has to be about how you feel when they do XYZ as opposed to blaming that person.

Question #10: Why Should We Hire You?

There are different versions of this question such as: why are you the best candidate or what value do you feel you bring? Interviewers ask the question because they want to hear how well you can impress them.

How articulate are you about yourself? If not you—then who? This question can be answered as a summary statement that combines your qualifications, the research you have done on the company, and what you have heard during the interview relative to the job and their needs. Think of it as closing the sale. What are the features and the benefits you can offer; what are your differentiators? It must be strong and convincing and all about the company's needs—not yours.

ANSWER TIPS

Job candidates have told me they want to work for me because they like me, they want the job, it sounds like a cool job, or they want to get their foot in the door of a large company. No, no, no! Not appropriate—it is not about you; it is about them. Remember, it is about the abilities you have to offer them. Take a look at your branding statement four boxes worksheet. You circled the skills and characteristics that matched the key or required job description requirements.
You will want to focus on those areas for your answer. Dazzle the interviewer with three messages in under two minutes:

1. You can do the work (based upon your skillset) and deliver excellent results

2. You fit into their culture
3. You are unique

If the interviewer talked about a problem they are facing and that is why they are hiring, be sure to highlight the skills you would use to solve it. Avoid using overused words—great team player, hardworking, trustworthy, reliable, and caring.

End with a question: do you think the qualities and skills I have are what you are looking for? At this point, they may ask you some more questions or merely answer yes. You want to leave them with no questions about your capabilities.

CHAPTER 4: IMPRESSIVE QUESTIONS TO ASK

At the end of every interview, they will always ask, "Do you have any questions for me?" Without a doubt, in some form or another, they are going to ask you this. Some people will think that this means the interview is over. They'll say something like, "Nope! I think I got it all, thanks!" This is the worst thing you can do!

When they ask this, the interview is not over. It's really the beginning of the second half of the interview. Never allow yourself to completely ignore this question. Always come up with at least one thing that you can ask. It shows that you are generally interested and that you want to become a part of the team, not just someone who wants the job to make money. Try to think of your own questions, but here are some good ones to ask in order to help you look professional and interested.

"What is the biggest challenge that other employees in the past have faced?"
This is a good question that can help show the employers that you aren't afraid of what might be coming your way in the position. You've accepted that there are going to be challenges but that you are prepared for this! When you open yourself up and are willing to embrace challenges, then it makes you look like a more hard-working employee.

It also gives you the opportunity to prove yourself. Whatever the issue is that they state previous employees have had, you can remind them that you are going to be able to overcome this uphill battle.

"Is there anything we've discussed that makes you concerned I'm not the right fit for the job?"
It can be challenging to keep track of everything you might have said throughout the interview. When you ask this, then you are covering all your bases. There might be something that you didn't explain well enough, stated in a way that they misunderstood, or there may be a topic that wasn't even covered in the interview.

They will respond by telling you that maybe it's your lack of experience or something else on your resume that they saw. This will give you the chance to explain yourself further so that they have the truth when making their final decision.

"What is the strongest quality needed for this position?"
This question is for you as well. If you are interviewing for a desk position because you enjoy computers and paperwork, but they tell you that customer service is actually the biggest role in the job, then this will give you the warning to show that this job might not be the right fit for you. It will also give you another opportunity to prove yourself, giving you the chance to remind them why you are actually a perfect fit for the job because you already have that strong quality that they are looking for.

"What is this position going to look like in the future?"
This is another question that is for you. In a way, you are taking the opportunity to see if this position has growth, or if it is something that will even be needed in five years. That will come in handy if you have to

pick between several positions you might be interviewing with. On top of that, it shows the person conducting the interview that you are dedicated and looking for something more long-term, proving that you are there for the long-haul.

"What is the most important responsibility that I will have?"
This is similar to the question about what the important quality is. You will be able to get a sense of what the real job you will be working on is. Those getting interviewed always focus on making themselves look as good as possible, but the person conducting the interview is going to do the same thing! They will want to make the position look good so that you might choose them if there are other prospective positions.

For example, it might be a fun "group coordinator" position at a museum, and throughout the interview, the person asking questions only takes time to discuss all the features of the museum. This can make the position seem fun, but then, the first day on the job, you may realize you are just a ticket-tearer at the front entrance and you have to stand for hours. This helps to show that you are concerned with your responsibilities, while also ensuring that it's the position you'll actually be wanting.

"What is your history with the company?"
You will want to know how long your interviewer has been there. If they say something like, "Just a year," then this tells you a few things. One, it is a good sign that there is room for growth within the company and that they provide new opportunities.

It also might be a sign, however, that there is a higher turnover rate and that some individuals might not enjoy working there for longer periods of time. If they say they've been there for a while, then you know it's a good place to work! It also helps to show your genuine interest in the company and the person that's asking you questions.

"Why do you enjoy working for this company?"
This is another question that lets the person conducting the interview know you are genuinely interested in this company. They might reveal some of the perks that you are wanting to ask about, such as an employee discount. You will be able to see the genuine quality of their response so that you can guess if they are really someone that likes the company or if it is just another job to them.

"I noticed something as I was researching the company. Can you explain that to me further?"
This is a great way to let the employer know that you were looking up the company and doing research before you came to the interview. When you can tell them that you were doing research, it lets them know that you are serious about this job and have a general interest in their company. It also shows that you are detail-oriented with a critical eye that can pick up on minor details hidden within their site. It can clear things up for you and also let them know that you are looking at the things that are shared about their company.

"What is the team like here? What is the dynamic among employees?"
This gives you a sense of the type of other employees that you might be working with. If you are looking for a

working environment where you can make friends or one where you don't have to talk to anyone at all, then this will give you an answer about whether or not it aligns with the kinds of things you are hoping for.

"Aside from what we've discussed, are there any tools you need from me, or any other research I can do in the meantime as the hiring process continues?"
This is a final way to make sure that you can fully prepare for the next step. They will likely tell you what the next steps will be. They might say something like, "I have four more interviews so I will let you know next week." This gives you the mindset needed to know if you should be nervous about what happened or be moving on and focusing on other jobs as well.

What Not to Ask
The following are all going to be legitimate questions that you might have, but don't ask them. Some you can find out on your own beforehand or they might be listed in the job description, such as what compensation or benefits there might be.

Though you might be curious about these, don't ask in the interview. It makes it look as though you believe you already have the position. They are also questioning that are focused on the wrong important things in the employer's eyes. Wait until you've been hired to ask these if they aren't already covered before that even happens.

"How much am I going to get paid?"
This is a top concern for many employees. There is this sort of idea that you are supposed to want the job regardless of what the pay is when you are going

through the interview process. While this would be true in the employer's perfect world, we have to face the fact that most of us wouldn't work at all if we didn't have to make money.

However, you don't want to ask this during the interview because it will make it seem like the only thing you care about. They might bring it up, but wait until they offer you the job to discuss salary.

"What kind of free stuff do employees get?"
Job benefits, like discounts or access to food/equipment, is a great perk for many positions. This can be the reason that you end up choosing one position over the other. You still want to ensure that you aren't asking this in the interview. The same with the salary question, it just makes it seem like that's the only thing that you are concerned about.

"Do you guys do drug tests?"
Of course, it's encouraged for you to not do drugs at all so that this is not an issue. However, if you are someone that partakes in recreational substances that might appear on a drug test, don't ask this in the interview process. It's basically saying, "I do drugs."

"What is the mission statement of the company?"
This seems like it would be a good question because you are showing interest in the company and what it stands for. However, this is a question that can easily be answered before you even arrive at the interview. They might include their mission statement in the actual application process, or they probably at least have it on their website. Asking this can indicate that you haven't done any research on the company beforehand.

"Will I have opportunities to work from home/how many sick days do I get?"
This is a real concern and something that you might want to consider before accepting the position. However, you don't want to ever make it look like you aren't willing to work. You will also never know how many sick days you will actually need since we can't always predict when we're sick. Asking this will end up being an obvious sign that you are planning on using some of those sick days for reasons other than having a cold or a fever.

CONCLUSION

Starting a new job can be exciting and nerve-wracking. Meeting new people, going to new places, and starting out with a blank slate, are all things which can make you feel insecure and uncertain. Remember that the choice to begin a new position is a choice that was made to help you take steps forward in your career. The fact that you have gained a new position over hundreds of other applicants is a testament not only to your interview skills but you as a person. You were the best fit for the position!

Take time out to enjoy the transition phase of starting a new job or career. Pat yourself on the back and be grateful at the opportunity before you. Many people wanted the job you have and were not offered a position. Now is the time to focus on showing your company they made the right choice in choosing you as their star candidate.

Do not be surprised if the position you take shifts and changes over time. It can very well be that as the company gets to know your skills better, they may shift your duties slightly to give you the best chance at success. Be sure to communicate openly with your supervisors, while you continue your work efforts, to be certain you are remaining on the same thought path for your career and involvement in the company.

If you find yourself becoming interested in other aspects of the company do not be afraid to vocalize this fact. The more in tune you are with your goals and desires, and the more you communicate with your superiors, the easier it will be to transition into other positions if the opportunity arises. There is nothing wrong with realizing you desire a completely different career path down the line than what you have accepted. It is best to try and remain in a position, unless given a promotion or are moved by the company itself, for at least three years.

The reason for this is because every company likes to see longevity and commitment to the positions you have already taken. People who move from one position to another quickly are also more likely to jump ship. You do not want your new employer to lose faith in your loyalty and excitement for the position you have taken.

Continue to practice your interview skills even if you are happy with your current position. Take time to practice with friends, even acting as the interviewer, and keep your resume up to date. When you have been in a position for a while it can become way too easy to become complacent and lose touch with what an interview is like. Should you desire to apply for a position higher up within the company you may attempt to rely solely on your work merits. Doing this may keep you from being the shining star you were when you gained the position which started you in the company to begin with. Even though you have started the position of your dreams it is always helpful to remain on your game.

Even if you are happy to remain in your position for the rest of your life be sure to take time for yourself and stay excited about your job and the company. Take your vacation time when you can and allow yourself rest and relaxation. Working too much is an easy trap to fall into as people with flourishing careers often feel they are unable to take time off as they are too pivotal to the company's function.

If you are constantly working and never taking time for your private life you will easily burn out and begin to hate the job you originally loved. Keeping the passion alive may require effort but it will not require as much effort as trying to rekindle the relationship you once had should it start to fizzle. Set clear boundaries with your workplace when you take your position so you are clear about the expectations of the hours you are required to work. If possible, take time to reaffirm these boundaries if they are being crossed over time because it will be a necessary practice to keep your heart in your work.

Remind yourself over time what aspects of your job you love. Keep positive affirmations at the ready to continue providing a positive attitude for yourself. There will be bad days at your job as every job has difficulties. No place of employment is perfect but you can be extremely happy if you have taken the time to apply for positions that truly fit who you are.

Your job does not define who you are but it is a big aspect of the building blocks that make you. Being in a position that you find fulfilling and rewarding will help you in your career path forward and keep you in a positive and happy mindset in the workplace. That positivity will then transfer over to your colleagues and will create an all-around better atmosphere.

Be grateful for the new opportunity and rejoice in the fact that you have taken another step closer to your achieved dreams and goals. Your hard work has finally paid off and will continue to do so as you keep bringing all of the wonderful talents you pose to the table.

Thank You

I would like to thank you from the bottom of my heart for coming along with me on this job searching and interview preparation journey. There are many books out there, but you decided to give this one a chance.

If you did expand your knowledge by reading this book, then I need your help! Please take a moment to leave an honest review for this book.

This feedback gives me a better understanding of the kinds of books and topics readers like yourself want to know more about.

It also gives my book more visibility to potential new readers. Leaving a review takes less than one minute and is much appreciated.

Lightning Source UK Ltd.
Milton Keynes UK
UKHW050653301219
355994UK00027B/578/P

9 781087 829326

KEY TOPICS IN

ACCIDENT A

EMERGENC

MEDICINI

The KEY TOPICS series

Advisors:

T.M. Craft *Royal United Hospital, Bath, UK*
C.S. Garrard *Intensive Therapy Unit, John Radcliffe Hospital, Oxford, UK*
P.M. Upton *Sir Humphry Davy Department of Anaesthesia, Bristol Royal Infirmary, Bristol, UK*

Key Topics in Anaesthesia

Key Topics in Obstetrics and Gynaecology

Key Topics in Accident and Emergency Medicine

Forthcoming titles include:

Key Topics in Paediatrics

Key Topics in Orthopaedic Surgery

Key Topics in Ear, Nose and Throat

KEY TOPICS IN
ACCIDENT AND EMERGENCY MEDICINE

PAUL A. HOWARTH
FRCS (Ed)
Consultant in Accident and Emergency Medicine, Treliske Hospital, Truro, Cornwall, UK

RUPERT J. EVANS
MRCP, FRCS (Ed)
Senior Registrar in Accident and Emergency Medicine, Cardiff Royal Infirmary, Newport Road, Cardiff, UK

Consultant Editor

GEOFF HUGHES
FRCP, FFAEM, DRCOG
Consultant in Accident and Emergency Medicine Bristol Royal Infirmary, Bristol, UK

*β*IOS
SCIENTIFIC
PUBLISHERS

© BIOS Scientific Publishers Limited, 1994

First published 1994

A CIP catalogue record for this book is available from the British Library.

ISBN 1 872748 67 8

BIOS Scientific Publishers Ltd
St Thomas House, Becket Street, Oxford OX1 1SJ, UK
Tel. +44 (0)865 726286. Fax +44 (0)865 246823

DISTRIBUTORS

Australia and New Zealand
  DA Information Services
  648 Whitehorse Road, Mitcham
  Victoria 3132

India
  Viva Books Private Limited
  4346/4C Ansari Road
  New Delhi 110 002

Singapore and South East Asia
  Toppan Company (S) PTE Ltd
  38 Liu Fang Road, Jurong
  Singapore 2262

USA and Canada
  Books International Inc
  PO Box 605, Herndon, VA 22070

Typeset by Herb Bowes Graphics, Oxford, UK.
Printed by Information Press Ltd, Oxford, UK.

CONTENTS

[a]Contributed by I.C. Grant BSc, MB, FRCS (Ed), FFAEM, Consultant in Accident and Emergency Medicine, Derriford Hospital, Plymouth, UK.
[b]Contributed by G. Johnson MBChB, FRCS, Senior Registrar in Accident and Emergency Medicine, Derriford Hospital, Plymouth, UK.
[c]Contributed by H.R. Guly MBBS, FRCP, MRCGP, DCH, DRCOG, Consultant in Accident and Emergency Medicine, Derriford Hospital, Plymouth, UK.
[d]Contributed by R.G.A. Choa MBBS, FRCS, Consultant Urological Surgeon, Derriford Hospital, Plymouth, UK.

ABBREVIATIONS

ABG	Arterial blood gases
A&E	Accident and emergency
ACLS	Advanced cardiac life support
AIDS	Acquired immunodeficiency syndrome
AIS	Abbreviated injury scale
ARC	AIDS-related complex
ARDS	Adult respiratory distress syndrome
ATLS	Advanced trauma life support
BLS	Basic life support
BP	Blood pressure
BSA	Body surface area
CBF	Cerebral blood flow
CCU	Cardiac care unit
CDC	Centers for Disease Control
CDH	Congenital dislocation of the hip
CMV	Cytomegalovirus
CO	Carbon monoxide
COHb	Carboxyhaemoglobin
CPAP	Continuous positive airway pressure
CPP	Cerebral perfusion pressure
CPR	Cardiopulmonary resuscitation
CSF	Cerebrospinal fluid
CT	Computerized tomography
CVA	Cerebrovascular accident
CVP	Central venous pressure
DF2	Dysgonic fermenter 2
DIC	Disseminated intravascular coagulation
DOA	Dead on arrival
DPL	Diagnostic peritoneal lavage
DSH	Deliberate self-harm
EMD	Electromechanical dissociation
ENT	Ear, nose and throat
ERC	European Resuscitation Council
ESR	Erythrocyte sedimentation rate
FBC	Full blood count
FEV_1	Forced expiratory volume in 1 second
GCS	Glasgow Coma Scale
GI	Gastrointestinal
Hb	Haemoglobin
HBIG	Hyperimmune gamma-globulin
HBsAg	Hepatitis B surface antigen
HBV	Hepatitis B virus

β-HCG	β-human chorionic gonadotrophin
HDCV	Human diploid cell vaccine
HDU	High-dependency unit
HIV	Human immunodeficiency virus
HRIG	Human rabies immunoglobulin
HSV	Herpes simplex virus
HVM	High-velocity missile
ICP	Intracranial pressure
IG	Immunoglobulin
INR	International normalized ratio
ISS	Injury severity score
ITU	Intensive therapy unit
IVU	Intravenous urography
LFT	Liver function test
LVF	Left ventricular failure
LVM	Low-velocity missile
MI	Myocardial infarction
MTOS	Major trauma outcome study
NAI	Non-accidental injury
NIBP	Non-invasive automated blood pressure
NSAID	Non-steroidal anti-inflammatory drug
PASG	Pneumatic antishock garment
PEF	Peak expiratory flow
PMH	Past medical history
PPF	Plasma protein fraction
PTSD	Post-traumatic stress disorder
RDS	Respiratory distress syndrome
RSI	Repetitive strain injury
RSV	Respiratory syncytial virus
RTA	Road traffic accident
RTS	Revised trauma score
RVA	Rabies vaccine absorbed
SAH	Subarachnoid haemorrhage
SCIWORA	Spinal cord injury without radiological abnormality
SIDS	Sudden infant death syndrome
T-RTS	Triage revised trauma score
T_3	Tri-iodothyronine
T_4	Thyroxine
TIA	Transient ischaemic attack
TRISS	Trauma score and injury severity score
TS	Trauma score
U&E	Urea and electrolytes
UTI	Urinary tract infection
VF	Ventricular fibrillation

PREFACE

Emergency Medicine is a young, emerging speciality which historically has developed to serve local needs. With the recent introduction of the Accident and Emergency Fellowship Examination of the Royal College of Surgeons, the formation of the Faculty of Accident and Emergency Medicine and expanding consultant numbers, the speciality will develop more strategically.

This book contains essential information regarding a number of key topics in accident and emergency medicine. We have attempted to bring together topics in a structured manner which will lend itself both to clinical practice and to the reader studying for their higher examinations. A common theme throughout the text is its adherence to the basic principles of resuscitation, namely those of the advanced cardiac life support, advanced trauma life support and advanced paediatric life support courses.

By the very nature of the speciality it is not possible for the text to be a comprehensive account and the reader is encouraged to further enhance their knowledge by referring to the topics of related interest and consulting the references at the end of each topic. It is a book written by emergency medicine clinicians specifically for all those involved in the speciality, including nurses and paramedics.

Paul Howarth
Rupert Evans

ABDOMINAL PAIN

Life-threatening illnesses requiring immediate management

Obtain as complete a history as possible from the patient, relatives and ambulance crew as the diagnosis can often be made from this alone. Enquire specifically about prodromal illness or symptoms, and the onset and nature of the acute illness, including pain, its site, radiation, nature and precipitating and relieving factors. Ask about the presence of gastrointestinal symptoms such as vomiting, diarrhoea, haematemesis and melaena and non-gastrointestinal symptoms such as dyspnoea, cough and haemoptysis. Take a urinary, sexual and menstrual history if appropriate.

Examination
- Vital signs.
- Smell for fetor and ketoacidosis.
- Look at the patient. Peritonitis is suggested by pallor, drawn-up legs and a reluctance to move.
- Rapid abdominal evaluation. Palpate for tenderness, guarding, rebound, rigidity, masses and aneurysms. Examine all hernial orifices (especially the femoral) and all peripheral pulses. Auscultate for bowel sounds and bruits and perform rectal examination in all patients and vaginal examination in females.

Differential diagnosis
Consider:
- Intra-abdominal catastrophe, such as peritonitis of any cause.
- Myocardial infarction.
- Haemorrhage from a ruptured ectopic pregnancy or gastrointestinal bleed, or an abdominal aortic aneurysm.
- Infection, commonly of the chest or urinary tract.

Resuscitate and investigate
Simultaneously:
- Oxygen, via mask.
- Commence vigorous shock therapy with two 14-gauge intravenous lines (but beware in cardiogenic shock).
- Bloods for full blood count (FBC), urea and electrolytes (U & E), amylase, glucose, liver function tests (LFTs), cardiac enzymes and cross-match.
- ECG.
- Arterial blood gases.
- Urinalysis.

- Pregnancy test.
- Radiography. An erect chest radiograph will demonstrate thoracic disease and free gas under the diaphragm. In the acute situation a supine abdominal film is often unhelpful.

Decisions

- Does the patient have an acute abdominal emergency? If so:
- Is immediate laparotomy required?
- Are further investigations and resuscitation required?
- Is there a non-abdominal cause for collapse, e.g. myocardial infarction?

Refer to surgeons for advice early but always consider a non-surgical cause. Ruptured ectopic pregnancy is not excluded by a negative pregnancy test, normal menstrual history and a denial of sexual activity and should be considered in all females of child-bearing age with lower abdominal pain or collapse. Always examine hernial orifices, especially in obese patients.

Less immediately life threatening illnesses and further evaluation

The causes of abdominal pain are legion, hence time and a full medical history and complete physical examination and appropriate investigations are required.

Surgical differential diagnosis

1. Gastrointestinal conditions

- Acute appendicitis (any age).
- Mesenteric lymphadenitis.
- Meckel's diverticulum.
- Intestinal obstruction.
- Perforated viscus.
- Diverticulitis.
- Colitis – infective or inflammatory.
- Biliary disease – colic and cholecystitis.
- Pancreatitis – acute and chronic.
- Vascular disease – aneurysm, ischaemia and infarction.
- Splenic rupture (infective mononucleosis or delayed rupture following trauma).

2. Urinary tract conditions

- Urinary retention.
- Renal and ureteric colic.

- Pyelonephritis.
- Prostatitis.
- Testicular torsion and epididymo-orchitis.

Gynaecological conditions
- Ruptured ectopic pregnancy.
- Miscarriage.
- Salpingitis.
- Ovarian cyst, rupture or torsion.
- Endometriosis.
- Mickleschmerz.

Obstetric causes
- Labour.
- Abruptio placentae.

Medical causes
- Referred pain, especially marked myocardial infarction, pericarditis, pneumonia and pulmonary embolism.
- Metabolic – diabetes and uraemia.
- Infective – gastroenteritis, infective mononucleosis, upper respiratory tract infection (in children), hepatitis, herpes zoster.
- Drug withdrawal or poisoning.

Psychiatric causes
- Hypochondriasis.
- Munchausen's syndrome.

Further reading

Browse NL. *An Introduction to the Symptoms and Signs of Surgical Disease.* London: Edward Arnold, 1991: 363–403.

Related topics of interest

ABDOMINAL TRAUMA

Unrecognized abdominal injury is a frequent cause of preventable death after trauma. A *high index of suspicion* is required as signs are often subtle, or masked by other injuries or alcohol. As many as 20% of patients with acute haemoperitoneum have benign abdominal findings when first examined in the accident and emergency department. Early evaluation by a surgeon is essential.

Examination

A positive examination is the most reliable clinical sign of abdominal trauma. However, a negative physical examination may hide significant intra-abdominal injury.

1. Inspect the lower chest, abdomen, flank, back and perineum.

2. Palpate for signs of pain, muscle guarding and rebound tenderness.

3. Percuss to elicit subtle rebound tenderness and peritoneal irritation.

4. Auscultate for bowel sounds and bruits.

5. Rectal examination. Look for evidence of blood and bony fragments and determine sphincter tone and prostate position.

6. Vaginal examination. Look for blood and bony fragments.

7. Urethral meatus. Look for evidence of blood.

Management

After the *ABC and initial resuscitation* the following are performed:

1. Blood sampling for blood group and cross-matching, together with samples for FBC including haematocrit and amylase.

2. Nasogastric tube insertion. A tube is inserted to remove gastric contents, relieve gastric distension and to detect the presence of blood in the aspirate. The tube is passed orally in those with a suspicion of basal skull fracture to prevent passage through the cribriform plate and into the cranial cavity.

3. Bladder catheterization will help decompress the bladder, detect haematuria and allow monitoring of urine output. A high-riding prostate, blood at the urethral meatus and scrotal haematoma are indicative of urethral trauma and the need for a urological opinion prior to catheterization.

4. Radiography. In addition to C-spine, chest and pelvic radiographs, an abdominal film may be helpful. Subdiaphragmatic air or extraluminal air in the retroperitoneum is a sign of hollow viscus injury, while loss of psoas shadow may suggest retroperitoneal blood.

5. Diagnostic peritoneal lavage (DPL). In adults the DPL is considered *98% sensitive* for intraperitoneal bleeding. The procedure should be performed by the surgeon caring for the patient. The *open technique* is preferred.

The only absolute *contraindication* is an existing indication for laparotomy. Relative contraindications include previous abdominal surgery, gross obesity, advanced cirrhosis, coagulopathy and pregnancy.

False negatives are found in 2% of patients and are usually related to injuries of the pancreas, duodenum, diaphragm, small bowel or bladder.

False positive results are caused by pelvic fracture, inadequate local haemostasis or accidental injury to intraperitoneal organs.

Complications include local haemorrhage, peritonitis, trauma to the abdominal and retroperitoneal structures and wound infection.

6. Ultrasound. Ultrasound is useful in detecting free intraperitoneal fluid in experienced hands and is often the investigation of choice in children. The ultrasound scan should be performed in the resuscitation room. This technique can also detect splenic and hepatic haematoma.

7. Computerized tomography (CT). The CT scan provides information regarding specific organ damage and its extent. It can also be used to visualize the retroperitoneal and pelvic organs. Hollow viscus injury is not readily detected. CT should only be performed in the stable patient.

Indications for laparotomy

(a) Hypotension with evidence of abdominal injury.
   - Gunshot wounds.
   - Stab wounds.
   - Blunt trauma with gross blood on diagnostic peritoneal lavage.
(b) Peritonitis – early or subsequent.
(c) Recurrent hypotension despite adequate resuscitation.
(d) Extraluminal air.
(e) Injured diaphragm.
(f) Intraperitoneal perforation of urinary bladder on cystography.
(g) CT evidence of injury to the pancreas or gastrointestinal tr`act, and specific injuries to the liver, spleen or kidney.
(h) Positive contrast study of upper and lower gastrointestinal tracts.
(i) Persistent amylase elevation with abdominal findings.

Further reading

American College of Surgeons Committee on Trauma. Abdominal Trauma. In: *Advanced Trauma Life Support*. Chicago: American College of Surgeons, 1993: 141–58.

Robertson, C, Redmond AD. *The Management of Major Trauma. Oxford Handbooks in Emergency Medicine*. Oxford: Oxford University Press, 1991.

Related topics of interest

AIRWAY

Safe and effective airway management is a fundamental skill in the accident and emergency department. Airway compromise can occur suddenly and unexpectedly.

Causes of airway compromise

- Obtunded state for whatever reason.
- Anatomical airway disruption.
- Compression from haematoma, tumour, retropharyngeal abscess.
- Oedema – burns, inhalation injury, angioneurotic oedema and allergy.
- Obstruction of lumen by blood, vomitus or foreign body, including sweets, chewing gum and teeth.
- Infection – epiglottitis and croup.
- Vocal cord paralysis.

Indications for airway intervention

- Airway obstruction.
- Airway risk.
- Ventilation.

Basic airway manoeuvres

Oxygen and suction must be available at all times. Call for anaesthetic assistance early.

Protect the cervical spine in all trauma patients. Open the airway using a chin lift or jaw thrust manoeuvre with head tilt if cervical injury is excluded. Remove foreign bodies manually or by suction. Oro- or nasopharyngeal airways may be passed. The nasopharyngeal route, although more unpleasant, is better tolerated once the airway is *in situ*. Having opened and cleared the airways assess breathing and ventilate if necessary using one of the following techniques:

(a) Mouth to mouth.
(b) Mouth to mask.
(c) Bag and valve mask.

- One-person technique.
- Two-person technique.

Advanced airway manoeuvres

Orotracheal intubation is the method of choice unless there is a high likelihood of cervical spine injury in the spontaneously breathing patient, in which case the nasotracheal route may be preferable (controversial and not widely practised in the UK as it may cause significant epistaxis). Avoid prolonged attempts at intubation and always reoxygenate between attempts.

Surgical airway   A surgical airway is indicated if attempts to establish an airway by any other route fail for any reason.

1. Needle cricothyroidotomy with jet insufflation of airway is indicated in children under 12 and as a temporizing measure in adults.

   Technique. Identify the cricothyroid membrane and pass a 14-gauge cannula through it into the tracheal lumen. Attach the cannula to wall oxygen administering 15 l/min via tubing with either a side vent or 'Y' connection. Ventilate by obstructing the side vent for 1 second in every 5. Ventilation can be continued for 35–45 minutes (limited by hypercarbia).

2. Surgical cricothyroidotomy is contraindicated in children under 12 when the cricoid is the only circumferential support for the upper trachea and when there is massive swelling in the neck or pre-existing anatomical abnormalities.

   Technique. An incision is made over the cricothyroid membrane, which is open under direct vision and through which can be passed a 5- to 7-mm tracheostomy tube or endotracheal tube.

3. Tracheostomy. This is a difficult procedure which is best performed electively and is almost never used in the emergency department.

Further reading

Latto IP, Rosen M, eds. *Difficulties in Tracheal Intubation*. London: Balliere Tindall, 1983.

Related topics of interest

ALCOHOL-RELATED PROBLEMS

Ethanol (C_2H_5OH) abuse is the most common, but methanol and ethylene glycol (antifreeze) are also alcohols of abuse.

The *standard unit of alcohol* is 8 g, which is equivalent to a half-pint of beer, a glass of wine, a glass of sherry or a measure of whisky. The recommended limit for males is 21 units per week, and for females 14 units per week. Intakes above these levels are associated with an increased risk of harm to the individual.

Alcohol is rapidly absorbed (90% within an hour). It is metabolized by liver alcohol dehydrogenase to acetaldehyde and then to acetate. Above a level of 1g/l liver metabolism is saturated, further intake thereafter resulting in a rapid increase in plasma concentration. Liver impairment, enzyme-inducing drugs and genetic factors may alter the rate of alcohol metabolism. The level of alcohol excreted by the lungs is in equilibrium with the blood concentration and allows estimation using breath alcohol analysis. In addition, salivary analysis allows qualitative analysis. The gold standard for estimation remains blood analysis.

Acute ethanol intoxication

The effects of ethanol vary with the plasma concentration, as summarized below:

1. Mild intoxication (0.5–1.5 g/l). Emotional lability, impaired muscle coordination and reaction time.

2. Moderate intoxication (1.5–3.0 g/l). Visual impairment, sensory loss, impairment of motor skills and slurred speech.

3. Severe intoxication (3.0–5.0 g/l). Marked impairment of motor skills, blurred vision, hypothermia, occasionally hypoglycaemia and convulsions.

4. Coma (>5.0 g/l). Coma, respiratory depression, hypotension, depressed reflexes and hypothermia. Death may result from respiratory or cardiovascular failure or from aspiration.

Management

Apply the ABCs. Pay particular attention to the possibility of cervical spine trauma, other occult injuries and respiratory complications. Exclude hypoglycaemia.

1. Hypoglycaemia. This is due to inhibition of gluconeogenesis. It is especially common in children, chronic alcoholics and the elderly. It is usually unresponsive to glucagon and intravenous glucose should be given.

2. *Thiamine* (100 mg i.v.) should be administered to chronic alcoholics prior to dextrose to prevent Wernicke's encephalopathy.

3. *Hypothermia.* Avoid overexposing the patient and inducing hypothermia.

4. *Occult injury.* Patients require admission and further assessment to exclude occult injury prior to discharge. Such injuries are easily missed. Continuous monitoring of the patient is necessary. *Radiographs* are taken as necessary. In the unconscious victim these should include the cervical spine, chest and pelvis if there is any possibility of trauma. CT scanning may be necessary to exclude head injury. Radiographs of facial bones etc. may be better performed when the patient is sober.

5. *Lactic acidosis* may complicate acute ethanol intoxication in patients with severe liver disease, pancreatitis or sepsis or in those prescribed biguanides. This will require correction of hyperglycaemia and hypovolaemia.

6. *Ketocidosis* may result from dehydration, glycopenia, increased lipolysis and ketogenesis and may develop in alcoholics who binge drink. It is usually corrected by infusion of 5% dextrose.

7. *Gastric lavage* should be performed in the unconscious patient, provided the airway can be protected.

8. *Naloxone.* Some patients may respond but the mechanism is unknown.

9. *Haemodialysis* should be considered if the blood ethanol exceeds 500 mg% or if metabolic acidosis is present.

10. If the level of consciousness does not improve, consider other toxins.

Alcohol withdrawal

Ethanol can cause physical dependence and hence withdrawal symptoms. Counselling after recovery from withdrawal is vital.

1. Early mild features occur within 6–12 hours of abstinence and consist of tremulousness (especially morning), anorexia, nausea, retching, sweating and irritability.

2. Late major features usually occur after 24–72 hours of abstinence but can take as long as 2 weeks to develop.

(a) Fits are common and tend to occur before delirium tremens:

- A single fit does not require specific treatment.
- Recurrent seizures and status epilepticus can be controlled by i.v. diazepam, chlormethiazole or phenytoin.

(b) *Delirium tremens* is a life-threatening emergency with a 10% mortality. It is associated with fever, tachycardia, tremulousness, agitation, and frightening and bizarre visual hallucinations. It may be associated with clouding of the senses or frank delirium.

(c) In *acute hallucinosis* auditory hallucinations occur but without clouding of the senses. The patient should be managed with haloperidol 5–10 mg intramuscularly repeated a few hours later. Oral therapy can then replace intramuscular treatment.

Management of withdrawal

Patients with fits, delirium tremens or acute hallucinosis should be admitted. Other indications for admission include concurrent physical illness or concurrent abuse of other drugs. The differential diagnosis includes head injury, Wernicke–Korsakoff syndrome and hepatic encephalopathy.

The drugs used in the management of withdrawal may result in the complications of oversedation, respiratory depression and circulatory collapse. Overhydration is to be avoided, and the osmolarity should be monitored regularly, using normal saline sparingly in those with severe liver disease, in whom sodium retention is common. Complications such as infection, pulmonary embolism and cardiac arrhythmias should be treated as they arise.

1. General measures. Calm, quiet and gentle, but firm, handling in subdued surroundings is essential, with constant monitoring of vital signs. The patient with status epilepticus or who is unconscious should be admitted to an intensive therapy unit (ITU) or high-dependency unit (HDU).

2. Investigations. Glucose, urea and electrolytes, blood gases, amylase, LFTs, calcium and magnesium. Blood cultures may be required. Chest radiography, brain scan and abdominal ultrasound may be required.

Blood glucose requires regular monitoring as hypoglycaemia is common, and easily missed.

3. Treatment.

(a) *Multivitamins* are given, but severe malnutrition or suspected Wernicke–Korsakoff syndrome requires intravenous high-potency vitamins (Parentrovite: one pair of ampoules given slowly over 10 minutes daily for 5–7 days) and thiamine hydrochloride 100 mg twice daily.

(b) *Sedative medication* should be prescribed in withdrawal.

- *Chlormethiazole* is widely used and is a powerful sedative, anticonvulsant and anxiolytic. In severe cases chlormethiazole may be administered by i.v. infusion titrated to the patient's needs. The patient will require monitoring on the ITU/HDU as the drug acts as a potent respiratory depressant. The aim is to replace agitation with light sleep. Early conversion to oral therapy is desirable.
- *Chlordiazepoxide.* Many regard chlordiazepoxide as the drug of choice. A suitable regimen would be to start with 20 mg four times daily and gradually wean the patient over a week.

(c) Other drugs used to treat ethanol withdrawal include paraldehyde, phenothiazines, barbiturates, beta-blockers and ethanol.

Chronic effects

1. Hepatic. Fatty liver, alcoholic hepatitis, cirrhosis.

2. Central nervous system. Alcoholic dementia, cerebellar degeneration, subdural haematoma, toxic amblyopia, seizures, peripheral neuropathies, myopathy, Korsakoff's psychosis and Wernicke's encephalopathy.

3. Abdominal. Gastric erosions, peptic ulcers, oesophageal varices, pancreatitis and diarrhoea.

4. Cardiovascular. Cardiomyopathy, arrhythmias and hypertension.

5. Haematological effects. Marrow depression, haemolysis, sideroblastic anaemia and macrocytosis.

6. Endocrine effects. Androgen deficiency, hypoglycaemia, pseudo-Cushing's, hyperlipidaemia and osteoporosis.

7. Psychological damage. Pathological jealousy, alcoholic hallucinosis and suicidal behaviour, marital problems, domestic violence, child abuse and work problems.

Prevention
The accident department can play a role in prevention. The *CAGE* questionnaire is a valuable screening test:

Ought to Cut down
Annoyed about advice
Guilty about drinking
Eye opener: the need for a drink first thing in the morning.

Two or more positive responses to the above indicate that the patient has a problem and should be advised to seek help. Communication to the GP is essential.

Further reading

Brunt P. Management of ethanol withdrawal. *Prescriber's Journal,* 1992; **32**: 2–8.
Paton A. *ABC of Alcohol.* London: BMJ Publishing Group, 1994.

Related topics of interest

ANAESTHESIA – GENERAL

Whenever possible general anaesthesia should be carried out as an elective procedure by a trained anaesthetist and following full assessment, premedication and optimization of the patient's condition. Emergency anaesthesia carries a particularly high perioperative risk and should be only carried out when absolutely necessary and after careful consideration of the benefits weighed against the potential dangers.

Indications for emergency anaesthesia

(a) To protect the airway:
- When the level of consciousness is impaired and protective reflexes are compromised, e.g. poisoning, cerebrovascular accident, head injury and major trauma with hypoxia and hypovolaemia.
- In cases of actual or potential respiratory obstruction, e.g. facial injuries, orofacial burns, angioneurotic oedema and epiglottitis.

(b) To optimize or control ventilation, e.g. in cases of head or chest injury.

(c) Primary treatment, e.g. carbon monoxide poisoning.

(d) Emergency surgery, e.g. laparotomy, thorocotomy, urgent fracture fixation and vascular repair.

(e) To render the patient immobile for radiological examination, e.g. CT scan.

Dangers of emergency anaesthesia

(a) Patients cannot usually be fully assessed or prepared for anaesthesia. They may have coexisting medical diseases such as hypertension or significant past medical conditions such as myocardial infarction. Drug history, allergies and response to previous anaesthetics are often not known. Moreover, there may be factors which predispose to difficult intubation such as a small jaw or a short fat neck.

(b) Full stomach. Patients are usually not starved and gastric emptying may be delayed by up to 24 hours following trauma or during pregnancy. Thus, even if the 6-hour rule is obeyed there is no guarantee that the stomach will be empty.

(c) Physiological optimization of condition is often not possible. The patient may be hypoxic, hypovolaemic, anaemic, uraemic or have a disturbed acid–base or electrolyte balance prior to induction of anaesthesia.

(d) Coagulopathy, especially following massive transfusions or in disseminated intravavascular coagulation.

(e) No premedication.

(f) Pain.

Assessment

(a) Urgency of anaesthesia.

(b) Risk of aspiration. Pass a nasogastric tube and give ranitidine 50 mg intravenously.

(c) Ease of intubation.

(d) Likelihood of pneumothorax (intermittent positive-pressure ventilation may precipitate tension pneumothorax).

(e) Investigations available or requested.

(f) Availability of blood or blood products.

(g) Availability of ancillary staff.

(h) Availability of surgeon and operating theatres.

Preparation

Check that all the equipment required is present and functioning normally, including bag, mask, laryngoscope, endotracheal tubes, introducers and suction, and make sure that the trolley has head-down tilt. Check the anaesthetic machinery and gases. Draw up drugs and check that resuscitation facilities are available. Establish monitoring and gain intravenous access.

Rapid sequence induction

Protect the cervical spine in all trauma patients. Where possible pre-oxygenate with 100% oxygen for 3–5 minutes but do not ventilate if the patient is breathing spontaneously as this can cause gastric dilatation. However, if ventilation is poor or apnoeic then hyperventilate with high-flow oxygen for 2 minutes while cricoid pressure is applied, making sure that the assistant is doing this correctly. Suction must be available at all times. Administer an induction agent such as thiopentone or etomidate followed immediately by a muscle relaxant. Suxamethonium is the drug of choice if it is not contraindicated (severe burns, major crush injuries or family history of cholinesterase deficiency), in which case vecuronium or atracurium may be used. Orally intubate the patient and do not allow release of cricoid pressure until the cuff has been inflated and it is established that both sides of the chest are being ventilated.

Further reading

Hickle RS. Administration of general anaesthesia. In: Firestone LL, Lebowitz PW, Cook CE, eds. *Clinical Anesthesia Procedures of the Massachusetts General Hospital.* Boston: Little, Brown and Co., 1988: 136–67

Related topics of interest

Airway (p. 7)
Anaesthesia – local and regional (p. 14)
Carbon monoxide poisoning (p. 53)
Inhalation injuries (p. 172)

ANAESTHESIA – LOCAL AND REGIONAL

Local anaesthetic agents reversibly block conduction of nerves by impairing propagation of the action potential. Small nerve fibres are more easily blocked than large ones and myelinated more than non-myelinated as agents need only produce blockage at the nodes of Ranvier. Most local anaesthetics in current use are amides (lignocaine, bupivacaine and prilocaine). Cocaine is an ester-type local anaesthetic which readily penetrates mucous membranes and has a vasoconstrictive action but, because of the dangers of dependence and systemic adverse effects, it is rarely used outside of ear, nose and throat (ENT) departments. The amide local anaesthetics are metabolized in the liver with elimination half-lives of about 2–3 hours. Although they are weak bases, most commercially available preparations have a pH adjusted to the acidic side in order to enhance chemical stability. Most cause vasodilatation, and the addition of adrenaline as a vasoconstrictive agent decreases local blood flow, reducing surgical bleeding and slowing the rate of absorption, thereby prolonging effect. The choice of agent and dose depends on the route of anaesthesia (surface, local infiltration or regional block), the length of anaesthesia required, the site of action and the patient's age, weight and fitness. It is important that local anaesthetic agents are not injected into inflamed or infected tissues, as this might result in rapid systemic absorption and hence toxicity. Preparations containing adrenaline should not be used in digits or appendages. The maximum dose of adrenaline used must not exceed 500 µg (1:200000 contains 500 µg per 100 ml).

Lignocaine	This is the most frequently used anaesthetic, and is available in 0.5 – 2% solutions with and without adrenaline. It has rapid onset but only a moderate duration, lasting between 1 and 2 hours. The speed of onset and duration of action are increased by the addition of adrenaline. The dose of plain lignocaine must not exceed 200 mg (3 mg/kg) or 500 mg (7 mg/kg) when given with adrenaline. A solution of 1% lignocaine contains 10 mg/ml. Doses must be reduced for the elderly, the infirm and children. Preparations are available for local infiltration, nerve block and also skin and mucous membrane anaesthesia. EMLA contains lignocaine 2.5% and prilocaine 2.5%. A lignocaine pump spray is available for mucous membrane anaesthesia; each dose contains 10 mg.
Bupivacaine	Bupivacaine is used for local infiltration, peripheral nerve block and epidural block. It has a slow onset, taking up to 30 minutes for full effect, but has a much longer duration of action than lignocaine, acting for up to 8 hours in nerve blocks. The maximum dose is 2 mg/kg (25 – 30 ml of 0.5% for local infiltration and

regional anaesthesia). Note that it is contraindicated as an intravenous regional anaesthetic as inadvertent systemic intravenous release may cause cardiac arrest that is resistant to therapy.

Prilocaine

This has a similar potency to lignocaine but is 40% less toxic. For this reason it is the drug of choice for intravenous regional anaesthesia. It is also available for local anaesthetic and nerve blocks. The maximum dose is 400 mg in the adult (1% solution contains 10 mg/ml). Methaemoglobinaemia may occur, especially if dosage exceeds 600 mg.

Adverse effects

1. CNS effects. Dizziness, perioral numbness and tinnitus, proceeding to grand mal seizures. CNS toxicity is exacerbated by hypercarbia, and if symptoms appear administration should stop and oxygen should be applied. Fits may be terminated by hyperventilation; if this fails intravenous diazepam should be administered.

2. Cardiovascular toxicity may be manifested as hypotension, arrhythmias, ventricular fibrillation or electrical standstill. Bupivacaine-related cardiovascular effects may be refractory to treatment. Hypotension is managed by the administration of intravenous fluids and adrenaline and, although the cardiac arrhythmias are difficult to treat, they may subside over time if the patient can be maintained haemodynamically, therefore in the case of cardiac arrest prolonged cardiopulmonary resuscitation is warranted.

3. Hypersensitivity reactions to the amide local anaesthetics are almost unknown.

Regional anaesthesia

1. Local infiltration. The intradermal or subcutaneous injection of local anaesthetic to produce anaesthesia at the site of surgery. The pain produced by infiltration can be minimized by slow administration and the use of a narrow-bore needle. The choice of agent depends on the desired duration and the volume required.

2. Haematoma block. The introduction of local anaesthetic into fracture haematoma prior to reduction.

3. Peripheral nerve block. The injection of local anaesthetic in the proximity of a peripheral nerve to provide anaesthesia in the area served by the nerve, e.g.

digital, median or femoral nerve blocks. The onset is usually rapid, but the duration depends on the agent used. Knowledge of the anatomy of the nerve is essential if anaesthesia is to be appropriate, effective and if intraneural injection is to be avoided.

4. Nerve plexus block. The injection of local anaesthetic in the proximity of a nerve plexus, e.g. brachial. Large volumes of local anaesthetic are required, and typically the onset is slow but a long duration may be achieved. Solutions containing adrenaline should be used to delay systemic absorption.

5. Intravenous regional anaesthesia (Bier's block). The injection of an anaesthetic agent into an arm vein after exsanguination with an Esmarch bandage and occlusion of the vein with a pneumatic tourniquet. Intravenous access must be obtained in another limb prior to administration of the local anaesthetic. Prilocaine is the agent of choice in the UK. The tourniquet must not be released less than 20 minutes after administration, and although anaesthesia persists as long as the tourniquet is applied this should not exceed $1\frac{1}{2}$ - 2 hours. Anaesthesia disappears rapidly after the tourniquet is removed.

Further reading

Katz J. *Atlas of Regional Anaesthesia.* Norwalk: Appleton-Centuary-Crofts, 1985
Loach A. New views on local analgesia. In: Atkinson RS, Adams AP, eds. *Recent Advances in Anaesthesia and Analgesia,* 16. Edinburgh: Churchill Livingstone, 1989: 65–81.

Related topic of interest

Anaesthesia – general (p. 14)

ANALGESIA

Pain is the commonest reason for presentation in accident and emergency departments. Not only is its treatment fundamental to a successful consultation, but research clearly demonstrates that untreated or inadequately treated pain affects the underlying disease process and may adversely influence outcome.

Requirements for successful analgesia

Analgesia should be effective and safe, and the appropriate agent, dose (where possible titrated with effect), route and frequency of administration should be chosen with care. Historically intramuscular analgesia has been a common route of administration, but this is painful and unpredictable in effect (as the onset is delayed and there is variable absorption from muscle which may be poorly perfused). Continuous intravenous infusion, small frequent intravenous aliquots, titration and patient-controlled analgesia are widely used methods for the in-patient management of pain and in future may be appropriate for use in A & E.

Pain evaluation

Many methods have been developed to try and measure pain objectively. The most commonly used is the visual analogue scale. However, pain and pain thresholds vary enormously and the practical principle should be that if the patient reports pain then the patient is in pain and analgesia is inadequate if it does not abolish the pain.

Agents

Non-opioid analgesics

Aspirin is the analgesic of choice for mild to moderate pain. It has anti-inflammatory and antipyretic properties and also reduces platelet aggregation. It is contraindicated in patients with aspirin hypersensitivity, children under the age of 12 (link with Reye's syndrome), breast feeding, active GI ulceration, asthmatics, and bleeding disorders.

Paracetamol is for mild to moderate pain. It has no anti-inflammatory action but is antipyretic. It is less irritant to the gastrointestinal tract than aspirin, but it is very dangerous in overdosage as it causes delayed onset of liver failure.

Non-steroidal anti-inflammatory drugs are used to treat mild to moderate pain, especially musculoskeletal. They are contraindicated in patients with known peptic ulceration and should be used cautiously in patients with known sensitivity to aspirin, asthmatics and renal failure. Common side-effects include indigestion and diarrhoea. Many different agents are available, some over the counter and others on prescription.

Opioid analgesics

Morphine is the standard narcotic for severe pain and the drug with which all others are compared. Given intravenously the peak action occurs in 2–3 minutes with a half-life of 2–4 hours. In addition to analgesia it increases venous capacitance and hence is used to treat pulmonary oedema. Side-effects include nausea, vomiting, drowsiness, respiratory depression and pupillary constriction. Diamorphine causes less nausea than morphine.

Fentanyl is a synthetic narcotic with a short half-life (90 minutes) but may cause severe respiratory depression. It is usually only used by anaesthetists.

Nalbuphine is for moderate to severe acute pain. It is a synthetic agonist–antagonist which causes limited respiratory depression and is not a drug of abuse. It is used in prehospital care by paramedics in the UK.

Pethidine is a short-lasting analgesic that is not as effective as morphine but causes less respiratory depression.

Codeine is good for mild to moderate pain, but it is not available for intravenous administration. Dihydrocodeine is similar to codeine.

Combination preparations

These are commonly used but they do not necessarily have any advantage over single agents and may complicate overdosage. They are not all the same and it is important to know what is contained in each one. Common agents include:

- CoCodamol (paracetamol 500 mg, codeine 8 mg).
- Codydramol (paracetamol 500 mg, dihydrocodeine 10 mg).
- Coproxamol (paracetamol 325 mg, dextropropoxyphene 32.5 mg).

Others

1. *Inhalation agents*, e.g. Entonox (50% nitrous oxide and 50% oxygen). Self-administered to cover short-duration, painful procedures. It is contraindicated in patients with pneumothorax.

2. *Regional anaesthesia*, including local, regional and epidural and spinal, produces analgesia as well as anaesthesia.

3. *General anaesthesia.*

Further reading

Reynolds JEF, ed. Analgesic and anti-inflammatory agents. In: *Martindale the Extra Pharmacopoeia*. London: The Pharmaceutical Press, 1989: 1–46.
Reynolds JEF, ed. Analgesic and opioid analgesics. In: *Martindale the Extra Pharmacopoeia*. London: The Pharmaceutical Press, 1989: 1294–321.

Related topics of interest

Anaesthesia – general (p. 14)
Anaesthesia – local and regional (p. 17)

ANAPHYLAXIS

Anaphylaxis is the syndrome elicited in a hypersensitive individual on subsequent exposure to the sensitizing antigen. Reactions range from mild pruritus and urticaria to anaphylactic shock and death.

Anaphylactoid reactions are similar, but are not IgE mediated and not related to prior sensitization. They require identical treatment.

Antibiotics (especially penicillin) and *radiographic contrast agents* are the most common causes of serious anaphylactic events, with rates of about 1 per 5000 exposures. They account for the majority of fatal reactions. Anaphylaxis also commonly results from reactions to *Hymenoptera stings (bee stings)*.

Aetiology

Anaphylaxis may arise in three ways:

(a) Exposure to a foreign protein results in the generation of an *IgE antibody response*. During re-exposure, antigen results in degranulation of mast cells and perhaps basophils, releasing chemical mediators such as histamine, prostaglandins, leukotrienes and platetet-activating factor.

(b) Immune complexes or other agents activate the *complement cascade*, resulting in the formation of anaphylatoxins which trigger the release of mast cells and basophils directly.

(c) Certain agents such as hyperosmolar solutions and radiocontrast mediums can stimulate the *release of mediators directly* by an as yet unknown mechanism.

Clinical features

Diagnosis of anaphylaxis relies on the association of the typical clinicopathological features in association with exposure to a foreign substance. Airway obstruction, hypotension, gastrointestinal symptoms and generalized cutaneous reactions, alone or in combination, should arouse suspicion.

The onset of symptoms and signs varies from *immediate to hours* with the majority occurring within 1 hour. The timing of onset depends on the sensitivity of the subject and the route, quantity and rate of delivery of the antigen. A biphasic reaction may occur.

1. General symptoms. Faintness, syncope, seizures, confusion or a feeling of impending doom.

2. Cutaneous. Pruritus, flushing, erythema, urticaria and in severe cases angio-oedema. Mucous membranes can also be involved.

3. *Respiratory symptoms.* Breathlessness, wheeze, chest tightness. In severe cases upper airway obstruction due to oedema of the larynx and epiglottis (angio-oedema) may result.

4. *Cardiovascular collapse.* Secondary to peripheral vasodilatation, increased vascular permeability and intravascular volume depletion. Arrhythmias and ischaemia may result.

5. *Gastrointestinal symptoms.* Nausea, vomiting, abdominal cramps and diarrhoea.

Differential diagnosis

The differential diagnosis includes those associated with:

(a) Loss of consciousness (e.g. syncope, epilepsy, myocardial infarction and arrhythmias).
(b) Acute respiratory conditions (asthma, epiglottitis, foreign body obstruction and pulmonary embolism).
(c) Disorders with cutaneous or respiratory manifestations (mastocytosis, carcinoid, hereditary angio-oedema and reactions to drugs).

Treatment

Avoidance and *prevention* are the mainstay of therapy.

Less severe reactions (urticaria alone) should be treated with oral antihistamines and/or steroids.

Severe reactions may not respond initially to treatment and patients should be admitted for at least 24 hours.

1. *Administration of the causative agent should be stopped* and the patient made to lie flat.

2. The *airway* is checked and oxygen given. If compromised by laryngeal or glottic oedema with stridor and severe respiratory distress, *endotracheal intubation* is required, and if this fails then resort to a *surgical airway.*

3. *Adrenaline* is the drug of choice for systemic reactions. It counteracts the vasodilatation, bronchospasm and other effects on target tissues and inhibits the further release of mediators from the mast cells and basophils. Intramuscular adrenaline (1 ml of 1:1000) should be given.

- Dose: 1-ml vial of 1:1000 adrenaline (1 mg)

Adult	1 ml
Child (0.01 ml/kg)	
< 1 year	0.1 ml
1–5 years	0.25 ml
6–10 years	0.5 ml
11–15 years	0.75 ml

4. Antihistamines (H_1-receptor and H_2-receptor antagonists) may prove useful in the treatment of histamine-induced cardiac arrhythmias and vasodilatation. Intravenous chlorpheniramine should be given over 1 minute.

- Dose

Adult	10–20 mg
Child	
1 year	2.5 mg
7 years	5 mg
Adolescent	10 mg

5. Intravenous fluids. If hypotension is present then colloid is initially infused rapidly at a dose of 10 ml/kg and after the initial bolus at an appropriate rate guided by monitoring. Inotropic support may be required.

6. Intravenous hydrocortisone may be helpful to prevent secondary inflammatory responses, especially those associated with bronchospasm, but has a delayed onset of action.

- Dose

Adult	200 mg immediately 100 mg i.v. every 6 hours or oral prednisolone 40–60 mg daily for 3 days
Child	50–100 mg immediately

7. Bronchospasm. Administer nebulized salbutamol and use aminophylline (intravenously) in a loading dose followed by an infusion if salbutamol is unsuccessful.

8. Glucagon is useful in patients taking beta-blockers in a dose of 1 mg as an infusion in 1 litre of 5% dextrose at a rate of 5–15 µg (5–15 ml/min).

Further reading

Bochner BS, Lightenstein LM. Anaphylaxis. *New England Journal of Medicine*, 1991; **324:** 1785–90.

Brueton MJ, Lortan JE, Morgan DJR, Sutters CA. Management of anaphylaxis. *Hospital Update*, 1991; **5**: 386–98.

Handley AJ. Special circumstances. In: *Advanced Life Support Manual*. London: Resuscitation Council (UK), 1992: 39–43.

Related topics of interest

Airway (p. 7)
Bites and envenomations (p. 43)
Cardiopulmonary resuscitation (p. 56)
Shock (p. 269)

ANKLE SPRAIN – ACUTE

A sprain is defined as the acute rupture of a ligament. It includes a spectrum of injury from the tearing of a few fibres to almost complete disruption. Injuries to the ankle ligaments are extremely common and occur in both sexes and at any age. They are the result of either forced overload or abnormally directed loads.

Lateral ligament

Sprains account for about 80–85% of injuries. The lateral complex comprises anterior talofibular and calcaneofibular ligaments. Injuries occur as the result of an inversion force, tearing the anterior talofibular ligament first. With additional force the calcaneofibular ligament tears; if these two are completely disrupted the posterior talofibular ligament may also become involved, resulting in complete lateral instability of the ankle.

Differential diagnosis

- Lateral malleolar fracture.
- Fractured base of fifth metatarsal.
- Achilles tendon rupture.

Medial ligament (deltoid)

Deltoid strain makes up about 15% of cases and may be complicated by high fracture of the upper fibula (Maisonneuve fracture). It usually follows an eversion injury. If the entire ligament is torn then medial instability may follow. If it is complicated by rupture of the inferior tibiofibular ligament then diastasis of the ankle occurs.

Anterior tibiofibular ligament

Injury does not usually occur in isolation but is usually associated with injuries to the anterior portion of the deltoid and the anterior talofibular ligaments.

The mechanism of injury will indicate the likely ligaments involved. There is pain associated with rapid swelling, which usually occurs within a few hours. The patient may be able to weightbear, but this is painful.

Examination

Swelling may be very marked, either localized to the affected area or around the whole ankle (particularly if presentation is delayed and the foot is left dependent). Tenderness is usually specific to the site of injury. Stress testing is unhelpful in the acute phase of injury because of the degree of pain. The entire length of the fibula should be palpated. The fifth metatarsal head and Achilles tendon should be examined to exclude injury to these structures.

Investigations

Anteroposterior and lateral radiographs are required to exclude fracture. Additionally, views of the whole tibia and fibula are required if a Maisonneuve fracture is suspected. Stress views are rarely indicated in the acute phase and require general anaesthesia if they are to be performed properly.

Treatment

Acute ankle injuries should be treated regardless of stability with:

- Rest.
- Ice.
- Compression.
- Elevation.
- Non-weightbearing exercises.
- NSAIDs.

Plaster immobilization should be avoided as it leads to loss of proprioceptive reflexes and when removed may lead to further injury and delayed healing.

Outcome

Most patients with stable ankles should be able to resume normal activities within about 6 weeks. In patients with unstable injuries return to normal may be delayed, but only a very few develop chronic instability. Operative treatment is usually reserved for top athletes.

Further reading

Petersen L, Renstrom P. *Sports Injuries*. London: Martin Dunitz, 1986: 341–7.

Related topics of interest

Calf pain – musculoskeletal causes (p. 50)
Overuse injury (p. 235)

ANTERIOR KNEE PAIN

Anterior knee pain is common among teenagers and young adults. An accurate diagnosis requires a careful history and examination.

History

The exact mechanism of injury should be ascertained with particular reference to immediate post-traumatic function, exact localization of pain, predisposing and relieving factors, presence of swelling and, if it occurred immediately following injury (suggesting haemarthrosis) or subsequent to it, locking and giving way.

Examination

Observe the position of limb, scars, wasting, swelling, deformity and colour. Palpate for swelling, noting effusion, tenderness, heat and crepitus. Observe the gait and active and passive movements. (The normal range of movement should be 0–150°.)

Specific tests

1. *Medial and lateral collateral ligaments.* Determine valgus and varus strain with the knee held at 0° and 30°. Laxity at 0° is always abnormal, however it is possible for there to be medial or lateral stability at 0° if the anterior cruciate is intact even if the collateral ligament is torn. Hence, the test should be repeated at 30° when the anterior cruciate is lax.

2. *Cruciate stability.* Flex the knee to 90° and observe the position of the upper leg. Sagging of the tibia backwards suggests a posterior cruciate tear, as does a positive posterior draw. Anterior draw laxity indicates anterior cruciate instability.

   Lachman's test. Flex the knees to 20–25°, grasp the upper tibia and attempt to glide it on the distal femoral condyles. If there is movement the test is positive and suggests anterior cruciate instability.

3. *Meniscal tears (McMurray's test).* Fully flex the knee and internally and externally rotate the tibia while slowly extending the knee in an attempt to trap a loose body or meniscus. In positive tests there may be a palpable or audible click, often associated with pain.

4. *Patella apprehension test (for recurrent dislocation of the patella).* The patella is pushed laterally while

flexing the knee. A positive test is indicated by apprehension, the patient resisting this movement.

Radiography

Any patient with a knee injury should have anteroposterior and lateral views of the knee taken. Horizontal beam lateral films should be performed if lipo-haemarthrosis is suspected, and tunnel views obtained if loose bodies or osteochondral fractures are suspected. Skyline views are useful in imaging the patellofemoral joint.

Chondromalacia

The exact pathogenesis of chondromalacia of the patella is unclear. It may be due to an overload of the patella caused by strenuous activity and/or malalignment of the patella. It is most common in adolescents and young adults, and is more common in females than in males. It presents with pain in the front of the knee and under the patella which is worse with physical activity and on climbing stairs and is relieved by rest. Examine specifically for patella malalignment and exclude recurrent subluxation of the patella with the apprehension test. Chondromalacia usually gets better with rest. If there is quadriceps wasting then physiotherapy is indicated. Patella malalignment may require surgical correction.

Osgood–Schlatter disease

This disease, traction apophysitis of the tibial tubercle, usually develops at 13–14 years and is more common in males. Patients present with pain and swelling of the tibial tubercle. Radiographs may show soft-tissue swelling over the tibial tubercle, however the diagnosis is made on clinical grounds. Treatment is rest, NSAIDs and to await fusion of the tibial tubercle.

Osteochondritis dissecans

Separation of a small fragment of bone and overlying articular cartilage, usually from the lateral side of the medial femoral condyle, is thought to be an overload injury, although it may be familial or can indicate an underlying endocrine illness. Radiographs may reveal a scalloped appearance of the femoral condyle. However, this may not be obvious and a MRI scan is sometimes required. The patient should be referred to an orthopaedic surgeon for consideration of fixation or removal of the fragment.

Patella dislocation

This may follow a specific injury or occur spontaneously, especially if there is predisposing patella malalignment or muscle wasting. It is more common in females. On examination the patella is often found to be lying laterally, although it may have spontaneously relocated. Treatment for first-time injury without predisposing factors is immobilization in a plaster cylinder followed by physiotherapy. Recurrent dislocation and subluxation requires referral for orthopaedic opinion.

Plica syndrome

The patients are usually teenagers or young adults and present with pain in the upper portion of the patella. A thickened fold may be palpable at this site. Pain is usually worse on exercise, and clicking or popping may be felt by the patient. It usually responds to rest and NSAIDs. If the condition is persistent, consider referral to an orthopaedic surgeon for arthroscopy and division of the plical fold.

Others

- Pre- and infrapatella bursitis.
- Meniscal lesions and cysts.
- Tumours (rare but always consider if symptoms are unusual or do not respond to treatment).
- Ruptured patella tendon.

Further reading

Bentley G, Dowd G. Current concepts of aetiology and treatment of chondromalacia patella. *Clinical Orthopaedics*, 1984; **189**: 209–28.

Related topic of interest

Overuse injury (p. 235)

ANTIBIOTICS

Antibiotics are routinely prescribed and administered in accident and emergency departments for both prophylaxis and the treatment of established infection. Antimicrobial chemotherapy is only one of the modalities available for the prevention and treatment of infection. Rest, elevation, wound toilet, surgical drainage and debridement continue to be the mainstay of therapy, and antibiotics must not be considered a substitute for them. Most therapy started in A & E will be 'blind', and it is important to ensure that wound swabs are obtained before treatment starts.

Choice of agent

It is essential to prescribe the most appropriate agent, dose, route of administration and duration of course. Consideration must be given to:

1. Pathogen factors

- Likely infecting organism.
- Known local antibiotic resistance pattern.
- Culture and sensitivity tests, if available.

2. Host factors

- Infection type, site and severity.
- Age.
- Immunosuppression.
- Pregnancy.
- Breast feeding.
- Prosthetic implants (e.g. heart valve).
- Previous or current antibiotic treatment.
- Known allergy.
- Likely compliance.

3. Antibiotic factors

- Local antibiotic policy.
- Available routes for administration.
- Side-effects.
- Contraindications.
- Cost.

Hazards

- *Anaphylaxis.* Antibiotics should not be administered if there is a known history of allergy (urticarial rash, bronchospasm, angio-oedema and cardiovascular collapse). Do not withhold antibiotics, especially in the presence of life-threatening infection such as meningitis, if the history of allergy is unreliable (many patients think that GI upsets or failure of antibiotic treatment to work constitute allergy).

- *Inappropriate or inadequate treatment* resulting in continuing infection of the development of resistance.
- *Superinfection* – resulting from alteration of normal flora, e.g. thrush.
- *GI upsets* are common. Pseudomembranous colitis may occur, especially with lincamycin and clindamycin.
- *Specific effects*, such as the effect of tetracycline on developing teeth or bone and the ototoxicity of aminoglycosides.

Further reading

Reynolds JEF, ed. Antibacterial agents. In: Martindale: *The Extra Pharmacopoeia*. London: The Pharmaceutical Press, 1989: 94–105.

Related topics of interest

Anaphylaxis (p. 23)
Bites and envenomations (p. 43)
Meningitis (p. 204)
Tetanus (p. 289)
Wound management (p. 307)

ASTHMA

Asthma affects over 5% of the population in industrialized countries, and there is evidence that the prevalence and severity are rising. The diagnosis and treatment are relatively straightforward, yet asthma is still *underdiagnosed and undertreated* with resultant avoidable deaths. The mortality from asthma is approximately 2000 patients per year in the UK.

Asthma is defined as widespread narrowing of the airways which changes in severity over periods of time due to bronchial hyperresponsiveness. Symptoms include intermittent wheeze, chest tightness, cough and shortness of breath. Pathologically it manifests as widespread airway narrowing with bronchial smooth muscle contraction, mucosal oedema and inflammatory cell infiltration.

Reversibility of airways obstruction is characteristic, and bronchial hyper-responsiveness is defined as a 20% fall in the 1-second forced expiratory volume in response to a provoking dose of histamine or methacholine of less than 8 μmol.

A number of stimuli may activate the inflammatory response, including inhaled allergens, infection, exercise, anxiety, cold and drugs.

Acute asthma

Patients with severe or life-threatening attacks may not be distressed and may not have all these abnormalities. The presence of any should alert the doctor.

1. Features of acute severe asthma include:

- Inability to complete sentences in one breath.
- Respiratory rate $\geq$ 25 breaths per minute.
- Pulse $\geq$ 110 beats per minute.
- Peak expiratory flow (PEF) $\leq$ 50% of predicted or best.

2. Life-threatening features include:

- PEF <33% of predicted or best.
- Silent chest, cyanosis or feeble respiratory effort.
- Bradycardia or hypotension.
- Exhaustion, confusion, or coma.
- Normal or high $PaCO_2$.
- Severe hypoxia: PaO_2<8 kPa (60 mmHg) irrespective of treatment with oxygen.
- Low pH (or high H^+).

Monitoring

1. Peak expiratory flow rate. Repeat measurement of PEF 15–30 minutes after starting treatment.

2. Pulse oximetry. Maintain SaO_2 >92%.

3. *Arterial blood* gases. Repeat blood gas measurements if:

(a) Initial PaO_2 <8 kPa (60 mmHg).
(b) $PaCO_2$ is normal or raised.
(c) Patient deteriorates.

Management

Acute severe asthma requires urgent and aggressive management based on clinical assessment and repeated *objective measurement* of respiratory function.

1. The aims of management are to:

• Prevent death.
• Restore the patient's clinical condition and lung function to the optimum levels as soon as possible.
• Maintain optimal function and prevent early relapse.

2. Treatment consists of:

• *High-flow oxygen* in all cases.
• *Bronchodilators.* Salbutamol 5 mg or terbutaline 10 mg via oxygen-driven nebulizer.
• *Steroids.* Prednisolone tablets 30 – 60 mg or hydrocortisone 200 mg i.v., or both.
• No sedative of any kind.

Mild asthma

PEF greater than 75% of predicted:

(a) Treat with oxygen and inhaled bronchodilators.
(b) Observe for 60 minutes and discharge if the patient is stable with PEF > 75%.
(c) Ensure that the patient has a supply of drugs, correct inhaler technique and written instructions. Arrange GP follow-up and inform of need to return if symptoms worsen.

Moderate asthma

PEF 50 – 75%:

(a) Treat with oxygen and a nebulized bronchodilator.
(b) Observe for 60 minutes, and discharge if the PEF is stable and >60%.
(c) Drugs should include prednisolone 30 – 40 mg for 7 days, regularly inhaled steroid and bronchodilator.
(d) Follow-up by GP and chest clinic, crisis plan and PEF monitoring.

Severe asthma	PEF 33 – 50%:
	(a) Measure arterial blood gases and monitor closely.
	(b) Admit.
Life-threatening asthma	PEF <33%:
	(a) *Seek senior help.*
	(b) Add ipratropium 0.5 mg to the nebulized β-agonist.
	(c) Give i.v. aminophylline 250 mg over 20 minutes or salbutamol or terbutaline 250 μg over 10 minutes. Do not give bolus aminophylline to patients already taking oral theophylline.
	(d) Chest radiography to exclude pneumothorax.
	(e) Admit to the intensive care unit.
Indications for ventilation	(a) Deteriorating PEF, worsening or persisting hypoxia, or hypercapnia.
	(b) Exhaustion, feeble respirations, confusion or drowsiness.
	(c) Coma or respiratory arrest.

Further reading

British Thoracic Society and others. Guidelines for the management of asthma: a summary. *British Medical Journal*, 1993; **306**: 776–82.

Related topics of interest

BABY CHECK

Baby check is a scoring system used to determine whether a baby of less than 6 months is acutely ill. It is not a substitute for clinical judgement and is not applicable to conditions such as injury and convulsions, which clearly warrant admission.

One version is to be used by parents and the other by doctors. A total of seven symptoms and 12 signs are checked, and these provide the user with individual scores derived from the regression coefficients. The total score provides the user with a risk assessment of the severity of illness. The higher the score the more likely the baby is to be seriously ill.

Parents

The score provides the parent with a guide to help decide whether medical advice should be sought:

1. Score 0 – 7. The baby is only a little unwell, and medical attention should not be necessary.

2. Score 8 –12. The baby is unwell, but is unlikely to be seriously ill Seek advice from your doctor, health visitor or midwife, as necessary.

3. Score 13 –19. The baby is ill. Contact your doctor and arrange for your baby to be seen.

4. Score 20 or more. The baby may be seriously ill and should be seen by a doctor straight away.

Doctors

A study has shown that the baby check is of some value in predicting those babies 'needing hospital admission', with a score over 20 resulting in a 100% admission rate. It also revealed that conditions such as apnoeic episodes, feeding problems, trauma and rashes often result in low scores despite the obvious need for admission. Conditions such as bacterial pneumonia, meningitis and intussusception all scored over 20.

Have these symptoms been present in the last 24 hours?

	Score
1. Has the baby vomited at least half the feed after each of the last three feeds?	4
2. Has the baby had any green-stained vomiting?	13
3. Has the baby taken less fluid than usual in the last 24 hours? If so score for the total amount of fluids taken as follows:	
• Taken slightly less than usual (more than two-thirds normal)	3
• Taken about half usual amount (one-third to two-thirds normal)	4
• Taken very little (less than one-third normal)	9

Breast-feeding mothers should estimate the amount taken.
Fluids that have been vomited should still be scored.

4. Has the baby passed less urine than usual?   3

5. Has there been any frank blood (not streaks) mixed with the baby's stools? 11

6. Has the baby been drowsy when awake? If so, score as follows:

   • Occasionally drowsy   3
   • Drowsy most of the time   5

   Do not score irritability or increased sleeping.

7. Has the baby had an unusual cry (sounds unusual to mother)?   2

Now examine the baby awake

8. Is the baby more floppy than you would expect?   4

9. Talk to the baby. Is the baby watching you less than you expect?   4

10. Is the baby wheezing (not snuffles or upper respiratory noises)
    on expiration?   3

11. Is the baby responding less than you would expect to what
    is going on around?   5

Now examine the baby naked for the following checks

12. Is there any indrawing (recession) of the lower ribs, sternum or upper
    abdomen? If so, score as follows:

    • Just visible with each breath   4
    • Obvious and deep indrawing with each breath   15

13. Is the baby abnormally pale or has the baby looked very pale
    in the last 24 hours?   3

14. Does the baby have blue fingernails or toenails?   3

15. Squeeze the big toe to make it white. Release and observe the
    colour for 3 seconds. Score if the toe is not pink within 3 seconds, or
    it was completely white to start with.   3

16. Has the baby got an inguinal hernia?   13

17. Has the baby an obvious generalized truncal rash or a sore and
    weeping rash covering an area greater than 5 × 5 cm?   4

18. Is the baby's rectal temperature 38.3°C or more?   4

19. Has the baby cried (more than just a grizzle) during this assessment?   3

Further reading

Morley CJ, Thornton AJ, Cole TJ, Hewson PH, Fowler MA. Baby Check: a scoring system to grade the severity of acute systemic illness in babies under 6 months old. *Archives of Disease in Childhood.* 1991; **66**: 100–5.

Thornton AJ, Morley CJ, Cole TJ, Green SJ, Walker KA, Rennie JM. Field trials of the Baby Check score card in hospital. *Archives of Disease in Childhood.* 1991; **66**: 115–20.

Copies of Baby Check for professionals and patients can be obtained at low cost from: Baby Check, PO Box 324, Wroxham, Norwich NR12 8EQ, UK; Tel. 0603 784400.

Related topic of interest

Trauma scoring and injury scaling (p. 297)

The authors wish to acknowledge Dr. Morley who gave his permission for Baby Check to be reproduced in this book.

BACK PAIN

Back pain is a common cause of presentation in accident and emergency. Eighty per cent of the population suffer from it at some time in their life, and a small percentage will continue to have chronic pain. There is no single definition or cause, but syndromes include sciatica (radicular pain caused by nerve root compression) and lumbago (non-radicular back pain). In addition, strains, lifting and twisting also result in local pain. Vertebral fracture and spinal cord injury must be excluded, particularly in the elderly, in whom minimal trauma and osteoporosis cause vertebral collapse. Back pain in children is frequently organic and should always be taken seriously; disc herniation is rare but conditions such as tumours and infection, including discitis and osteomyelitis, should be considered and excluded.

Causes

- *Soft-tissue injury.* Usually muscular or ligamentous strains.
- *Disc prolapse* of nucleus pulposus through the annulus fibrosis. This ranges from bulging of the disc to extrusion of the disc contents. Symptoms result from nerve root compression and possibly from nerve root inflammation due to the release of enzymes from the nucleus of the disc. Central disc prolapse may cause cauda equina compression causing bilateral sciatica, saddle sensory changes and bladder and bowel dysfunction.
- *Facet joint pain.* This is usually the result of degenerative joint conditions.
- *Spondylosis* is associated with degenerative changes of the vertebral column and disc degeneration.
- *Congenital and developmental.* Ankylosing spondylosis or spondylolysis (defect in the pars intra-articularis) may lead to spondylolisthesis (slippage of the anterior border of a vertebral body forwards onto the one below).
- *Metabolic bone disease* such as osteoporosis and Paget's disease.
- *Spinal stenosis* is caused by narrowing of the spinal canal, causing pain referred to either or both lower limbs precipitated by walking and relieved by rest.
- *Inflammatory arthritis*, especially rheumatoid and ankylosing spondylitis.
- *Vertebral fracture* may be spontaneous or follow minimal trauma, especially in the elderly osteoporotic spine.
- *Malignancy.* Secondaries are most common, especially from prostate, breast, lung, kidney and thyroid.

Multiple myeloma is the most common primary bone tumour.
- *Referred pain.* Important conditions include abdominal aortic aneurysm, peptic ulcer, pancreatitis, renal disease, pelvic inflammation and pregnancy.
- *Functional.*

Management

1. History. This must be careful and complete and include duration, distribution and nature of onset of symptoms, bladder and bowel dysfunction.

2. Examination

- *Observation.* With the patient standing, any obvious deformity should be noted. Test the range of movement of the spine and observe the gait.
- *Motor examination,* including abdominal reflexes and anal tone
- *Sensation,* including perineum.
- *Passive straight-leg raising.* If the symptomatic leg is lifted, a positive test is indicated by pain radiating down the back of the leg. Note that if pain is perceived on the symptomatic side when the good leg is lifted, this constitutes a positive cross-over test, which is a useful sign of nerve root compression. Back pain without leg pain does not constitute a positive straight-leg test.

3. Lumbar radiographs. These are often unhelpful but should be performed if there is a history of trauma and when organic disease other than disc prolapse or musculoskeletal pain is suspected. They should also be performed in children and the elderly.

4. Special imaging

- CT scan.
- CT myelography.
- MRI (especially useful for imaging soft tissues and spinal cord).
- Isotope bone scan.

Disposal

Indications for admission include:

- Cauda equina compression – this constitutes a neurosurgical emergency.
- Severe pain or inability to move.
- Unable to cope at home owing to social or domestic circumstances.

Out-patient management can be achieved in the majority of patients with moderate pain and equivocal or minimal nerve root signs:

- Advise the patient to rest on a firm flat surface until the pain subsides and then to mobilize as early as symptoms allow. There is evidence that prolonged bed rest may delay recovery.
- Prescribe NSAIDs.
- Instruct the patient to seek urgent medical attention if neurological symptoms develop or progress, if bladder or bowel dysfunction occurs or if there is no significant improvement within 5 days.

Further reading

Jayson MIV, ed. *The Lumbar Spine and Back Pain*. Edinburgh: Churchill Livingstone, 1992.

Related topic of interest

Spine and spinal cord trauma (p. 278)

BITES AND ENVENOMATIONS

Bites and stings are commonly considered minor injuries but may cause extensive tissue damage, infection and specific complications. In the UK bee stings cause more deaths than snake bites, but worldwide the latter cause at least 40 000 deaths each year.

Non-venomous bites
- Contaminated crush injuries with haematoma and devitalization (dogs, humans and herbivores).
- Puncture wounds with inoculation of organisms with possible deep penetration (cats and rodents).

Risk of infection

This depends on:

- Animal species: human bites are particularly high risk.
- Location: hands, wrists and feet are high-risk areas, particularly if joints are involved. Head and face are low risk (except in infants).
- Wound type.
- Host factors: the old, the immunocompromised, diabetics, alcoholics and those with peripheral vascular disease are more susceptible.

Microbiology

The most common pathogens causing clinical infection are streptococci and *Staphylococcus aureus*. *Pasteurella multocida* also commonly causes clinical infection, particularly from cat bites and scratches. Infection is usually manifest locally with abscess formation, cellulitis, lymphangitis and lymphadenopathy. Osteomyelitis and tenosynovitis may occur if bones and tendons are penetrated. Fulminating septicaemia is uncommon. If it does occur consider Dysgonic Fermenter 2 (DF2) infection. Hepatitis B, syphilis and rabies have been transmitted by bite. HIV transmission is a potential problem.

Investigation

Radiograph bites over joints and hands and if the animal's teeth may have broken off in the wound.
   Culture of fresh wounds is not indicated. Swab clinically infected wounds.

Management

Careful surgical toilet with thorough cleaning, irrigation and excision of devitalized tissue is the mainstay of treatment. Low-risk wounds and wounds over the face may be sutured; others should be allowed to granulate or treated with delayed primary closure.

Antibiotics are not a substitute for wound care. They are used as prophylaxis for high-risk wounds and hand injuries. Penicillin and flucloxacillin are usually adequate for most bites. Consider tetracycline for *Pasteurella multocida* infections and metronidazole for anaerobic infection.

Rabies

Latency of the rhabdovirus allows post-inoculation prophylaxis against CNS invasion, so consider this in at-risk patients. If the patient has been previously vaccinated do not give human rabies immunoglobulin (HRIG). Give either human diploid cell vaccine (HDCV) or rabies vaccine absorbed (RVA). If the patient has not previously been vaccinated, give HRIG, infiltrating half the dose around the wound and half intramuscularly. HDCV and RVA are given intramuscularly. Note that local reactions to vaccine are very common.

Venomous bites and stings

Identify the perpetrator. This is important but often difficult. In the UK the only indigenous venomous snake is the adder, but imported exotic pets are also implicated.

Adder bites

The incidence of adder bites in the UK is estimated to be 100 per year but this is probably underreported. Fourteen deaths occurred in the period 1900–1976, at least one of which was due to anti-venom. Local pain and swelling occur rapidly. If there is no swelling after 2 hours this suggests mild envenomation. Haemorrhagic oedema and brawny swelling extend proximally for 48 hours. Blistering is common but necrosis is rare. Systemic symptoms such as abdominal pain, nausea, diarrhoea, hypotension, tachycardia and confusion suggest envenomation and may precede collapse. Haemorrhage is rare but suggests severe envenomation.

Management:

• Keep calm.
• Observe and monitor.
• Provide analgesia.

- Give anti-tetanus toxoid if indicated.
- Zagreb anti-venom is indicated for systemic envenomation, especially if hypotension persists or if there is rapid and progressive swelling of a limb. The anti-venom is produced from horse serum and can cause anaphylaxis.

Bee sting
The effects are usually dose dependent, however anaphylaxis may occur, usually within 30 minutes, although hypersensitivity delayed for up to 10 days has been reported. Treatment is supportive. Anti-venom is not available.

Weaver fish sting
Weaver fish are found in UK coastal waters. The venom is heat labile. Treatment is to remove the spine (which might be difficult) and to apply hand-hot water to the wound.

Further reading

Otten EJ. Venomous animal injuries. In: Rosen P, Barkin RM, eds. *Emergency Medicine*. St Louis: Mosby Yearbook, 1992: 875–93.

Related topics of interest

Antibiotics (p. 32)
Tetanus (p. 289)
Wound management (p. 307)

BURNS

Each year in the UK burns kill over 600 people and injure more than 10 000 others, causing varying degrees of disfigurement and disability. The mortality from burns can be estimated by adding the patient's age to the percentage body surface area (BSA) of burns: if this exceeds 100, the chances of survival are poor.

Early stabilization and management of the burn patient follows the ABCs and specifically includes:

(a) Identifying the *extent and depth of the burn.*
(b) Commencing i.v. *fluids.*
(c) Obtaining *baseline blood and radiography investigations.*
(d) Performing emergency *escharotomy* if necessary. (Deep circumferential burns to the limbs can restrict the circulation and in the neck and chest interfere with airway control and ventilation.)
(e) Identifying and arranging *transfer* to a burns unit as required.

Airway

A high index of suspicion for the presence of thermal injury to the airway and smoke inhalation is required. Mortality in burns patients is most commonly associated with smoke inhalation. Signs of airway obstruction may not be immediately obvious, but develop rapidly.

Indicators of smoke inhalation are:

• Facial burns.
• Singeing of the eyebrows and nasal vibrissae.
• Carbon deposits and acute inflammatory changes in the oropharynx.
• Carbonaceous sputum.
• History of impaired mental state and/or confinement in a burning environment.
• History of explosion.

All patients should be given humidified high-flow oxygen. If smoke inhalation is suspected, 100% oxygen is necessary to allow carbon monoxide to dissociate rapidly. Full-thickness thoracic burns causing restriction to ventilation require an escharotomy.

Stop the burning process

(a) Remove all clothing.
(b) If the clothing is still hot, apply liberal amounts of cold water.
(c) Cover burn with sterile towels or Clingfilm.
(d) Ensure that the patient is kept warm and do not

apply wet soaks as these induce hypothermia, especially in children.

(e) Consider the danger of toxic chemicals.

Intravenous lines

Patients with burns lose plasma, fluid and electrolytes, and adults with greater than 15% burns and children with greater than 10% burns require intravenous fluids.

(a) Ideally site two peripheral lines (needle gauge 14 – 16) in the forearm or antecubital fossa.

(b) Occasionally, alternative sites, e.g. femoral vein or central veins, or cutdowns or intraosseous infusion may be required. If necessary venous access may be made through a burnt area.

(c) Fluid resuscitation requirements are calculated by the use of a burns formula, of which there are many. The time of the burn is the time used to calculate fluid needs.

- *Muir and Barclay formula.* The volume required for the first 4 hours after injury is:

$$\frac{\% \text{ BSA burn} \times \text{Body weight (kg)}}{2}$$

- *Advanced trauma life support (ATLS) guideline.* 2 – 4 ml of Ringer's lactate/kg/%BSA in first 24 hours; one half in the first 8 hours and one half in the next 16 hours.

(d) *Urinary catheter.* Insert and measure hourly urinary output. Urine output should be 1 ml/kg/h. Observe for myoglobinuria.

(e) Full-thickness burns of greater than 10% will require blood later (500 ml for each 10% of deep burn).

Assessment of burn

1. Body surface area can be calculated as follows:

(a) The *'rule of nines'*.

(b) The area covered by the patient's palm is 1% of the patient's body surface area.

(c) The *Lund and Browder chart* (corrects for age).

(d) Do not include simple erythema in this calculation.

(e) In patients with almost complete burns it is simpler to assess the unburned area and subtract from 100.

2. Depth of burn

(a) *Erythema.* Erythema only, no significant damage.
(b) *Partial thickness.* Associated swelling and blister formation. Plasma loss.
(c) *Deep dermal.* Patchy white, decreased sensation. Plasma loss. May need grafting.
(c) *Full thickness.* Damage to all skin layers. The skin appears pale and leathery and is painless. Needs excision and grafting. Plasma and red blood cell loss.

Investigations

(a) *Blood*
  • Full blood count.
  • Group and cross-match.
  • Arterial blood gases including carboxyohaemo-globin.
  • Serum glucose
  • Urea and electrolytes.
(b) *Chest radiography.*
(c) *Peak expiratory flow rate.*
(d) *Twelve-lead ECG.*
(e) *Core temperature.*

Analgesia

The severely burnt patient will be restless and anxious from hypoxia and hypovolaemia. These should be urgently corrected. Analgesics should be used sparingly and titrated to the patient's needs.

1. Entonox (50% nitrous oxide and 50% oxygen mixture) is useful for the conscious patient, especially before reaching hospital.

2. Opioids. Give intravenously in small aliquots titrated to the patient's needs, e.g. morphine 0.1 mg/kg.

Criteria for transfer

The following patients require transfer to a burns unit:

(a) Patients under 10 or over 50 years of age with partial-thickness and full-thickness burns greater than 10% of BSA.
(b) Patients in other age groups with burns greater than 15% BSA.
(c) Patients with burns involving the face, eyes, ears, hands, feet, genitalia or perineum or those with burns involving skin overlying major joints.

(d) Patients with full-thickness burns greater than 5%.
(e) Patients with electrical burns including lightning injury.
(f) Patients with significant chemical burns.
(g) Patients with inhalation injury.
(h) Patients with burn injury and pre-existing illness.

Complications
- Scarring and contractures.
- Adult respiratory distress syndrome.
- Wound infection and septicaemia.
- Renal failure, gastric and duodenal ulceration (Cushing's ulcer).
- Myoglobinuria.
- Sickle-cell syndrome.
- Glycosuria and hyperglycaemia.
- Tetanus.
- Rarely liver failure, necrosis of pancreas and gall bladder.

Further reading

American College of Surgeons Committee on Trauma. Injuries due to burns and cold. In: *Advanced Trauma Life Support*. Chicago: American College of Surgeons, 1993: 245–59.

Muir IFK, Barclay TL, Settle JAD. *Burns and their Treatment*, 3rd edn. London: Butterworths, 1987.

Robertson C, Fenton O. ABC of Major Trauma. Management of severe burns. *British Medical Journal*, 1990; **301**: 282–6.

Related topics of interest

CALF PAIN – MUSCULOSKELETAL CAUSES

Ruptured tendoachilles

This most commonly occurs in males in their 30s and 40s indulging in athletic activity, commonly badminton and squash but also while running to cross roads or catch buses. It also occurs in young athletes, especially following recurrent minor injuries or episodes of Achilles tendinitis. The most common site of rupture is 5 cm proximal to the calcaneal insertion of the tendon. Rupture may occasionally occur at the musculotendinous junction.

History	The patient presents with sudden onset of pain in the lower calf, sometimes described as like a blow or kick in the back of the leg, often causing the patient to fall to the ground. Walking is painful and difficult with the patient unable to lift the heel off the ground while weightbearing.
Examination	Examination reveals a palpable tender boggy gap in the tendon at the site of rupture. The functional continuity of the Achilles mechanism can be demonstrated by Simmonds test: with the patient prone, squeeze the calf and observe plantar flexion of the foot in the intact tendon. This test is particularly useful for differentiating complete from partial ruptures. (The terms Simmonds test positive and negative should be avoided as this can lead to confusion and it is best to simply record whether plantar flexion occurs when conducting the test.)
Predisposing factors	• Oral steroid therapy. • Local steroid injection (especially if intratendinous). • Gout.
Differential diagnosis	• Partial rupture • Gastrocnemius tear. • Ankle sprain.
Treatment	*1. Non-operative.* Plaster of Paris initially with the foot in full equinus. Later the foot can be moved into the neutral position. Mobilization will require intensive physiotherapy. *2. Operative.* This is especially appropriate for active sportspersons.

Local protocols should be consulted or orthopaedic opinions should be sought for specific advice as to the management of individual cases.

Achilles peritendinitis

This often occurs in athletes, in males more commonly than in females.

Pathology	There is acute inflammation of the tendon sheath leading to healing with fibrosis and thickening. With continuing physical activity a vicious circle of continuing inflammation leading to further fibrosis can occur.
History	The patient presents with pain in the Achilles region precipitated by physical activity and relieved by rest.
Examination	Examination reveals tenderness and swelling over the affected segment.
Differential diagnosis	• Partial rupture of the Achilles tendon. • Tendon degeneration. • Deep vein thrombosis.
Treatment	• Rest. • Heel elevation. • NSAIDs. • Physiotherapy. • Local steroid injection into the tendon sheath (for experienced practitioners only as intratendinous injection must be avoided). • Operative decompression of the tendon and division of adhesions.

Achilles tendinitis

This presents with similar features to peritendinitis except that there is usually no swelling around the affected tender segment. It is important to recognize this as a discrete entity as it may lead to partial or complete rupture of the Achilles tendon.

Treatment	Treatment is similar to that of Achilles peritendinitis, although for resistant cases rest in a below-knee plaster with the foot in the neutral position followed by intensive physiotherapy may be required.

Gastrocnemius tear

This occurs most commonly in the older, active sportsperson and usually involves the medial head.

History	There is severe pain in the calf during physical activity and the symptoms may initially mimic Achilles tendon rupture. Walking is extremely painful and swelling may be rapid and severe.
Examination	Examination reveals maximal tenderness at the site of rupture. The swelling and bruising may be extensive.
Differential diagnosis	• Achilles tendon rupture. • Ruptured Baker's cyst. • Deep vein thrombosis. • Intermittent claudication.
Treatment	• Rest, ice, compression, elevation. • Physiotherapy. • NSAIDs. This injury may take many months to recover and persistent or recurrent symptoms are common, especially if physical activity is resumed prematurely.

Posterior tibial compartment syndrome

There is pain in the posterior compartment during and after physical activity. Intracompartment pressure testing will confirm the diagnosis.

Further reading

Gillies H, Chalmers J. The management of fresh ruptures of the tendo-achilles. *Journal of Bone and Joint Surgery*, 1970; **52a**: 337–43.

Related topic of interest

Compartment syndrome (p. 77)

CARBON MONOXIDE POISONING

Carbon monoxide (CO) is a colourless, odourless, tasteless, non-irritant gas produced by the incomplete combustion of carbon-containing compounds. Important sources include car exhaust fumes, inadequately ventilated or improperly maintained heating appliances and all types of fires. In addition methylene blue (a solvent in paint strippers) is metabolized by the liver to CO. The normal endogenous production of CO will produce levels of 0.7%. Levels of 9% in smokers and 20% in urban joggers have been recorded.

Although the incidence of poisoning has declined since the introduction of natural gas, it is still responsible for about 1500 deaths each year in England and Wales. In 1989 it was the single most common cause of death by poisoning in Scotland.

Pathophysiology

CO has an affinity for haemoglobin 200 – 250 times that of oxygen. In the past it was assumed that the principal effect of tissue hypoxia was caused by the consequent failure of oxygen delivery, however the degree of anoxia is now known to be greater than can be explained by the loss of oxygen-carrying capacity alone. The three major factors are now thought to be:

(a) Binding with haemoglobin (Hb) to form carboxy-haemoglobin (COHb), reducing the oxygen-carrying capacity and shifting the oxygen dissociation curve to the left (as above).
(b) In binding to Hb it produces a modification of the remaining oxygen binding sites, distorting the shape of the oxygen dissociation curve.
(c) At a tissue level it inhibits cellular respiration by binding with other haem proteins such as cytochrome oxidase.

Clinical features

The severity of poisoning depends on:

• Concentration of CO breathed.
• Duration of exposure.
• Level of activity of the victim.
• General health of the victim.

Chronic CO poisoning may present with vague symptoms ranging from flu-like illness, headache, malaise, abdominal pain and diarrhoea to almost every neurological syndrome ever described. In order to make the diagnosis it is necessary to have a high index of suspicion. COHb levels are not usually helpful.

Acute CO poisoning is usually recognized by the circumstances of the incident, clinical features ranging from headache to confusion, coma and death. Careful clinical examination is required which may include psychometric tests. The classic cherry-red appearance is not a reliable sign of poisoning.

Investigations

- COHb levels are an indication of exposure not of severity: it is possible to be comatose with a level of 20%. Therefore management decisions must be made on clinical status not COHb levels.
- ECG. Ischaemic changes are common; arrhythmias are uncommon.
- Chest radiograph. Baseline.
- ABG. Metabolic acidosis.
- U & E. Hypokalaemia may occur.
- Cardiac enzymes.

Treatment

The key to treatment is delivery of high concentrations of oxygen. The elimination half-life of CO is reduced from 250 minutes breathing air to 50 minutes breathing 100% oxygen and to 22 minutes breathing hyperbaric oxygen at 2.5 atmospheres.

- 100% oxygen via a tight-fitting face mask or endotracheal tube.
- Cardiovascular support including inotropes if indicated.
- Hyperbaric oxygen. Consider transfer to the nearest centre with hyperbaric oxygen if there is clinically severe poisoning, i.e. altered neurological function, confusion, disorientation, coma, chest pain, an abnormal ECG or metabolic acidosis. Partial resolution of minor symptoms despite oxygen therapy or a recurrence of symptoms after treatment is also an indication to consider hyperbaric treatment.

Outcome

If untreated, COHb levels over 66% are usually fatal. Neuropsychiatric problems, including intellectual impairment and memory loss, are common in survivors, but treatment with hyperbaric oxygen can reduce the frequency of this from 43% to less than 5%.

Further reading

Meredith T, Vale A. Carbon monoxide poisoning. *British Medical Journal*, 1988; **296**: 77–8.

Polson CJ, Green MA, Lee MR. *Clinical Toxicology*, London: Pitman Press, 1983.

Related topics of interest

Burns (p. 46)

Inhalation injuries (p. 172)

CARDIOPULMONARY RESUSCITATION

The *UK Resuscitation Council*, established in 1982, produces guidelines and recommendations on *basic life support* (BLS) and *advanced cardiac life support* (ACLS). They also coordinate an *Advanced Life Support Course* (established in 1993). The primary aim is to save human life by improving and coordinating standards of resuscitation in the UK.

The *European Resuscitation Council* (ERC), established in 1989, performs a similar function in Europe.

Survival from cardiac arrest is improved if:

- The event is witnessed.
- Bystander cardiopulmonary resuscitation is given.
- Ventricular fibrillation is the rhythm.
- Early defibrillation is given.

Basic life support

Basic life support (BLS) refers to airway maintainence and support of circulation without the use of equipment other than a simple airway. There is no evidence to date for the transmission of the human immunodeficiency or hepatitis B viruses during mouth-to-mouth ventilation, the ERC recommends that the use of simple and effective mouth-to-mouth barrier devices be taught in BLS.

Guidelines introduced in 1992 stress the importance of telephoning for help in adult cardiopulmonary arrest, since with BLS alone the chances are remote that spontaneous cardiac action will be restored.

The ERC recommends:

- Training in BLS should be compulsory in all European medical and dental schools and nurse training institutions.
- Hospitals within Europe should provide programmes to ensure that all hospital doctors remain up to date in the practice of BLS skills.
- Hospitals within Europe should provide programmes to ensure that all staff involved in direct patient care receive compulsory training and retraining in BLS skills.
- Similar accreditation should be in force for general medical and dental practitioners and other health care staff practising in the community.
- Emergency service personnel should receive in-service training and retraining in BLS.
- All professional drivers should be examined in BLS as part of their requalification test.

- In those countries in which road users are required to take a driving test, BLS testing should be part of that test.
- All European schools should include a graded programme of BLS training within their curriculum.

Advanced cardiac life support

Cardiac arrest occurs with four underlying disorders of heart rhythm:

(a) Ventricular fibrillation (VF).
(b) Pulseless ventricular tachycardia (usually degenerates into VF).
(c) Asystole.
(d) Electromechanical dissociation (EMD).

Ventricular fibrillation is the most important, as it is the most common cause of sudden cardiac death and is the most amenable to treatment. *Emphasis is now placed on:*

- Precordial thump
- Early defibrillation
- Antiarrhythmic drugs and alkalizing agents assuming a more background role

The BRESUS study

This multicentre study determined the circumstances, incidence and outcome of cardiopulmonary resuscitation (CPR) in 12 British hospitals and included 3765 patients in whom resuscitation was performed. In 927 patients CPR was initiated outside the hospital and in 580 it occurred in the accident and emergency (A & E) department. Patients were followed up for 1 year.

The study concluded that 71% of the deaths occurred during the initial resuscitation and that hospital resuscitation was life-saving, cost-effective and justified appropriate training.

The results of the study are summarized below:

- 12.5% survival overall.
- The average hospital had 30 one-year survivors each year:

  (a) Three who had an arrest outside hospital.
  (b) Seven in the A & E department.
  (c) Seven in the cardiac care unit (CCU).
  (d) Ten in the general wards.
  (e) Three in other, non-ward areas.

- Patients below age 65 who had a cardiac arrest in specialized hospital areas – A & E and CCU – had an

initial success rate of 57% and 1-year survival of 31%: much better than average.
- For every 1-year survivor there were eight attempted resuscitations, three initial survivors, two surviving at 24 hours and 1.5 leaving hospital alive.
- In patients who arrested in the pre-hospital setting, the survival rate after 1 year was only 40% of the study average survival. Prehospital arrest was also associated with greater attrition after 24 hours.

Further reading

A statement by the Basic Life Support Working Party of the European Resuscitation Council, 1992. *Guidelines for Basic Life Support. Resuscitation*, 1992; **24:** 103–10.

A statement by the Advanced Life Support Working Party of the European Resuscitation Council 1992. *Guidelines for Advanced Life Support. Resuscitation*, 1992; **24:**111–21.

Tunstall-Pedoe H, Bailey L, Chamberlain DA, Marsden AK, Ward ME, Zideman DA. Survey of 3765 cardiopulmonary resuscitations in British hospitals (the BRESUS study): methods and overall results. *British Medical Journal*, 1992; **304**:1347–51.

Related topics of interest

Airway (p. 7)
Drowning and near-drowning (p. 96)
Drug overdose and accidental poisoning (p. 99)
Electrical injury (p. 111)
Hypothermia (p. 168)
Intraosseous infusion (p. 177)
Organ donation (p. 231)

CEREBROVASCULAR SYNDROME – ACUTE

Acute stroke is a condition with 'rapidly developing clinical signs of focal (or global) disturbance of cerebral function, with symptoms lasting 24 hours or longer or leading to death, with no apparent cause other than of vascular origin'.

Stroke is the third commonest cause of death in the UK, accounting for 12% of all deaths, with over 100 000 first strokes occurring every year. The incidence of first ever stroke is 2 per 1000 population per year, with over half the patients aged over 70 years.

Risk factors for stroke include:

- Hypertension.
- Hypercholesterolaemia.
- Smoking.
- Increasing age.
- Male sex.
- Obesity.
- Diabetes.
- Oral contraception.

The main types of stroke are:

- Cerebral infarction   85%
- Primary cerebral haemorrhage   10%
- Subarachnoid haemorrhage   5%

Prognosis depends on the underlying cause. In cerebral infarction the mortality is 10%, with 25% of survivors being dependent at 1 year. With intracranial haemorrhage 50% of patients die within 30 days.

Aetiology	There are numerous causes of stroke:

- *Cerebral embolism*, e.g. carotid, vertebral and basilar arteriosclerosis.
- *Cardiac embolism*, e.g. post-myocardial infarction, mitral valve and atrial fibrillation.
- *Artherosclerosis*
- *Hypercoagulable states*, e.g. polycythaemia.
- *Small-vessel disease*, e.g. diabetes mellitus.
- *Haemodynamic stroke*, e.g. hypotension.
- *Vasculitis*.
- *Subarachnoid haemorrhage*.
- *Primary intracerebral haemorrhage*.

History	A history should establish the sudden onset of a focal neurological deficit and the associated risk factors such as heart disease and smoking.

Examination

The neurological examination may allow identification of the territory of the lesion, while the general examination should concentrate on the aetiology of the stroke, such as heart murmurs, carotid bruits and atrial fibrillation. The blood pressure should be taken both lying and standing and in both arms, as a significant difference suggests aortic dissection or subclavian steal.

Differential diagnosis includes:

- Space-occupying lesions

  (a) Subdural haematoma.
  (b) Cerebral tumour.
  (c) Cerebral abscess.

- Multiple sclerosis.
- Focal epilepsy.
- Intracranial vascular lesion such as an arteriovenous malformation.
- Migraine.
- Hypoglycaemia.
- Hysteria.

Investigations

The following investigations should be considered:

1. Blood glucose. To exclude hypoglycaemia or diabetes.

2. Full blood count and erythrocyte sedimentation rate (ESR).

3. Urea and electrolytes.

4. Blood lipids. Except in the very elderly.

5. Blood clotting tests. In all patients with cerebral haemorrhage. In young patients test for prothrombotic disorders including anticardiolipin antibodies, protein S and antithrombin III deficiency.

6. Syphilis serology.

7. Blood cultures. If bacterial endocarditis is suspected.

8. Autoantibody screening.

9. Sickling tests in appropriate ethnic groups.

10. Cardiac investigations

(a) *ECG.*

(b) *Chest radiography.*

(c) *Echocardiography* – indicated in patients with:
  - Abnormal cardiac findings on clinical examination, chest radiography or ECG.
  - Raised ESR or positive blood cultures, suggesting endocarditis.
  - Stroke in a young patient (aged < 40 years) with no obvious cause.

(d) *Carotid duplex scanning* – indicated in those with:
  - Transient ischaemic attack or CT-confirmed ischaemic stroke with good recovery.
  - Hemiparesis or monocular visual loss or aphasia (event in the carotid artery distribution).
  - Patients fit for carotid surgery.

(e) *Cerebral arterial angiography* – in those with greater than 70% stenosis.

11. CT scanning. This enables differentiation between ischaemic or haemorrhagic stroke and indications include:

- Doubt regarding the diagnosis.
- Need to exclude haemorrhage.
- Suspected cerebellar stroke with obstructive hydrocephalus. This most commonly presents with acute onset of unsteadiness with rapid deterioration, but with no focal neurology. Neurosurgical intervention can be life-saving.

Management

Admission to hospital in the acute phase of stroke allows appropriate investigation and treatment, however patients with transient ischaemic attacks (TIAs) and mild strokes with rapid recovery can be investigated as outpatients.

There is no treatment that should routinely be given to most patients with acute stroke.

- *Antiplatelet drugs (aspirin) and anticoagulants (heparin).* If a cardiac source for emboli is identified, and anticoagulants are used, treatment should be delayed for a few days after a small ischaemic stroke and for 1–2 weeks if there is a persistent neurological deficit. The risk of haemorrhage if given earlier is high. Consider anticoagulation in patients with frequent TIAs or stepwise progression or if an angiogram has shown thrombus in a major artery.

- *Thrombolytics.* Not recommended as yet for the acute ischaemic stroke.
- *Neuroprotective agents.* Calcium antagonists (nimodopine 60 mg 4-hourly) improve outcome after subarachnoid haemorrhage but have not shown clear benefit in ischaemic stroke
- *Others.* Glycerol, high-dose steroids and mannitol have shown no clear benefit.

Complications

1. Cerebral

(a) *Oedema.* If symptomatic use mannitol and hyperventilate.
(b) *Haemorrhagic transformation.* If symptomatic treat raised intracranial pressure (ICP) and consider neurosurgical evacuation of the haematoma.
(c) *Seizures.* Treat repetitive seizures or status epilepticus with anticonvulsants.
(d) *Depression.* Consider antidepressants.

2. Systemic

(a) *Hyperglycaemia.* Maintain normoglycaemia as hyperglycaemia is harmful.
(b) *Inappropriate antidiuretic hormone secretion.* If symptomatic restrict fluid intake.
(c) *Hypertension.* If associated with hypertensive encephalopathy or if the systolic blood pressure is persistently >200 mmHg or diastolic >120 mmHg, consider cautious lowering with oral agents such as labetolol and nifedipine.
(d) *Pyrexia.* Exclude infection and reduce core temperature.
(e) *Dysphagia.* Swallowing difficulties are best recognized to prevent aspiration.
(f) *Deep vein thrombosis.* Consider prophylaxis with subcutaneous low-dose heparin and antithromboembolism stockings.

3. Cardiac

(a) *ECG repolarization changes.* Monitor for arrhythmias.
(b) *Sudden cardiac death (6%).*

Further reading

Brown M. Cerebrovascular disease. *Medicine International*, 1992; **99:** 4158–67.
Oppenheimer S, Hachinski V. Complications of acute stroke. *Lancet*, 1992; **339:** 721–7.
Sandercock PA, Lindley RI. Management of acute stroke. *Prescribers' Journal*, 1993; **33:** 196–205.

Related topics of interest

Coma (p. 73)
Diabetic emergencies (p. 86)
Headache (p. 142)

CERVICAL SPINE – ACUTE NECK SPRAIN

The term *whiplash* was coined by Harold Crowe in 1928 and describes the *mechanism of injury* of hyperextension of the neck followed by forward flexion. It is often used incorrectly to refer to the cluster of symptoms that follows this event when the term acute neck sprain or soft-tissue injury is more appropriate (by definition bony damage and other serious injury are excluded). Injury occurs typically in a rear impact collision (almost twice as likely) but may also result from front or side impacts, and occurs in 15–30% of car accidents. Symptoms are delayed for up to 24 hours in up to half of those who injure their necks.

The incidence of neck sprains rose after the introduction of compulsory seat belts in January 1983. Head restraints protect the neck but only if designed and fitted correctly. The incidence by position is as follows:

- Front seat passenger (19%).
- Driver (15%).
- Rear seat passenger (10%).

The injury causes stretching of the muscles and ligaments of the neck, the severity of symptoms depending on the relative movements of the head and neck on the torso and the forces involved.

Symptoms

1. Cervical pain and stiffness which may extend into the shoulders and interscapular region.

2. Headache (82%), usually of the muscle contraction type, often associated with greater occipital neuralgia and less often temperomandibular joint syndrome.

3. Paraesthesiae in up to one-third, but less commonly cervical root radiculopathy, even in the absence of spondylosis.

4. Dizziness often occurs and can result from vestibular, central or cervical injury.

Management

There is no consensus on the treatment of acute neck sprain. A pragmatic approach is:

1. Ice for 24 hours followed by heat applications.

2. Analgesia or anti-inflammatory medication.

3. Application of a soft collar, which should be removed every few hours to allow gentle mobilization of the neck.

4. Early passive mobilization and a range of movement exercises to accelerate recovery.

5. Review a few days later. Those with persistent pain and neck stiffness need *physiotherapy* in combination with cautious mobilization and measures for pain relief. Physical therapy and transcutaneous nerve stimulation may be helpful in reducing pain and improving movement.

Prognosis

Disability occurs commonly after acute neck sprain, 26% of patients experiencing intermittent pain in the neck 1 year after injury and 4% experiencing continuous pain.

Litigation is common and raises the question of secondary gain in patients with persistent neck pain, but most patients are not cured by a verdict.

Poor prognostic features include:

- Objective neurological signs.
- Sharp reversal of the cervical lordosis on radiography.
- Restricted motion at one level on flexion/extension radiographs.
- The use of a cervical collar for more than 12 weeks.
- Relapse necessitating a further course of physiotherapy.
- Pre-existing degenerative changes.

Further reading

Evans R. Some observations on whiplash injuries. *Neurologic Clinics,* 1992; **10**: 975–97.

Related topics of interest

Analgesia (p. 20)
Spine and spinal cord trauma (p. 278)

CHEST PAIN

Acute chest pain is a common presentation to the accident and emergency department. Diagnosis may be difficult, but a detailed accurate history will reduce the risk of missing a potentially treatable condition. The differential diagnosis is extensive and includes:

- Myocardial ischaemia or infarction.
- Pericarditis.
- Dissecting aortic aneurysm.
- Pleurisy or pneumonia.
- Pneumothorax.
- Pulmonary embolism.
- Oesophageal pain (reflux, spasm, rupture).
- Peptic ulcer.
- Gall bladder inflammation.
- Chest wall (ribs, myalgia and herpes zoster) pain.
- Thoracic and cervical spine pain.

Dissecting aortic aneurysm

This typically occurs in middle-aged patients with a history of hypertension. It is associated with Marfan's syndrome and trauma.

The pain is severe, tearing in character and radiates through to the back.

A myocardial infarct may coexist with dissection if the coronary arteries are affected. If the carotid, vertebrobasilar or spinal arteries are involved then neurological symptoms and signs will be present. Haematuria, intestinal ischaemia or bowel infarction may occur.

Loss of peripheral pulses or inequality of blood pressure between the arms and aortic regurgitation support the diagnosis. A haemopericardium may result in a pericardial rub or cardiac tamponade.

A chest radiograph reveals a widened mediastinum, but further investigation with *echocardiography* (transoesophageal), *CT scanning* or *aortography* is necessary.

Treatment takes two forms:

(a) *Medical* – relieve pain with intravenous opiates and reduce elevated blood pressure.
(b) *Surgical* – refer the patient immediately to the cardiothoracic surgeons for repair.

Pulmonary embolism   This is defined as obstruction of pulmonary arterial vessels by thrombus, which usually originates from the deep systemic vessels. In the UK approximately 20 000 patients die each year in hospital from it, and 40 000 have non-fatal episodes. Predisposing factors include:

- Major trauma.
- Recent surgery.
- Obesity.
- Immobility.
- Smoking.
- Increasing age.
- Malignant disease, oral contraception and pregnancy.
- Hypercoagulable states.

1. History

(a) *Acute minor emboli* often result in a pulmonary infarction. Symptoms include tachypnoea, pleuritic chest pain and haemoptysis. Examination is often normal, but may reveal a tachycardia, pleural rub and mild pyrexia.
(b) *Acute large emboli* cause central chest pain and dyspnoea with cyanosis, tachycardia, hypotension and a raised jugular venous pressure. If sudden and severe, syncope and death may occur.

2. Investigations

(a) The *ECG* can show:
  - Sinus tachycardia.
  - Right-axis deviation.
  - Right atrial P waves.
  - Right bundle branch block.
  - Right ventricular hypertrophy.
  - Classically the S1, Q3, T3 pattern in 25%.
  - Atrial fibrillation.

(b) *Chest radiographic* features are usually non-specific but useful to exclude other diagnoses such as pneumonia and pneumothorax. Findings include oligaemia (with central embolus) or linear or wedge-shaped shadows (with peripheral emboli) and small pleural effusion.
(c) *Isotope radionuclide ventilation–perfusion lung scan.* A normal scan rules out a pulmonary embolus.

(d) *Pulmonary angiography.* The gold standard and useful in difficult cases if available.

3. Treatment

(a) *Acute minor.* Oxygen, analgesia, heparin and warfarin.
(b) *Acute major.* Resuscitation with oxygen. If the patient is hypotensive, haemodynamic monitoring to allow restoration of the central venous pressure with colloid is necessary. Consider inotropic support.

- *Thrombolysis.* Unless contraindicated a loading dose of streptokinase 250 000 – 600 000 IU should be given over 30 minutes followed by 100 000 IU/hour for up to 72 hours, followed by warfarin.
- *Pulmonary embolectomy.* For the small group of patients who have contraindications to thrombolysis with massive emboli. Pulmonary angiography allows the site and extent of thrombus to be visualized.

Pericarditis

Typical pericardial pain is continuous, retrosternal and sharp and is relieved by sitting up and leaning forwards. A *pericardial friction rub* (often louder in inspiration) is a characteristic physical finding.

1. Investigations

(a) The *ECG* may reveal symmetrically raised ST segments (concave upwards), supraventricular ectopics, atrial flutter or atrial fibrillation.
(b) *Chest radiography* is usually normal, but may reveal cardiac enlargement.
(c) An *echocardiogram* will detect a pericardial effusion.

An underlying cause should be considered. Look for evidence of co-existent myocarditis. Causes of pericarditis include:

- Myocardial infarct.
- Viral infection.
- Rheumatic fever.
- Pyogenic infection.
- Tuberculosis.
- Neoplasm.
- Connective tissue disorders.

2. Treatment. Idiopathic acute pericarditis is self-limiting and requires symptomatic treatment. As it may coexist with myocarditis, the patient should rest. Pain relief with a non-steroidal anti-inflammatory drug may be necessary. Pericardial effusions may require drainage. Arrhythmias are treated conventionally. Specific treatment depends on the cause.

Gastrointestinal pain
Reflux oesophagitis causes a burning retrosternal pain that is exacerbated by eating and stooping and relieved by antacids.

Spontaneous rupture of the oesophagus following vomiting (Boerhaave's syndrome) results in severe, central pain, often radiating to the back. It may be associated with haematemesis and surgical emphysema. The chest radiograph reveals a widened mediastinum, pneumomediastinum and classically a hydropneumothorax. A *gastrograffin swallow* will confirm the diagnosis. Treatment is surgical.

Peptic ulcer and gall bladder inflammation may also cause gastrointestinal pain and should be excluded.

Further reading

Hampton J. The patient with chest pain and breathlessness. *Medicine International*, 1993; **21:** 288–329.

Related topics of interest

CHILD ABUSE

Child abuse (non-accidental injury, NAI) is the act of harm to a child by parent, relative, sibling, carer or other person either as a direct act or by a failure to provide proper care or protection or both. There are about 40 000 children on child protection registers in England, a prevalence of 3.5 per 1000 children. The mortality rate is not known as cases may go undetected.

Types of abuse

- Neglect.
- Physical injury.
- Sexual abuse.
- Emotional abuse.

The role of the A & E department is to identify potential cases and to activate local procedures for the protection of the child. Confirmation of the diagnosis is usually only made after a multidisciplinary investigation and case conference.

Features of NAI

- Failure to seek or delay in seeking medical attention.
- Vague or inconsistent history.
- Injury not consistent with history.
- The child is sad, withdrawn or frozen.
- Abnormal relationship between child and parent.
- Inappropriate parental behaviour.
- Attendance out of usual catchment area.
- A clear history of abuse may be given.

None of these features is itself diagnostic of NAI, but the presence of one or more should raise the possibility.

Common injuries

1. Burns

- Scalds will map out the involved regions, e.g. feet and buttocks after immersion in hot water.
- Brands.
- Cigarette burns.
- Radiation burns.
- Friction burns.

2. Fractures. When caused by NAI fractures usually present before the child is able to walk. A skeletal survey to detect multiple fractures should only be performed after discussion with a consultant paediatrician.

Osteogenesis imperfecta and birth-related injury may be mistaken for NAI. Features suggesting abuse are:

- Multiple fractures, often at different stages of healing.
- Single fractures with multiple bruises.
- Rib fractures.
- Spiral long bone fractures in infants.

3. Head injury. This is the single most important cause of death following NAI. There is no characteristic mechanism of injury, but shaking, swinging, hurling, pushing or direct blows may all result in brain injury and intracerebral bleeding. Skull fractures may not be present. A torn upper lip frenulum and retinal haemorrhages are highly suggestive of NAI.

4. Asphyxia. This may present as apnoea attack (especially if recurrent), cot death or near-miss cot death.

Management

A detailed history should be obtained from the child and all other available sources. All children should be completely undressed and fully examined, but internal examinations should be omitted. If NAI is suspected then local procedures must be followed. In most centres it is the duty consultant paediatrician who will assess the child in A & E, arrange further care and perform internal examinations if indicated.

The Children Act 1989

This sets out a comprehensive code of law regarding children and replaces or limits previous statutes.

Principles

- *Paramountcy* of the child's welfare.
- *Parental responsibility.*
- *Judicial non-interference*: courts cannot make an order unless to do so would be better than no order.
- *No delay* in court proceedings.
- *Welfare.* Courts must consider the range of powers available, the child's wishes, feelings and needs, actual or potential harm, the effect a change of circumstances will have and the capacity of others to meet the child's needs.

Further reading

An Introduction to the Children Act 1989. London: HMSO, 1989.
Meadow R, ed. *ABC of Child Abuse*. London: BMJ Publishing Group, 1989.

Related topics of interest

Burns (p. 46)
Fractures – principals of treatment (p. 125)
Limping child (p. 186)
Sudden infant death syndrome (p. 283)

COMA

Coma (Greek for a deep sleep) is defined as a prolonged state of unconsciousness. Consciousness is maintained by activity of the reticular formation in the brain stem, and thus coma is due to global suppression of nerve function or a lesion in the brain stem.

Coma is best assessed using the *Glasgow Coma Scale*, and a total score of *8 or less indicates coma*. Since all patients in coma have their eyes closed and do not speak, the nature of the motor response is the best guide to the depth of coma. The common causes of coma are listed below:

(a) *Structural brain damage*
  - Tumour.
  - Haematoma (traumatic, spontaneous).
  - Trauma.
  - Infarction.
  - Infection (abscess, encephalitis, meningitis, cerebral malaria).

(b) *Metabolic disorders*
  - Hypoxia.
  - Hypoglycaemia and hyperglycaemia.
  - Renal and hepatic failure.
  - Hypothermia and hyperthermia.

(c) *Drugs*
  - Alcohol.
  - Sedatives, narcotics and hypnotics.
  - Carbon monoxide.

(d) *Endocrine*
  - Diabetic coma.
  - Hypopituitarism.
  - Hypothyroidism.
  - Adrenal cortical failure.

(e) *Miscellaneous*
  - Epilepsy.
  - Hysteria.
  - Hypertension.

History

As full a history as available should be taken, but the unconscious patient requires treatment prior to attempting diagnosis. Whatever the aetiology, the patient may suffer further deterioration owing to airway obstruction, respiratory depression or circulatory failure.

Examination

1. Respiratory pattern

- *Cheyne–Stokes* suggests bilateral hemisphere lesions or a high brain-stem lesion.
- *Sustained deep breathing* suggests a midbrain lesion.
- *Irregular breathing* with deep sighing breaths suggests pontine or medullary lesions.

2. Head. Examine for evidence of head injury.

3. Neck. Look for signs of meningism, except in cases of suspected cervical injury.

4. ENT. Examine for signs of a basal skull fracture or infection.

5. Tongue. May have been bitten during an epileptic fit.

6. Breath. May reveal alcohol, acetone, uraemia or hepatic fetor.

7. Skin. Examine for:

- Injection sites of addict or diabetic.
- Pupura of meningococcal septicaemia.
- Spider naevi, palmar erythema, jaundice of liver failure.
- Pigmentation of Addison's.
- Cherry-red colour of carbon monoxide poisoning.
- Coarse, dry skin of myxoedema.
- Fine, supple skin in hypopituitarism.

8. Neurological

(a) *Focal neurology:*
   - Facial asymmetry.
   - Limb weakness.
   - Plantar responses.
   - Corneal reflexes.
   - Deep tendon reflexes.

(b) *Pupils.* Examine pupil size and reaction to light:
   - *Fixed dilated pupils.* Irreversible brain damage, drugs (atropine, adrenaline).
   - *Unilateral dilatation with fixed pupil.* Tentorial herniation, III nerve palsy, rapidly expanding ipsilateral lesion (e.g. subdural), epileptic seizures.

- *Pinpoint fixed pupils.* Opiate poisoning, barbiturates, organophosphates, metabolic disorders.
- *Small reactive pupils.* Metabolic disorders, pontine lesion.
- *Fixed mid-size pupils.* High midbrain lesion.

(c) *Fundi*
- Papilloedema.
- Hypertensive retinopathy.
- Subhyaloid haemorrhage.

(d) *Eye deviation.* In cerebral lesions the eyes deviate towards a destructive lesion and away from an irritative lesion. In brain-stem lesions, the eyes deviate away from a destructive lesion.

Investigations

1. Hypoglycaemia. The blood glucose must be checked immediately using a BM Stix test in every unconscious patient. Hypoglycaemia is reversed with intravenous glucose or glucagon. Plasma glucose is taken prior to treatment to confirm the diagnosis.

2. Arterial blood gases.

3. Drug screen. A rapid drug screen for alcohol, aspirin and paracetamol is appropriate. Consider a complete toxicological screen if clinically indicated. Specifically consider *opiate toxicity*. A trial of *naloxone* should be given to those patients with suspected opiate toxicity.

4. Others. U&E, plasma osmolality, FBC, LFTs, blood smears for parasites, blood ammonia, urinary metabolic screen and other drug analysis as necessary. *Chest radiography* and/or CT may be required.

Outcome

Recovery is often complete from life-threatening coma secondary to metabolic disorders or drugs. Structural lesions have a poorer prognosis. Prevention of secondary brain damage from hypoxia, hypotension or hypoglycaemia is important so as not to worsen prognosis.

Further reading

Advanced Life Support Group. Coma. In: *Advanced Paediatric Life Support. The Practical Approach.* London: BMJ Publishing Group, 1993: 111–20.
Jennett B. Coma. *Medicine International*, 1992; **99**: 4120–3.

Related topics of interest

COMPARTMENT SYNDROME

Compartment syndrome is any condition in which high pressure within a closed fascial space (muscle compartment) reduces capillary blood perfusion below the level necessary for tissue viability. It may be acute or chronic and can be secondary to a variety of causes. The leg and forearm muscles are most frequently involved, with 45% due to fractures.

The lower extremity consists of four compartments:

(a) Anterior (most commonly affected).
(b) Lateral.
(c) Deep posterior.
(d) Superficial posterior.

The forearm consists of two compartments:

(a) Volar (most commonly affected).
(b) Dorsal.

However, any limited osseofascial space may be affected, including the hand, foot, thigh, shoulder and buttocks.

Causes

1. Decreased compartment size

- Tight-fitting dressing and/or plaster of Paris.
- Thermal injury and frostbite.
- Application of military anti-shock trousers.

2. Increased compartment size

(a) *Primarily oedema accumulation*
- Post-ischaemic swelling.
- Drug overdose or other unconscious limb compression.
- Thermal injury and frostbite.
- Intensive muscle use (exercise, seizures).
- Venous disease.
- Venomous snakebite.
(b) *Primarily haemorrhage accumulation*
- Coagulation disorders e.g. disseminated intravascular coagulation, haemophilia.
- Anticoagulation.
- Arterial injury.
(c) *Combination of oedema and haemorrhage*
- Fracture.
- Soft-tissue injury or muscle tear, including crush injuries.

Pathophysiology

The compartments are confined by osseofascial boundaries. Within these compartments, tissue perfusion is dependent upon the balance of hydrostatic and oncotic pressures across the capillary membranes. Significant pathophysiological changes occur when intracompartmental pressures are greater than $30 - 40 \, mmHg$. This compromises the circulation, which leads to ischaemic changes in the muscles and nerve. Anoxic capillary damage with resultant leakage is the major cause of post-ischaemic swelling. When the damaged area is reperfused, large quantities of fluids can leak into the compartment. Myoglobin and potassium released from dying muscle cells will be absorbed and may lead to renal failure and/or cardiac dysfunction. Eventually various amounts of muscle regenerate and fibrous tissue replacement occurs, leading to a contracture deformity.

The precise pressure and time thresholds for irreversible nerve or muscle injury are not defined and thus criteria for surgical decompression are controversial.

Diagnosis

Diagnosis on clinical grounds is difficult, therefore a high index of clinical suspicion required. Early findings of acute compartment syndrome can be summarized by the *'six Ps'*. Additionally, swelling, tenseness and tenderness on palpation of the involved compartment may be present.

- *Pain* is the most important symptom and is a deep, aching and unrelenting feeling of pressure. The pain is frequently out of proportion to the primary injury, and is often exacerbated by passive stretch of the affected muscle group.
- *Pressure.*
- *Paresis.*
- *Paraesthesia* is a common early finding, while anaesthesia is a late finding.
- *Pink colour.*
- *Pulses* are generally present because central arterial flow is rarely occluded.

The differential diagnosis includes:

- Vascular occlusion.
- Neuropraxia or other nerve injury.

Investigation

Objective measurement of the intracompartment pressure is essential for accurate diagnosis. The normal resting compartment pressure is 4 ± 4 mmHg. Most methods involve the transmission of intramuscular hydrostatic pressure in a fluid medium to a pressure transducer. There are four types of device:

(a) The needle manometer.
(b) The slit catheter.
(c) The wick catheter.
(d) The electronic digital fluid pressure monitor.

Indications for fasciotomy are controversial:

- A compartment pressure of more than 30 mmHg represents a relative indication for immediate fasciotomy in normotensive patients.
- An alternative criterion is based on a critical difference between blood pressure and the compartment pressure that is necessary for a compartment to be adequately perfused (ΔP):

ΔP = mean arterial blood pressure - compartment pressure

A safe ΔP is 40–50 mmHg.

Treatment

Treatment is aimed at reducing the intracompartment pressure and improving tissue perfusion.

- Remove any compressive elements that may themselves be adequate to decompress the limb.
- Measure the compartment pressure if suspicion exists. Repeated or continuous measurement may be necessary. Extreme elevation of the limb should be avoided as this may result in decreased distal arterial pressure and diminished tissue perfusion.
- Check the serum potassium, U&E and the urine for myoglobin.
- Keep the patient well hydrated and monitor for systemic effects such as renal impairment or cardiac dysfunction.
- Surgery must be definitive and adequate to decompress the entire compartment. An intraoperative compartment pressure measurement may be useful to assess adequacy.

Further reading

Murbarak SJ, Pedowitz RA, Hargens AR. Compartment syndrome. *Current Orthopaedics*, 1989; **3**: 36–40.

Ward KR. *Critical Decisions in Emergency Medicine*, Vol. 5, Lesson 16, Compartment syndrome. Dallas: American College of Emergency Physicians, 1990: 125–33.

Related topics of interest

CONVULSIONS

A convulsion is the clinical manifestation of disordered cerebral activity. The exact nature of the seizure depends on the anatomical location of the neuronal activity. A generalized motor seizure is commonly called a grand mal fit. Status epilepticus represents a prolonged seizure or series of seizures without interval recovery. If untreated, fits can lead to further cerebral damage due to hypoxia, hypercarbia, lactic acidosis, hypoglycaemia and hyperpyrexia.

Management

The principle of treatment is to:

(a) *Control the fit.* Diazemuls 5 to 10 mg i.v. Repeat if the patient is still fitting at 5 minutes or has a second seizure.
(b) *Prevent hypoxia.* Oxygen via a face mask.
(c) *Seek an underlying treatable cause*:

- Hypoglycaemia. Check urinary glucose with BM Stix. If it is low take blood for glucose determination and administer 50 ml of 50% dextrose i.v.
- Meningitis. Consider if there has been a prodromal illness, recent fever, photophobia, neck stiffness or rash. Take blood cultures and commence chemotherapy.
- Rigors due to sepsis.
- Subarachnoid haemorrhage.
- Eclampsia.
- Metabolic disorders such as uraemia, Addison's disease, hyperosmolar states or fluid and electrolyte disorders.
- Alcohol withdrawal.
- Hypertensive encephalopathy.
- Non-compliance – consider serum anticonvulsant levels.

Disposal

Most known epileptic patients who have had a short fit not associated with head injury and in whom there has been a full recovery may be discharged, providing there is a responsible adult to look after them. Consider admission for a first fit or if an underlying cause may be present, following or causing a head injury or if the patient has not fully recovered.

Status epilepticus

Initial management is as above. If the patient does not respond, start an intravenous infusion of saline and monitor the ECG, BP and oxygen saturation. Consider:

- Chlormethiazole i.v. infusion.
- Phenytoin, slow i.v. injection (beware cardiovascular collapse) with an appropriate loading dose.
- General anaesthesia if seizure continues.

Further reading

So EL. Update on epilepsy. *The Medical Clinics of North America*, 1993; **77**: 203–14.

Related topics of interest

DELIBERATE SELF-HARM

Deliberate self-harm (DSH) is intentional self-injury by either poisoning or trauma irrespective of motive. The term is more appropriate than attempted suicide, which implies an intention which is not always present.

Epidemiology

Rates for admission to hospital following acts of deliberate self-harm have fallen during the 1980s. The reasons for this are unknown. It is most common in young adults, females, those in lower socioeconomic groups, the divorced or unmarried and teenage brides.

Causes

Compared with the general population DSH patients are four times more likely to have had a stressful life event in the 6 months prior to the episode, e.g. bereavement, unemployment, divorce, etc. Common precipitating events are:

- Argument with partner.
- Sexual rejection.
- Illness of close family member.
- Court appearance.
- Physical illness.

Predisposing factors

Many patients have a background history of long-term health, work or relationship problems. Fifty per cent of men and 25% of women admit to infidelity. Unemployment, personality disorders, alcohol and drug dependency and a psychiatric disorder which often falls short of full-blown depressive illness are all predisposing conditions.

Motive

The motive is usually mixed and difficult to identify with precision. Only a minority of patients admit to premeditation, and only about 25% say they actually wanted to die at the time of the act. There is often an attempt to influence somebody else.

Types

1. Deliberate self-poisoning. This accounts for 90% of cases of DSH. It usually results from drug overdosage, commonly anxiolytics, paracetamol (which is particularly dangerous because of delayed hepatotoxicity) and antidepressants.

2. Deliberate self-injury accounts for 10% of cases of DSH. The commonest form of injury is laceration, however jumping from heights or in front of trains, drowning, shooting and self-immolation also occur.

3. Deliberate self-laceration presents with:

- Deep dangerous wounds with true suicidal intent.
- Acts of self-mutilation.
- Superficial (often multiple wounds) not endangering life. These are especially common in patients with severe personality disorders and in those with low self-esteem and with impulsive, aggressive personalities. Patients are often young, have difficulty maintaining relationships and abuse drugs or alcohol.

Assessment

The aims of assessment are to determine:

- The risk of immediate suicide.
- The risk of subsequent deliberate self-harm or completed suicide.
- Social or medical problems.

Factors suggesting suicidal intent include planning, precautions to prevent discovery, no attempt to seek help, known fatal or violent method and organizing affairs (making a will or leaving a note).

Factors suggesting subsequent likelihood of completed suicide include evidence of serious intent (as above), depressive illness, drug abuse, personality disorder (especially if antisocial), social isolation and unemployment. Older males are particularly at risk.

Disposal

Those patients requiring medical or surgical admission should be referred to the appropriate specialty. However, those who pose a significant risk to themselves or others or who appear to have a psychiatric illness should have formal psychiatric assessment. Patients who fall into this category but who do not wish to stay or state intention of completed suicide may be detained under common law while awaiting a Mental Health Act assessment by psychiatrists. No patient should be discharged without being offered community follow-up, by a psychiatrist, community organization or general practitioner depending on the patient's need and local availability of services.

Outcome

Between 15 and 25% of patients will repeat the act of deliberate self-harm in the first year. The risk of repetition increases if there is an underlying psychiatric illness, anti-personality disorder or alcohol or drug abuse and in those with a criminal record. The risk of subsequent completed suicide is 1–2% in the first year (100 times the rate of the general population). A non-dangerous episode of self-harm such as oral contraceptive overdosage does not necessarily indicate a low risk of subsequent suicide.

Further reading

Gelder M, Gath D, Mayou R. *Oxford Textbook of Psychiatry*. Oxford: Oxford University Press, 1989: 478–506.

Related topics of interest

DIABETIC EMERGENCIES

Diabetes mellitus affects 3–7% of the population. The diagnosis is usually made on clinical grounds with biochemical confirmation. In *symptomatic patients* (symptoms include polyuria, polydipsia and weight loss) a single fasting (overnight and for more than 10 hours) or random venous plasma glucose level is often diagnostic. The patient is diabetic if:

• Fasting plasma glucose ≥ 7.8 mmol/l or
• Random plasma glucose ≥ 11.1 mmol/l.

In *asymptomatic patients* diabetes is unlikely if:

• Fasting glucose < 5.5 mmol/l or
• Random glucose ≤ 7.8 mmol/l.

The disease is classified into five categories:

(a) *Insulin-dependent diabetes mellitus.*
(b) *Non-insulin-dependent diabetes mellitus*
    • Non-obese.
    • Obese.
(c) *Malnutrition-related diabetes mellitus.*
(d) *Secondary*
    • Pancreatic disease.
    • Hormonal aetiology.
    • Drug induced.
    • Abnormalities of insulin or its receptors.
    • Genetic.
    • Other.
(e) *Gestational diabetes mellitus.*

Hypoglycaemia

Symptoms and signs   Symptoms and signs are secondary to the *neurogly-copenic* or *neurohumoral (autonomic)* responses.
Symptoms include:

• *Neuroglycopenic*
  Dizziness.
  Confusion.
  Tiredness.
  Speech difficulties.
  Impaired concentration.
  Drowsiness.

- *Autonomic*
  Tremor.
  Sweating.
  Anxiety.
  Nausea.
  Palpitations.

Signs include:

- Sweating.
- Pallor.
- Tachycardia.
- Tremor.
- Aggressive/irrational behaviour.
- Decreased conscious level.

Neurological sequelae include seizures and focal defects. Permanent neurological deficit may occur after prolonged hypoglycaemia. Recurrent severe hypoglycaemic episodes may impair intellectual function.

Precipitants of hypoglycaemia include:

- Missed, delayed or inadequate meal.
- Excess exercise.
- Timing error or excess dose of insulin.
- Alcohol intake.

Hypoglycaemic unawareness occurs in 25% of long-standing diabetics and is due to impaired adrenergic responses. There is no current evidence to suggest that human insulin increases this phenomenon.

Sulphonylureas (which stimulate insulin secretion), with a long half life (e.g. chlorpropamide), a prolonged action on the β-cells (e.g. glibenclamide) or excreted via the kidneys (if there is renal impairment) are prone to cause hypoglycaemia.

Treatment

If hypoglycaemia is clinically suspected, rapidly check the blood sugar with a BM Stix and treat if hypoglycaemia is present, having first taken a blood specimen for formal estimation. Hypoglycaemia is unusual unless the plasma glucose is less than 2.5 mmol/l, however the threshold varies from patient to patient, e.g. a diabetic with prolonged hyperglycaemia may experience symptoms if the plasma glucose is rapidly lowered towards a normal level. Rapidly reverse the hypoglycaemia. Determine the cause of the episode and give appropriate advice.

Mild episodes are treated by giving the patient a sugared drink (e.g. three or four lumps of sugar with a little water), which may be repeated 10 – 15 minutes later. This will raise blood glucose rapidly. The patient should then eat some biscuits.

Severe episodes may be treated using:

(a) *Glucose gel* applied to the buccal lining.
(b) *Glucagon.* Glucagon mobilizes hepatic glycogen stores and thus is not effective in the starved patient. It is useful in the combative patient or other patients with poor venous access.

- *Dose.* 1 mg i.v., i.m. or s.c.
- *Contraindications.* Insulinoma, phaeochromocytoma and glucagonoma.
- *Side-effects.* Nausea, vomiting, rarely hypersensitivity reactions.

(c) *Glucose*

- *Dose.* Glucose 50% i.v., up to 50 ml, into a large vein. This dose may need to be repeated. An infusion of 5% or 10% glucose may be needed to maintain normoglycaemia.
- *Side-effects.* Hypertonic and may cause venous irritation and thrombophlebitis.

Patients with hypoglycaemia secondary to sulphonylurea ingestion should be admitted to hospital as prolonged hypoglycaemia is likely.

Children are treated with 10% glucose 5 ml/kg, as higher concentrations of glucose may cause hyperglycaemia.

Diabetic ketoacidosis

This complication of diabetes mellitus may result from failure to take adequate doses of insulin or present as the first manifestation of diabetes. The patients are typically hyperglycaemic but not always. The mortality in specialist units is < 5%. Causes of death include hypokalaemia, cerebral oedema and the precipitating illness (such as an infection, aspiration or myocardial infarct). The differential diagnosis includes alcoholic ketoacidosis, hyperglycaemic hyperosmolar coma and hypoglycaemic coma.

Symptoms and signs Polydipsia, polyuria and unexplained weight loss are the cardinal symptoms. The patient is dehydrated owing to osmotic diuresis, with Kussmaul's breathing and acetone on the breath. The patient may have a depressed level of consciousness or be in coma (10%). Nausea, vomiting and abdominal pain may result. Hypothermia may be an associated finding. Signs of infection or other precipitant should be sought.
Complications include:

- Cerebral oedema.
- Venous thrombosis.
- Rhabdomyolysis.
- Aspiration.

Investigations *1. Plasma glucose.* This is typically elevated about 25 mmol/l but may be normal.

2. Urinalysis. Marked glycosuria and ketonuria.

3. Acid–base balance. Arterial blood gases should be measured. Acidosis with an elevated plasma anion gap is expected. To confirm the identity of the anion, serum ketones should be measured. The nitroprusside test (Acetest or Ketostix on plasma or urine) measures acetoacetate and acetone, but not hydroxybutyrate. If ketones are not present, then diagnoses such as renal failure and poisoning with methanol or ethylene glycol need to be considered.

4. Electrolytes.

(a) *Sodium* concentration is expected to be low owing to the shift of water out of the intracellular fluid because of the osmotic effects of glucose. The Na^+ concentration is expected to fall by 2.4 mmol/l for every 10 mmol/l rise in the plasma glucose. If, after this correction, the Na^+ concentration is below 140 mmol/l, free water should be restricted. If it is higher, care must be taken to avoid hypernatraemia.

(b) *Potassium* concentration is usually around 5 mmol/l. There is, however, an overall total body deficit of K^+ because of the osmotic diuresis.

(c) *Urea and creatinine* may be altered as a result of prerenal effects or pre-existing diabetic nephropathy. Creatinine may be falsely elevated in some assays.

5. *Blood, urine and sputum cultures.*

6. *Chest radiography.*

7. *ECG.*

Treatment

Pay attention to the ABCs and monitor in a high-dependency area.

1. Extracellular fluid volume replacement. Initially rapidly infuse 1–2 litres of normal saline over the first hour, and then according to clinical assessment. Central venous pressure monitoring may be required. A large-volume deficit may be present, but once the tissues are adequately perfused half-strength normal saline is required.

2. Hyperglycaemia. In the absence of hypokalaemia, soluble insulin should be added to the intravenous fluids as an initial bolus of 0.1 units/kg, followed by an infusion of 0.1 units/kg/h. Once the glucose is < 14 mmol/l, glucose (5–10%) with insulin is infused to maintain plasma glucose at 10–14 mmol/l.

3. Potassium. Supplements are required if the K^+ concentration falls below 4.5 mmol/l, or 5 mmol/l if the patient is excreting urine rapidly. It is given in a concentration of 10–40 mmol/l initially. Once insulin is started and the patient is passing urine, potassium can be given at the following hourly rate:

- 20 mmol/l if K^+ 4–5 mmol/l.
- 40 mmol/l if K^+ 3–4 mmol/l.
- 40–60 mmol/l if K^+ 3 mmol/l.

4. Acidosis. The use of bicarbonate is controversial and should be decided by the specialist team. The dangers include hypokalaemia, Na^+ load, increased carbon dioxide production, late metabolic acidosis and cerebral oedema.

5. A nasogastric tube is required in the nauseated, vomiting or unconscious patient. Gastric atony and retention are common.

6. A urinary catheter is required in the comatose or incontinent patient or the patient who has not passed urine.

7. Treat any *underlying cause* such as sepsis, myocardial infarction, trauma, etc.

Hyperosmolar non-ketotic coma

This typically occurs in non-insulin-dependent diabetics. It is often associated with a precipitant such as sepsis and drugs such as diuretics.

Dehydration is very severe, and profound hyperglycaemia with an associated hyperosmolar state but without ketosis and acidosis distinguishes the condition from ketoacidosis.

Treatment is initially the same as for ketoacidosis but:

• Dehydration is more profound and careful fluid balance is essential.
• Hypotonic saline is preferred.
• Less insulin is required.

Thrombotic events are common and prophylactic anticoagulation is necessary.

Complications of diabetes

1. Ocular. Retinopathy, cataracts, vitreous haemorrhage.

2. Neurological. Peripheral neuropathy, mononeuritis multiplex, autonomic neuropathy and cerebrovascular accident.

3. Renal. Hypertension, nephropathy, pyelonephritis and renal failure.

4. Vascular. Small- and large-vessel disease may cause ischaemia of the myocardium, brain, kidneys and feet.

5. Dermatological. Fat atrophy, fat hypertrophy, ulcers, infections, xanthomata and necrobiosis lipoidica diabeticorum.

6. Infections. Urinary tract infections, *Candida*, pneumonia, tuberculosis and cutaneous infection.

Further reading

Amiel SA. Hypoglycaemia in diabetes mellitus. *Medicine International*, 1993; **21:** 279–81.

Goguen JM, Josse RG. Management of diabetic ketoacidosis. *Medicine International*, 1993; **21:** 275–8.

Related topics of interest

Alcohol-related problems (p. 9)
Coma (p. 73)
Endocrine emergencies (p. 115)

DISASTER PLANNING

Disasters are incidents (natural or man-made) on a scale sufficient to overwhelm a community by physically and psychologically traumatizing its population and devastating its homes and businesses. Contingency planning should optimize resources, personnel and facilities to enable a community to respond as efficiently as possible.

Major disasters

The phases of a response include:

- Initial response.
- Search and rescue.
- Triage.
- Establishing a casualty clearing station.
- Transportation.
- Treatment in A & E departments and hospitals.
- Establishing a temporary mortuary.
- Record keeping.
- Post-disaster actions.

Major disaster plan

To have a successful *major disaster plan* hospitals need to:

- Document the potential disasters that may occur within their own area or in adjacent areas.
- Develop a flexible protocol to respond to each of these disasters with an organized, realistic plan that uses existing resources.
- Establish communication and cooperation with regional disaster agencies.
- Carry out disaster drills to rehearse and evaluate the plans. These may range from a tabletop exercise to a full rehearsal in the field with simulated patients. A realistic exercise allows the major disaster plan to be accurately and objectively evaluated by impartial observers. Practise, evaluate and update the plan on a regular basis.
- Educate the public about the correct response to a disaster.
- Test communications equipment. A frequent difficulty encountered is communication failure due to equipment malfunction or human error. Accurate information from the scene is essential for predicting demand and communicating with victims, relatives and the media.
- Anticipate the need for supplies, both basic, e.g. food and blankets, and esoteric, e.g. specific antidotes to

toxic chemicals, and arrange for these to be transported and distributed optimally.

- Establish mobile medical teams which can operate on site. These require experienced personnel, who must be fully equipped, easily identifiable and able to work well within their own team and with the other teams in the prehospital setting. Regular training will overcome the difficulties of working in unusual environments.
- Be aware of the potential and limitations of sophisticated search and rescue equipment, which is continually being developed.
- Accurately document events. Patients must be correctly identified and their location recorded. Mobile teams should try to provide the receiving hospital with a record of the condition of the victims, detailing treatment and response to treatment.
- Have a triage procedure. Triage in a disaster is based on the likelihood of survival, given the resources available at the time. The mobile medical team assesses each patient's injuries and designates priorities for treatment and extrication. Three factors helpful in decision making are:

  (a) The patient's condition and accessibility.
  (b) The availability of personnel, time and supplies.
  (c) The presence of actual and potential dangers.

- Know that psychological trauma is an important cause of morbidity. Potential victims of *post-traumatic stress* include families and close friends of the deceased, the injured, non-injured participants, spectators, rescue workers and other members of the community whose lives have been affected or disrupted. The provision of social and psychological support should be included in major incident planning.
- Have a procedure for the recovery, transportation and final disposition of the dead as well as the collection of forensic evidence.

Further reading

Miles S. ABC of major trauma. Major accidents. *British Medical Journal*, 1990; **301**: 919–23.
Waeckerle, J.F. Disaster planning and response. *New England Journal of Medicine* 1991; **324**: 815–21.

Related topics of interest

Major injuries – Royal College of Surgeons of England Report (p. 194)
Post-traumatic stress disorder (p. 245)
Trauma scoring and injury scaling (p. 297)

DROWNING AND NEAR-DROWNING

Drowning is defined as suffocation due to submersion in a liquid medium; near-drowning implies survival, at least temporarily. Wet drowning, which occurs when fluid has been aspirated, accounts for 85% of cases. Dry drowning, when no fluid is found in the lungs, is thought to be caused by laryngospasm *or* absorption of water into the bloodstream before the circulation stopped and occurs in 15% of cases. Drowning should be differentiated from the immersion syndrome, in which sudden death occurs immediately following submersion in very cold water, thought to be caused by vagally mediated bradysystolic cardiac arrest or ventricular fibrillation resulting from an intense noradrenergic reflex drive to the ventricle. Secondary drowning, when the patient deteriorates following apparent recovery, is due to the respiratory distress syndrome (RDS) and usually occurs in the first 4–24 hours but may rarely develop up to 72 hours after the event. Up to 15% of patients who are conscious on arrival in the A & E department will die from RDS.

Epidemiology

Drowning is responsible for 700 deaths each year in the UK. It is the third most common cause of death by accident. Children under 4 years account for up to 50% of all submersion incidents. The number of near-drowning incidents is not known as many of those affected do not present to hospitals.

Predisposing factors include lack of responsible supervision, alcohol or drugs, suicide, injury, epilepsy and sudden illness such as myocardial infarction/cardiovascular accident.

Pathophysiology

In the past the differences between freshwater and saltwater submersions have been emphasized, however the majority of patients do not aspirate enough water to cause significant changes in serum electrolyte concentrations or intravascular volume. The principal effect is of hypoxia, the main causes being:

- Decreased pulmonary compliance due to inactivation and dilution of surfactant.
- Intrapulmonary shunting due to bronchospasm, and pulmonary collapse and oedema.
- Alveolar obstruction by water, vomit and debris.

Management

At the scene:

- Remove the victim from the water.
- Check vital signs.
- Start basic life support.

Forcible removal of water from the lungs should not be attempted as it may cause aspiration.

- Immobilize the cervical spine if there is any possibility of injury to it.

On arrival in A & E:

- Continue resuscitation and re-evaluate vital signs.
- Give 100% oxygen.
- Start ACLS, including intubation if indicated.
- Administer continuous positive airway pressure by mask if only hypoxia is present.
- Positive end-expiratory pressure in intubated patients with persistent hypoxia:

    (a) Will reduce pulmonary shunting, thus reducing ventilation–perfusion mismatch and increasing the functional residual capacity.
    (b) Will help prevent RDS.
    (c) May exacerbate cerebral oedema by reducing venous return.

- Insert a nasogastric tube.
- Prevent further heat loss by warmed i.v. fluids and inspired air, overhead heating and a space blanket.

Investigations
- Rectal temperature, low-reading thermometer.
- ABG.
- Pulse oximetry.
- Chest radiographs will typically show either:

    (a) Normal appearance or
    (b) Perihilar oedema or
    (c) Generalized pulmonary oedema.

- ECG.
- Laboratory tests: FBC, U&E, LFTs, glucose and cardiac enzymes.

Resuscitation should be continued until the core temperature is greater than 32°C as the diagnosis of brain death cannot be made in the hypothermic patient. Rewarming may prove difficult as the brain-dead patient is poikilothermic; attempts to actively rewarm using peritoneal dialysis and cardiopulmonary bypass have been used to warm very hypothermic patients. Prophylactic antibiotics and anticonvulsants may be used empirically but have not been shown to improve survival. There is no evidence that corticosteroids reduce pulmonary oedema in near-drowning.

Disposal   Patients resuscitated after a near-drowning and those who have had a significant submersion or have symptoms or signs of RDS should be admitted to the intensive care unit. All patients should be observed for a minimum of 6 hours however trivial the event, and then only discharged with caution if examination, ABG and chest radiographs remain normal. All other patients should be admitted for a minimum of 24 hours because of the danger of RDS.

Outcome   This depends on the duration of immersion, water temperature, the age of the patient, associated medical conditions and the promptness and effectiveness of BLS. In a recent UK survey of children who nearly drowned respiratory effort appeared to be the most accurate prognostic indicator. All children who were unconscious but with established respiratory effort did well.

Further reading

Kemp AM, Sibert JR. Outcome in children who nearly drown: a British Isles Study. *British Medical Journal*, 1991; **302**: 931–3.

Related topics of interest

Cardiopulmonary resuscitation (p. 56)
Hypothermia (p. 168)

DRUG OVERDOSE AND ACCIDENTAL POISONING

Adults

Adult poisoning results in approximately 3500 deaths annually in the UK. The majority of poisoned patients recover with supportive care. In certain cases it is imperative that health care providers protect themselves against contamination by toxic substances while stabilizing the patient, e.g. cyanide, hydrogen sulphide, corrosives and organophosphates.

The immediate priorities in the treatment of patients who have ingested toxins are:

- Establish an airway, provide ventilation and maintain adequate vital signs.
- Assess the level of consciousness.
- Contact the poisons information service.
- Consider an antidote.
- Take measures to prevent absorption and measures for elimination of the poison.
- Analyse drugs.
- Assess the need for admission or follow-up.

History	It is often difficult to obtain a reliable history from the patient, and thus all sources must be utilized. Relatives, friends, paramedics, the GP, pharmacists and empty containers are all invaluable.
Examination	A thorough evaluation for trauma and a neurological examination to exclude other causes of coma are essential. Signs of drug addictions should be sought, e.g. needle tracks. Drugs may be hidden within the rectum or vagina or visible on plain radiographs.

The patient's *breath* may yield helpful information:

- The faint odour of ketoacidosis or ketones (suggestive of ethanol, isopropyl alcohol and petroleum distillates).
- The garlic-like odour of arsenic or organophosphates.
- The almond-like odour of cyanide.
- The rotten-egg odour of disulphiram or hydrogen sulphide.
- The glue-like odour of toluene abuse.

Complications of acute poisoning

- *Pulmonary oedema.*
- *Renal failure.*
- *Cerebral oedema.*
- *Convulsions.* The treatment of toxin-induced epilepsy is similar to conventional therapy, but often more

difficult to control. Drug or alcohol withdrawal should be considered as a cause of otherwise unexplained seizures.
- *Rhabdomyolysis.*
- *Compartment syndrome.*
- *Hypothermia and hyperthermia.* These treatable conditions may be missed if an accurate temperature is not taken. *Core temperature* is preferable and should be monitored continuously if abnormal. Hyperthermia can occur after an overdose of cocaine, amphetamines or ecstacy, and aggressive cooling methods may be life-saving.
- *Complications of specific poisons.*

Basic life support

1. Airway and breathing. In the unconscious patient remove dentures and clear the oropharynx. If the patient has no cough reflex, a cuffed endotracheal tube is necessary. Otherwise insert an oropharyngeal airway. If there is inadequate ventilation, administer oxygen. Check arterial blood gases.

2. Circulation. Treat hypotension by:

- Treating the cause (e.g. arrhythmia).
- Elevating the foot of the bed.
- Volume expansion.
- Inotropes, e.g. dobutamine and dopamine.
- If hypotension persists, enhancement of removal of poison may reduce the negative inotropic effect.

Assessment of coma (Edinburgh Coma Scale)

Grade 0 Fully conscious.
Grade 1 Drowsy but obeys commands.
Grade 2 Responds well to pain.
Grade 3 Responds minimally to pain.
Grade 4 Completely unresponsive.

In patients with an altered level of consciousness consider:

1. Hypoglycaemia. Test with BM stix before giving dextrose if this can be done without delaying treatment.

2. Naloxone. This is another drug to consider in the unconscious patient who has taken an overdose. It is a competitive opiate antagonist. The initial dose of naloxone should be 0.4–2 mg. Occasionally more will be required to reverse the effects of the synthetic narcotics, and an infusion may even be necessary. If the patient is a known or suspected drug addict, a lower dose of naloxone (0.2 – 0.4 mg) may be used in non-life-threatening circumstances to prevent violent withdrawal symptoms. Other side-effects include hypertension, cardiac arrhythmias and even cardiac arrest.

3. *Thiamine* (100 mg i.v. or i.m.). This should be given to all alcoholic patients with altered mental states in order to prevent or treat Wernicke's encephalopathy. Thiamine should be given before dextrose is administered.

4. *Other medical causes* of coma, e.g. head injury, subarachnoid haemorrhage.

Preventing further drug absorption

Empty the stomach within 4 hours of ingestion (up to 12 hours with mefenamic acid, opiates, anticholinergics, tricyclics or salicylates).
Do *not* use lavage when:

- The airway is not protected.
- A corrosive agent has been ingested.
- A petroleum distillate has been ingested.
- The patient refuses.

Always insert a cuffed endotracheal tube in uncon scious patients. Lavage is performed in the left lateral position using a large-bore (e.g. 14 mm external diameter) Jaques tube and warm tap water until the returned fluid is clear of particles.

Oral adsorbents (charcoal)

This is most effective early after ingestion. Administer 50 g of activated charcoal orally or via nasogastric tube initially, then 25 g every 4 hours.
Side-effects include:

- Pulmonary aspiration, empyema and bronchiolitis obliterans.
- Gastrointestinal obstruction and perforation.
- Nausea, vomiting, constipation and diarrhoea.
- Corneal abrasions.

Drugs for which charcoal may prevent absorption include aspirin, carbamazepine, dapsone, digoxin, phenobarbitone and other barbiturates, phenytoin, quinine and theophylline.

Induced emesis	*Syrup of ipecacuanha* is the treatment of choice for emptying the stomach in conscious children. The dosage is 10 ml for children aged 6 – 18 months, and 15 ml for older children and 30 ml for adults.
Eliminating poisons	*1. Gastrointestinal dialysis*, i.e. repeated oral charcoal to transfer drug from the circulation back to the gut. The procedure is useful in cases of poisoning with theophylline, phenobarbitone, amitriptyline, carbamazepine, dapsone, dextropopoxyphene, digitoxin, nadolol, nortriptyline, quinine and sotalol. Give 50 g of charcoal followed by 10 g every 4 hours, with an initial dose of sorbitol (50 ml of a 70% solution). Use cholestyramine for digitoxin and warfarin.

2. Haemodialysis. Salicylates, phenobarbitone, methanol, ethanol, ethylene glycol, lithium and salt poisoning.

3. Haemoperfusion. Salicylates, short- and medium-acting barbiturates, glutethimide, meprobamate, trichloroethanol derivatives, disopyramide, theophylline, phenytoin, carbamezapine and chloroqine. |
| **Investigations** | *1. ECG.* Dysrythmias and conduction defects.

2. Chest radiography. Non-cardiogenic pulmonary oedema.

3. Electrolytes and arterial blood gases will indicate metabolic acidosis.

4. Toxicology. Knowledge of this rarely alters decisions about clinical management and generally it is recommended that a complete toxicological screen (of serum, urine and rarely gastric contents) be ordered in cases of major toxicity.
  (a) Blood. Heparinized tubes for specific drug analysis.
  (b) Urine or gastric contents. 50 ml in a clean container with no preservatives for a drug screen.
  (c) Alternatively, qualitative screening of urine for street drugs, measurement of specific drug levels in serum and storage of specimens until it becomes clear what tests might prove useful. |

(d) Specific serum or plasma drug levels are most useful when the patient has taken:
- Anticonvulsants.
- Aspirin.
- Digoxin.
- Ethanol.
- Ethylene glycol.
- Iron.
- Isopropyl alcohol.
- Lithium.
- Methanol.
- Paracetamol.
- Theophylline.

Antidotes

Some antidotes may be harmful if used inappropriately, and unless you are familiar with their proper use and possible complications a poisons centre should be consulted. Stabilizing the patient takes precedence over attempting to determine which antidote is required, with rare exceptions.

An unexplained metabolic acidosis should prompt consideration of substances such as salicylates, methanol or ethylene glycol as possible causes, as they are common in overdose and early haemodialysis improves prognosis.

The antidotes to be used in the first hour of management are:

- *Acetylcysteine.* See Paracetamol (p. 237).
- *Flumazenil.* This is a specific benzodiazepine antagonist but may induce acute benzodiazepine withdrawal symptoms and induce seizures (avoid in epileptics) or ventricular arrhythmias.
- *Desferrioxamine* is an iron antidote that is left in the stomach after gastric lavage (5–10 g of desferrioxamine mesylate in 50–100 ml water). The serum iron concentration is measured and parenteral desferrioxamine given to chelate absorbed iron in excess of the expected iron-binding capacity.
- *Dicobalt edetate.* In cases of severe cyanide toxicity. This antidote reacts with the cyanide ion to form a less toxic cyanide–cobalt complex. Side-effects include vomiting, anaphylactoid reactions, cardiac arrhythmias and chest pain. The antidote should only be prescribed when there is a clear history of cyanide exposure.

- *Sodium thiosulphate.* In cases of *moderate* cyanide toxicity.
- *Pralidoxime.* Antidote to organophosphate toxicity, it is a cholinesterase reactivator. It is indicated in moderate and severe poisoning but is only effective if given within 24 hours. The dose is 1 g i.m. or i.v., but repeated doses by i.v. infusion may be necessary in severe cases. Side-effects include CNS disturbances, muscle weakness and convulsions.
- *Viper antivenom.* Adder (*Vipera berus*) venom may cause systemic symptoms, especially hypotension, or swelling at the bite site. The Zagreb antivenom may need to be given. After dilution it is slowly infused intravenously over 20 – 30 minutes. Side-effects include anaphylaxis.
- *Fuller's earth.* For treatment of paraquat poisoning. After stomach washout 300 ml of a suspension containing 30 g of fuller's earth and 15 g of magnesium sulphate should be left in the stomach. Avoid oxygen therapy after paraquat ingestion as this may exacerbate pulmonary fibrosis.
- *Glucagon.* Beta-blocker poisoning.
- *Calcium gluconate gel 2.5%.* Hydrofluoric acid burns.
- *Ethanol.* Methanol and ethylene glycol poisoning.
- *Methylene blue injection.* Drug-induced methaemoglobinaemia.
- *Folinic acid.* Folic acid antagonist poisoning.
- *Phentolamine.* Hypertension due to α-agonist drugs.
- *Propranolol.* Poisoning with β_2-agonists, thyroxine and ephedrine.
- *Dimaval.* Heavy metal poisoning.
- *Digoxin-specific antibody fragments.* Digoxin.
- *Prussian blue.* Thallium poisoning.
- *Pyridoxine.* Isoniazid poisoning.
- *Thioctic acid. Amanita phalloides* poisoning.
- *Atropine.* Organophosphate insecticide poisoning.
- *Benztropine.* Phenothiazine overdosage.
- *Vitamin K.* Oral anticoagulant poisoning.
- *Sodium bicarbonate.* Tricyclic overdose.

Children

Accidental poisoning, despite the impact of child-resistant containers, remains a problem. In 1986, approximately 36 000 children presented to A & E departments after accidental poisoning. Most of these children did not have serious symptoms, having taken either a relatively non-toxic substance or too small an amount of a toxic substance to cause problems.

Classification

Classify poisons taken by children into one of four categories:

(a) *Low toxicity.* Children who have actually taken a substance of low toxicity can be sent home.

- Antibiotics (except ciprofloxacin, sulphasalazine and chloramphenicol).
- Oral contraceptives.
- Vitamins which do not contain iron.
- Antacids.
- Washing powder (except dishwasher powder).

(b) *Intermediate toxicity.* Observe for a short period in either the A & E department or the paediatric ward.

- Ibuprofen.
- Lignocaine gel.
- Laxatives.
- Paracetamol elixir.
- Rat or mouse poison.

(c) *Potential toxicity.* Admit for treatment and observation. If there is any doubt about the toxicity of the substance the local poisons centre should be contacted.

- Barbiturates and tricyclics.
- Iron.
- Mefenamic acid.
- Opiates.
- Theophyllines.

(d) *Uncertain toxicity.* If there is doubt the child should be admitted for observation.

Children who have deliberately taken poisons will need full *psychiatric and social* assessment and should be admitted to hospital. Those that have been poisoned deliberately by their parents or carers will need admission for full assessment, both medically and socially, and may require local child abuse procedures (*Munchausen-by-proxy*) to be implemented.

Prevention of further accidents may be achieved by advice and health visitor follow-up.

Further reading

Kulig K. Initial management of ingestions of toxic substances. *New England Journal of Medicine*, 1992; **326**: 1677–81.

Sibert JR, Routledge PA. Accidental poisoning in children: can we admit fewer children with safety? *Archives of Disease in Childhood*, 1991; **66**: 263–6.

Related topics of interest

EAR, NOSE AND THROAT

Non-traumatic ear conditions

Otitis externa

This is a bacterial (often *Pseudomonas*) or fungal infection of the external auditory canal commonly precipitated by minor trauma or swimming. The patient presents with earache, often with conductive deafness and discharge which may become purulent.

Mild cases can be treated with simple analgesia, aural toilet and topical antibiotics. Neomycin should be avoided if the tympanic membrane is ruptured, as this is associated with an increased risk of sensorineural deafness. More severe cases require systemic antibiotics (flucloxacillin is the drug of first choice) and may require admission for analgesia and formal aural toilet.

Otitis media

This most commonly occurs in children aged 3–6 years, often accompanying viral upper respiratory tract infection. In 70% of cases it is caused by bacterial infections secondary to blockage of the eustachian tube (usually *Streptococcus pneumoniae* or *Haemophilus influenzae*). It presents with severe earache, conductive deafness and pyrexia. On examination the tympanic membrane is injected with loss of the light reflex, and as the condition progresses bulging and eventual rupture occur.

There is no place for topical antibiotic therapy. Give analgesia for pain and oral antibiotics (amoxycillin or erythromycin for children and penicillin for adults). Severe cases may necessitate admission for treatment with intravenous antibiotics.

Mastoiditis

Mastoiditis occasionally follows otitis media with extension of infection into the mastoid air sinus. The signs are redness, tenderness and swelling over the mastoid process. Patients should be admitted for aggressive intravenous antibiotic therapy. The condition may be complicated by meningitis.

Earache

In addition to local causes of earache consider referred pain from dental abscess or caries, the temporomandibular joint, tonsils, pharynx and larynx.

Traumatic ear conditions

Subperichondrial haematoma

This follows local trauma to the ear, especially in boxing and rugby. It presents with a cherry-red swelling in the pinna. Small haematomas require aspiration followed by application of a pressure dressing. Larger haematomas should be drained surgically to prevent necrosis of the underlying cartilage and the development of cauliflower ear.

Foreign body

A foreign body in the ear is found usually, but not exclusively, in children. Only attempt removal in the accident department if the child is cooperative, the object is superficial or easily grasped, no attempt has been made to remove it before and you have sufficient expertise and equipment to perform the task. Otherwise refer to ENT surgeons. A general anaesthesic may be required.

Barotrauma

Most commonly the result of scuba diving; it is also seen in airline passengers. Caused by failure of equibration of the middle ear pressure with ambient pressure, usually on descending although it may occur less commonly on ascent. Patients usually present with pain, also conductive deafness, tinnitus and nose bleed.

Management. Visualize the tympanic membrane looking for congestion, blood in the middle ear and tympanic membrane rupture. Treat with oral decongestants and antibiotics if the tympanic membrane is ruptured. Most episodes will resolve. However, the patient should be reviewed by an ENT surgeon.

Epistaxis

Most cases of epistaxis follow minor local trauma, although it may be spontaneous (especially in children). In adults consider bleeding disorder or trauma as these are common predisposing causes.

Anterior epistaxis

Anterior epistaxis usually arises in Little's area over the anterior part of the nasal septum, which is served by branches of the nasopalatine and anterior ethmoidal vessels.

Sit the patient forward and apply pressure, firmly, for 10 minutes. If the bleeding stops then discharge the patient with advice not to pick or blow the nose. If the bleeding is persistent, the mucosa may be anaesthetized with lignocaine and adrenaline and cauterized with silver nitrate. If this fails, proceed to nasal packing or tamponade using a Foley catheter or nasal tampon. If the nose is packed the patient must be admitted.

Posterior epistaxis   Posterior epistaxis usually occurs in older patients and may be very profuse, leading to hypovalaemic shock. It is often diagnosed only after treatment for anterior epistaxis has failed.

Anticipate hypovalaoemia and treat accordingly. Tampon the posterior nasal space with a Foley catheter or nasal pack.

Nasal fracture

Examine for swelling, deformity, septal deviation and septal haematoma. Radiographs are unhelpful, and treatment is based on clinical findings. If there is minimal swelling and no deformity and no evidence of septal haematoma, then simple analgesia is all that is required. Nasal deviation should be reduced within 5–10 days. Septal haematoma requires urgent surgical drainage to prevent necrosis of the nasal cartilage with subsequent collapse of the nasal bridge. The squashed nose may require reconstruction and the patient should be referred for urgent ENT opinion.

Sore throat

Tonsillitis. Clinically, it is not possible to identify the aetiology which may be viral or bacterial although the beta haemolytic streptococcus is a common agent. Treatment includes analgesia and if antibiotics are considered then Penicillin V is the drug of choice. Avoid Ampicillin if glandular fever is suspected.

Peri-tonsillar abscess (Quinsy). This may follow tonsillitis, the patient is systemically unwell, the tonsillar bed is enlarged and the soft palate swollen on the affected side. Referral to an ENT surgeon is required for surgical drainage.

Other causes of sore throat include a foreign body and the prodromal phase of a variety of upper respiratory tract infections. Diphtheria is rarc but still seen, especially in immigrants from the Third World who may not have been immunized.

Swallowed bone

A swallowed bone, usually fish or chicken, may lodge in the pharynx or cause local trauma as it passes, giving the feeling of something being stuck. The patient is often able to localize the level of the foreign body. Examine the oropharynx thoroughly, especially the tonsillar bed and the base of the tongue. If the obstruction is lower down, indirect laryngoscopy should be performed. On a lateral radiograph of the neck look for a foreign body, prevertebral swelling or air. There is a spectrum of symptoms from mild discomfort to inability to swallow saliva. If you think there is *no* foreign body the patient can be discharged with advice to return if symptoms do not improve or get worse. Superficial foreign bodies can usually be removed in the accident department. If there is evidence that the foreign body is in the oesophagus surgical referral is necessary for endoscopy and removal.

Further reading

Edmunds C, Lowry C, Pennefather J. *Diving and Sub-aquatic Medicine.* Oxford: Butterworth-Heinemann, 1992: 115–39.

Related topics of interest

Maxillofacial injury (p. 198)
Respiratory distress in children (p. 257)

ELECTRICAL INJURY

Electrical injuries are arbitrarily divided into *high voltage* (>1000 V) and *low voltage*. More than 90% of cases occur in young males. Electric burns account for less than 5% of admissions to major burns units. The mortality (3–15%) and morbidity (20%) are high.

The spectrum of injury ranges from a transient unpleasant sensation to instant cardiac arrest. The mechanism of tissue damage is complex and not completely defined, but includes the *direct effects* of current on cell membranes of nerves, blood vessels and muscles and the conversion of electric energy into *heat energy* as current passes through the body.

High-voltage injuries are generally more serious, although fatal electrocution may occur with low-voltage household current (110 V). Most household and commercial electrical sources are alternating current at 60 cycles/second and may cause tetanic contractions that prevent the victims from releasing themselves.

Factors that determine the nature and severity of electric trauma include:

- Amperage.
- Voltage.
- Resistance to current, e.g. reduced by water.
- Type of current.
- Duration of contact.
- Current pathway.

Basic life support	Rescuer safety is paramount, and only after the power is switched off by an authorized person or the source is safely cleared may the victim's cardiopulmonary status be determined. Additionally, consider the possibility that high-voltage electricity can arc or pass through the ground.
	If the victim is located above ground, rescue breathing should be started at once and the victim lowered to the ground as soon as possible.
	Associated trauma may be a feature so spinal protection is required.
Advanced life support	Arrhythmias are treated as per European Resuscitation Council guidelines. Patients with electrical burns of the face, mouth and neck may require special airway techniques, as extensive soft-tissue swelling may develop and compromise the airway.
Cardiac effects	• Ventricular fibrillation (VF), asystole and ventricular tachycardia progressing to VF are the arrhythmias most likely to occur.

- Alternating current increases the likelihood of precipitating VF. Transthoracic current flow (hand-to-hand) is more likely to be fatal than a vertical (hand-to-foot) or straddle (foot-to-foot) current path.
- *ECG changes* include ST and non-specific ST–T wave changes.
- *Systemic hypertension* is common with high-voltage injuries and possibly due to catecholamine release.
- *Dysrhythmias* and conduction defects may occur.
- *Myocardial* damage occurs rarely.
- *Hypovolaemia* may occur secondary to fluid and blood loss into the tissues.
- *Major vessel thrombosis,* delayed rupture of large vessels and *aneurysms* have been reported.

Respiratory effects

Respiratory arrest may occur as a result of:

- Inhibition of the medullary centre by a direct effect.
- Tetanic contraction of the diaphragm and chest wall muscles.
- Prolonged paralysis of respiratory muscles.

Trauma related

- *Skeletal muscle.* This tends to dominate the clinical picture of electrical injury and is often the *'hidden'* tissue damage that accounts for the greatest morbidity, functional impairment and cosmetic disfigurement. Skeletal muscle cells are particularly vulnerable to injury. A massive release of intracellular contents with cell lysis occurs.

  (a) Fluid requirements are often massive.
  (b) Devascularization over the next 3 – 4 days is caused by injured blood vessels which thrombose.
  (c) Compartment syndrome and compressive neuropathies may require escharotomy and fasciotomy.
  (d) Infection may occur.
  (e) Amputation may be required.
  (f) Chronic effects include muscle atrophy and fibrosis.
  (g) Release of K^+.
  (h) Release of muscle enzymes resulting in myoglobinuria and renal failure.
  (i) At initial operation necrotic muscle is difficult to distinguish and it is often necessary to reinspect and debride necrotic tissue every 48 hours.

- *Fractures.*
- *Dislocations.*
- *Haemorrhage.* Spleen, liver, bladder.
- *Head injury.*

Cutaneous effects

- *Entry and exit wounds.* Usually the current path in electric shocks is predictable but:

  (a) A skin contact may serve as both an entry and exit point.
  (b) It is possible in very high-voltage shocks to have several entry and exit points.

- *Burns.* Gross inspection of the cutaneous injury does not give any indication of the extent of involved underlying tissue damage.

  (a) *Electrothermal burns.* Low voltage, limited, rarely more than 10%.
  (b) *Arc burns.* Treat as thermal burns (temperature 2000–4000°C). Mostly they involve a very small area (<1%) and are caused by low-voltage shock.
  (c) *Mixed burns.* High voltage, often extensive and cause major sequelae.

Neurological effects

1. Acute

- Coma.
- Epilepsy.
- Motor and sensory deficits.
- Headache.
- Dizziness, lassitude, mood and personality disturbances.

2. Delayed

- Peripheral nerve injury.
- Sensory, motor and vasomotor nerve injury.
- Spinal cord injury rarely.

Ocular effects

- Conjunctivitis.
- Corneal burns.
- Retinal burns (may cause decreased vision).
- *Cataract* (rare). Onset may be delayed for weeks to years and associated with electrical contact with head.

Auditory effects	• Ruptured eardrums. • Delayed tinnitus. • Reduced hearing.
Lightning	A high-voltage direct current shock. Around five people are killed in England and Wales annually from lightning. For every fatality, four or more are injured. Hills, open country and open stretches of water are dangerous places in thunderstorms – and included in this category are golf courses. The advice to take is to get indoors or inside a car. If caught outdoors, throw away any metal or conductive object – a golf club, a carbon fibre fishing rod, a gun or umbrella. Do not shelter under a tree, especially an isolated tree. A warning sign of impending strike is one's hair standing on end. If this occurs crouch into a ball with your legs together. Indoors, unplug your TV aerial and do not use the telephone. Patients who do not suffer cardiorespiratory arrest have an excellent chance of recovery.

- The primary cause of death is *cardiac arrest* due to asystole or ventricular fibrillation.
- *Respiratory arrest* may occur as a result of respiratory muscle spasm or suppression of the respiratory centre.
- *Transient loss of consciousness* and *temporary blindness* or *deafness* may occur.

Further reading

Lee RC *et al. Electrical Trauma. The Pathophysiology, Manifestations and Clinical Management.* Cambridge University Press, 1992.
Smith T. On lightning. *British Medical Journal*, 1991; **303**: 1563.

Related topics of interest

ENDOCRINE EMERGENCIES

Acute adrenal crisis

Acute adrenal crisis may occur in either *primary* or *secondary adrenal insufficiency*. The acute event is often precipitated by acute stress (e.g. infection, trauma) in a patient with pre-existing chronic adrenal insufficiency or abrupt cessation of glucocorticoid therapy in patients with adrenal atrophy, secondary to chronic steroid administration.

Acute destruction of the adrenal cortex as a result of haemorrhage is most commonly caused by septicaemia in children (Waterhouse–Friderichsen syndrome) and anticoagulant therapy in adults. The diagnosis should be considered in cases of hypotension, collapse, non-specific abdominal pain, confusion and spontaneous hypoglycaemia.

Symptoms and signs

1. Primary adrenal insufficiency (Addison's disease)

- Hyperpigmentation of skin creases, buccal mucosa and scars.
- Weakness and fatigue.
- Nausea, vomiting and diarrhoea.
- Anorexia and weight loss.
- Postural hypotension or hypotension.
- Decreased level of consciousness.

2. Secondary adrenal insufficiency may be preceded by symptoms of hypopituitarism, hypogonadism, hypothroidism and symptoms of hypothalmic or pituitary tumour (headaches, visual defects).

Biochemical findings

- Hyponatraemia.
- Hyperkalaemia.
- Raised blood urea.
- Hypoglycaemia.
- Plasma cortisol of <600 nmol/l in the acutely ill patient.

Treatment

- Correct hypoglycaemia.
- Replace fluid volume with normal saline (1 litre over the first hour and thereafter according to clinical state). Correct electrolyte deficits, e.g. serum potassium. Initially serum K^+ is increased, however there is a deficit of total body K^+ and replacement should be started when serum K^+ falls after hydration and cortisol administration.

- Give hydrocortisone – 100 mg i.v. then 100 mg 6-hourly.
- Mineralocorticoid replacement with fludrocortisone is required in those with primary adrenal insufficiency.
- Treatment of underlying cause, e.g. infection.
- Look for associated conditions such as hypothyroidism and panhypopituitarism.

Thyroid crisis

This is a life-threatening emergency usually precipitated by stress (e.g. infection, trauma) in a poorly treated or untreated thyrotoxic patient. Death occurs from hypovolaemic shock, coma, congestive cardiac failure and tachyarrhythmias.

Symptoms and signs
- *General.* Fever, sweating, warm skin and dehydration.
- *Cardiovascular.* Hyperdynamic circulation, wide pulse pressure, sinus tachycardia, atrial arrhythmias, congestive cardiac failure, myocardial ischaemia and infarction.
- *Central nervous.* Agitation, tremor, weakness, proximal myopathy, confusion, psychosis and coma.
- *Abdominal.* Nausea, vomiting, diarrhoea, abdominal pain and jaundice.

Investigations
- Take blood for measurement of tri-iodothyronine (T_3) and thyroxine (T_4), plasma glucose, electrolytes and FBC.
- ECG monitoring and 12-lead ECG.

Treatment
1. General. Parenteral fluids, treatment of arrhythmias or cardiac failure, antipyretics and identification of any precipitant such as underlying infection.

2. Specific.

- *Block hormone action.* Beta-blockers block the peripheral effects of the thyroid hormone, e.g. propranolol 1 – 5 mg i.v. or 20–80 mg orally, to control tachycardia, fever, tremor and restlessness.
- *Block hormone synthesis.* Propylthiouracil (600 – 1200 mg loading dose) blocks thyroid hormone synthesis and peripheral conversion of T_4 to T_3.
- *Block hormone release.* Iodine compounds in high dose decrease thyroid hormone release. T_3 to be given 2 – 4 hours after propylthiouracil.

3. *Plasmapheresis can be considered.*

4. *Give hydrocortisone* (100 mg i.v.) to treat relative adrenal insufficiency, which may be present.

Myxoedema coma

This is due to thyroid hormone deficiency that results in encephalopathy. It can develop insidiously or precipitated by exposure to cold, infection, drugs (phenothiazines) or other stress. Mortality is high (50%), especially in the elderly.

Symptoms and signs	• *General.* Cold intolerance, dry skin, constipation, weakness, lethargy, slow speech, weight gain. Facial puffiness, coarse dry skin, yellow pigmentation (carotenaemia), hair loss, thinning of eyebrows, enlarged tongue. • *Central nervous.* Disorientation, progression to coma, grand mal epilepsy, ataxia, myxoedema madness (psychosis). • *Cardiovascular.* Bradycardia, cardiomegaly, distant heart sounds.
Investigations	• *Chest radiography* may reveal cardiomegaly and a pericardial effusion. • *ECG* shows bradycardia, low-voltage changes, flat or inverted T waves and J waves.
Biochemical features	• Core temperature – hypothermia. • Arterial blood gases – hypoxaemia, hypercapnia and respiratory or mixed acidosis. • Hyponatraemia. • Hypoglycaemia. • Low thyroid hormones and elevated thyroid-stimulating hormone. • Hypercholesterolaemia. • Elevated creatinine phosphokinase (CPK).
Treatment	*1. General* • Treat respiratory failure as necessary. • Correct hypoglycaemia. • Treat hypotension with crystalloid. • Treat hypothermia with passive rewarming. • Insert a nasogastric tube and urinary catheter. • Administer cortisol. • Correct hyponatraemia. • Identify and treat precipitant.

2. Specific

Initial replacement of thyroid hormone is with Liothyroxine sodium, 5–20 μg by slow intravenous injection. Take care in patients with known ischaemic heart disease (IHD) as the drug may precipitate arrhythmias, angina or myocardial infarction.

Hyponatraemia

Asymptomatic hyponatraemia is often benign. Symptomatic hyponatraemia with CNS manifestations (hyponatraemic encephalopathy) requires treatment to prevent brain damage as a result of brain oedema, respiratory insufficiency and hypoxaemia. The morbidity depends more on the age and sex of the patient (highest in children and menstruant women) than the magnitude or duration of the hyponatraemia.

Causes of hyponatraemia

- Post-operative.
- Intravenous hypotonic fluid administration.
- Inappropriate antidiuretic hormone secretion.

    (a) Lung and cerebral tumours.
    (b) Adrenal insufficiency.
    (c) Hypothyroidism.

- Drugs including diuretics, sedatives, oral hypoglycaemics, etc.
- Acquired immunodeficiency syndrome (AIDS).
- Psychogenic polydipsia.

Symptoms and signs

1. Early hyponatraemic encephalopathy

- Headache.
- Nausea / vomiting.
- Weakness.

2. Advanced hyponatraemic encephalopathy

- Reduced level of consciousness.
- Bizarre behaviour.
- Visual / auditory hallucinations.
- Incontinence.
- Hypoventilation.

Very advanced hyponatraemic encephalopathy results in manifestations secondary to increased intracranial pressure including focal or grand mal epilepsy, coma and respiratory arrest.

Treatment   Ideally treat the underlying cause:

1. Asymptomatic hyponatraemia generally does not require aggressive treatment with hypertonic saline, as symptomatic measures combined with fluid restriction are usually sufficient. In volume-depleted patients isotonic (154 mM) sodium chloride is usually the fluid of choice.

2. Symptomatic hyponatraemia is best treated with hypertonic (usually 514 mM) sodium chloride, often in conjunction with a loop diuretic. Aim to raise the sodium to around 130 mmol/l, by about 1 mmol/l/h. This is best performed in the ITU, where neurological, respiratory and haemodynamic monitoring can be performed.

Further reading

Anonymous. Endocrine emergencies. *Bailliere's Clinical Endocrinology and Metabolism*, 1992; **6**: 1–228.
Arieff AI. Management of hyponatraemia. *British Medical Journal*, 1993; **307**: 305–8.

Related topic of interest

Diabetic emergencies (p. 86)

FACTITIOUS DISORDERS

Factitious disorders are characterized by physical or psychological symptoms produced by an individual under voluntary control. An essential characteristic is that there is no apparent goal other than to assume the patient role, the most florid example being *Munchausen's syndrome.*

Factitious disorders should be distinguished from malingering, in which symptoms are also under voluntary control but the goal is personal gain (e.g. narcotics, compensation).

The diagnosis can be confirmed only by the patient's confession, and careful history taking and gentle confrontation may be effective in securing this. Factitious illness is often misdiagnosed but should be considered in patients with perplexing clinical problems and in dramatic presentations with no obvious organic cause.

It can be difficult to diagnose in the setting of an A & E department; an incorrect diagnosis of factitious illness may prove costly to both patient and doctor. It must not be forgotten that the patient who suffers from factitious illness is still at risk from organic disease.

Munchausen's syndrome

The Munchausen syndrome was coined by Asscher to describe patients who repeatedly present to hospitals with dramatic symptoms suggesting serious physical illness. It is most frequently seen in men.

Common presentations include:

- Patients who feign surgical illness, hoping for a laparotomy (*laparotimorphilia migrans*).
- Patients with alarming symptoms of bleeding (*haemorrhagica histrionica*).
- Patients who present with curious fits (*neurologica diabolica*).
- Patients who present with false heart attacks (*cardiopathia fantastica*).

Other evidence of deception (i.e. the use of many aliases and addresses) may be discovered. Occasionally extreme measures to deceive doctors are used.

Patients presenting with simulated illness should be confronted tactfully and offered referral to a psychiatrist. Unfortunately, psychiatric treatment is seldom helpful and the patient will often discharge himself when confronted with the diagnosis.

Munchausen's syndrome by proxy is a form of child abuse in which a parent (usually the mother) fabricates symptoms and signs in the child.

Neurological symptoms	• *Pseudocoma.* May result in patient intubation. Spontaneous flickering of the eyelids and resistance to passive attempts at opening them and the upward eye sign (with upward rolling of the eye and gaze avoidance) are suggestive of pseudocoma. • *Pseudoseizures.* There is often bizarre motor activity, with unusual precipitants, but no loss of consciousness.
Metabolic symptoms	• *Hypoglycaemia.* Often related to self-administration of insulin or oral hypoglycaemic drugs, especially in diabetics, health care professionals or relatives of diabetics. • *Brittle diabetes.* Some cases of brittle diabetes may be factitious. • *Phaeochromocytoma* can be simulated by administration of catecholamines and presents with palpitations, sweating and hypertension. • *Thyrotoxicosis.* • *Diuretic abuse.* • *Water intoxication.*
Cardiac symptoms	• *Chest pain.* Patients may present with myocardial type chest pain and demand analgesia. There may be signs of previous investigations such as cardiac catheterization. • *Arrhythmias.* Both bradycardias and tachycardias have been faked, resulting in insertion of pacemakers or cardioversion.
Respiratory symptoms	• *Asthma.* • *Upper airway obstruction with stridor.* • *Haemoptysis.*
General symptoms	• *Dermatitis artefacta.* Skin lesions are produced deliberately. • *Factitious pyrexia of unknown origin.* The patient produces symptoms of a febrile illness and will even tamper with the recording of the temperature. • *Factitious AIDS.* A recently described condition in which patients feign AIDS.

Further reading

Sutherland AJ, Rodin GM. Factitious disorders in a general hospital setting: clinical features and a review of the literature. *Psychosomatics*, 1990; **31**: 392–9.

Related topics of interest

Child abuse (p. 70)
Deliberate self-harm (p. 83)

FEBRILE CONVULSION

A febrile convulsion is a seizure usually occurring between the ages of 3 months and 5 years which is associated with fever but without evidence of intracranial infection or recognized neurological illness. The peak incidence is at 18 months. About 2–5% of children will be affected. The fit is a generalized tonic–clonic event lasting between 1 and 10 minutes. It is usually associated with a temperature over 39°C but may occur on the upswing of the rising fever. There is no antecedent neurological illness and the post-ictal examination will not reveal any focal neurological signs. The CT scan and EEG, if performed, are normal. It is essential to take a careful history and make a thorough physical examination with a view to identifying the source of a fever and recognizing the presence of CNS infection, in particular meningitis.

Treatment

Many seizures will have stopped before the child reaches the accident and emergency department. These patients require simple treatment:

- Reassurance, especially of the parents.
- Tepid sponging.
- Antipyretics, paracetamol.

Prolonged febrile convulsions require more active treatment. Diazepam is the drug of choice and is given by slow i.v. infusion of 0.25–0.4 mg/kg (as Diazemuls) or 0.4 mg/kg rectally (as Stesolid). These doses may be repeated after 5 minutes if necessary.

Paraldehyde, 0.4 ml/kg rectally, can be given if the seizure is resistant to treatment or if the child has status epilepticus.

It is customary UK practice to admit all patients with first-time febrile fits to confirm the diagnosis and reassure and educate the parents about what may appear to them to be a very frightening illness.

Routine anticonvulsant prophylaxis is not indicated following simple febrile convulsion. Parents should be instructed how to manage future fevers with tepid sponging and antipyretics to reduce the risk of recurrence.

Investigations

These should be performed on the basis of the clinical findings.

- Lumbar puncture is indicated when meningitis is suspected and in children under 18 months, in whom signs of meningitis may be absent. It is contraindi-

cated in the presence of raised intracranial pressure and focal neurological signs.
- Chest radiography, if underlying pathology is suspected.
- Laboratory investigations: FBC, CRP, blood cultures and septic screen if a severe infection is suspected.

There is no indication for routine CT scanning or EEG following simple febrile convulsion.

Prognosis
Febrile seizures are seldom associated with long-term cerebral damage. About 33% of children will have subsequent seizures, and these too are generally benign. Only 3% of children will go on to have non-febrile seizures. Children with prolonged or non-focal fits, pre-existing neurological disorder or a history of fits in parents or siblings are more at risk for subsequent fits and other neurological conditions.

Further reading

Ferry PC, Banner W, Wolf RA. *Seizure Disorders in Children*. Philadelphia: JB Lippincott, 1986: 143–152.
Menkes JH. *Textbook of Child Neurology*, Philadelphia: Lea & Febiger, 1985: 654–6.
Convulsions. In: *Advanced Paediatric Life Support*. London: BMJ Publishing Group, 1993: 105–9.

Related topics of interest

FRACTURES – PRINCIPLES OF TREATMENT

No two fractures are exactly the same; moreover, the treatment of orthopaedic injury is advancing rapidly, particularly in the field of operative intervention. It is therefore necessary to follow local procedures and protocols when dealing with fractures. However, the principles of treatment are common to all.

Clinical assessment

A full history is essential, especially the mechanism of injury.

Examine for the cardinal signs of fractures; tenderness, swelling, deformity and loss of function. Determine whether the fracture is closed or compound.

Classification of compound fractures

Grade I	Wound less than 1 cm punctured from within.
Grade II	Laceration less than 5 cm not contaminated, crushed and without soft-tissue loss or flaps.
Grade II	Greater than 5 cm long associated with wound contamination, crush or extensive soft-tissue damage.
Grade IIIA	Soft tissue stripped from bone.
Grade IIIB	Periosteum stripped from bone.
Grade IIIC	Major vascular injury.

If the skin is intact it may be compromised by pressure from bony fragments. Examine the soft tissues and look for vascular injury, nerve injury, other injuries and the general status of patient.

Radiological assessment

Always radiograph in two planes. The type of fracture may be simple (transverse, oblique or spiral), comminuted, crushed or impacted. Note the alignment: displacement, angulation, rotation and bony continuity.

Consider:

- Joint involvement.
- Likely stability.
- Bone quality.

Treatment

The aim of treatment is restoration of normal function. There are a number of ways achieving this. The principles are to reduce, immobilize and rehabilitate.

1. Reduction. Is it required? Treat the patient and not the radiograph and consider cosmesis and function. Angulation and displacement are likely to require reduction. As long as there is bony continuity and good alignment displaced fractures do not necessarily require reduction. Reduction may be open or closed and performed under sedation, regional or general anaesthesia. Always consider the status of the soft tissues, including skin, vessels, nerves and tendons.

2. Immobilization. This is not required for all fractures. Some can be mobilized as soon as pain allows. If immobilization is required consider the method – strapping, sling, splint, plaster of Paris, traction, external bony fixation and internal bony fixation – and consider the length of immobilization required. This varies according to age, fracture type, site and method of immobilization.

3. Rehabilitation. Aim to restore normal function. This may be achieved by the patient alone or with the aid of physiotherapy.

Fractures in children

1. Greenstick fracture. This can occur at any age up to puberty. It is an incomplete fracture, the bone being buckled and bent but the periosteum remaining intact. A torus fracture is another form of incomplete fracture in which the cortex is buckled. Healing is usually quick and uncomplicated.

2. Epiphyseal fractures. Salter–Harris classification.

Type I   Fracture through the epiphyseal plate. The radiographic appearance may be normal but this type of fracture should be suspected if there is tenderness over the growth plate.

Type II   As type I but the fracture extends to include a fragment of the metaphysis. Type II fractures constitute 75% of epiphyseal fractures.

Type III   As type I but the fracture extends into the epiphysis.

Type IV   Involves both metaphysis and epiphysis.

Type V   Crush injury of the epiphyseal plate. It is
          rare but important to recognize as growth
          arrest is the usual sequela.

Further reading

Charnley J. *The Closed Treatment of Common Fractures*. Edinburgh: Churchill
    Livingstone, 1970.

Related topics of interest

Compartment syndrome (p. 77)
Scaphoid fracture (p. 263)
Wrist injury (p. 311)

GASTROINTESTINAL HAEMORRHAGE – UPPER

District hospitals each year admit 50–80 patients with upper gastrointestinal haemorrhage per 100 000 of the population, of whom more than two-thirds are aged over 60 years.

Peptic ulcers account for 50% of bleeds, and about one-third of patients have recently taken non-steroidal anti-inflammatory drugs (NSAIDs). In 80% of patients bleeding stops spontaneously without therapeutic intervention. Mortality rises with age. The death rate has been reported at 10%, but in recent series has fallen to 4%.

Patients with massive lower gastrointestinal (GI) bleeding should be suspected of having upper GI bleeding and undergo endoscopy of the upper tract as up to 11% of patients will be bleeding from the upper GI tract.

Accurate diagnosis is essential, and flexible endoscopy is the mainstay of diagnosis. Radionuclide scanning and arteriography have a place in diagnosis when endoscopy fails.

History and examination

Important *historical features* include:

- Past medical history (PMH) of peptic ulcer.
- PMH of previous bleed.
- PMH of bleeding disorder.
- Liver disease.
- Alcohol intake.
- Aspirin or NSAIDs intake.
- History of vigorous retching or vomiting (Mallory–Weiss syndrome).

The *examination* includes assessment of the patient's general condition and degree of blood loss. Examine for signs of hepatic disease and alcohol abuse.

Severity of GI haemorrhage

1. Mild to moderate haemorrhage is defined as:

- Patient < 60 years.
- No PMH.
- No hypovolaemia.
- Hb > 10 g/dl.

2. Life-threatening haemorrhage is defined as:

- Patient > 60 years.
- Hypovolaemia (systolic blood pressure 100 mmHg or diastolic blood pressure falls on sitting and standing).

- Hb < 10 g/dl.
- Severe disease, e.g. liver, cardiovascular, respiratory.

Investigations
- FBC, blood urea.
- LFTs, coagulation screen, hepatitis B serum antigen in liver disease.
- Blood group and save serum (some laboratories like to cross-match) if Hb is normal or if bleed is considered mild or moderate.
- Cross-match blood if Hb < 10 g/dl, or with a life-threatening bleed.

Management

1. Mild to moderate haemorrhage

- Admit to a medical ward.
- Allow fluids only on day 1, food thereafter.
- Nil by mouth for 6 hours before endoscopy.
- Observe for continued haemorrhage or rebleeding.
- Put the patient on the next routine endoscopy list.

2. Severe haemorrhage

- Restore blood volume; consider using a central venous pressure (CVP) line.
- Admit to a high-dependency unit.
- Inform the consultant physician and consultant surgeon.
- Observe for continued bleeding or rebleeding.
- Sips of water only until endoscopy, which should be performed preferably within 12 hours of the bleed.
- If liver disease is present, avoid sedation; clear the bowel with magnesium sulphate mixture 10 ml t.d.s. or lactulose 20 ml t.d.s. or an enema.
- Start the patient on a diet containing 20 g of protein per day.

3. Transfusion

- Oxygenate with high-flow oxygen.
- Insert a large-bore intravenous cannula.
- If there is supine or postural hypotension, tachycardia or reduced capillary refill, a plasma expander, followed by whole blood, should be given as soon as possible.
- CVP measurement should guide replacement, especially in those with cardiovascular disease.
- Packed cells may be required if there is anaemia but a normal or increased blood volume.

• Group O Rh– blood may be required in emergencies.

Investigations

Flexible *endoscopy* should be the first diagnostic test in patients who present with upper GI bleeding. Endoscopy allows accurate diagnosis of the cause of bleeding in up to 90% of patients when undertaken within 48 hours of a bleeding episode, but is only 33% accurate when performed after more than 48 hours. The procedure should be performed in the stable patient within 48 hours, but if bleeding is severe and continued, then early endoscopy is indicated.

If signs of recent bleeding from an ulcer are present at endoscopy, haemostasis may be achieved using thermal coagulation or direct injection of a vasoconstrictor and/or sclerosant. The death rate is reduced by about one-third after such procedures.

Surgery

Operation is the mainstay of treatment of patients with persistent bleeding from peptic ulcer disease. It may not always be possible to pinpoint the source of upper GI bleeding before operation, but endoscopy should be attempted prior to surgery either in the endoscopy suite or in theatre, depending on the urgency of the case.

Delayed operation usually results in greater blood loss and higher morbidity and mortality rates in patients aged > 60 years, but early operation in younger patients leads to unnecessary operations.

Indications for surgery include:

• A patient who requires more than 4 units of whole blood to maintain blood volume over 24 hours.
• A patient who continues to bleed or rebleeds.

Variceal bleeding

Oesophageal varices account for 2–4% of bleeds but carry a 30% mortality. Upper GI bleeding is associated with cirrhosis and accompanying liver compromise.

There is a high recurrence rate, so long-term therapy such as repeated sclerotherapy, propranolol therapy, shunt surgery and liver transplantation should be considered.

Management:

• *Injection sclerotherapy.* This is the best method of arresting the acute bleed with a success rate of 90%.
• *Sengstaken–Blackmore or Minnesota balloon tamponade.* In those in whom injection sclerotherapy is hampered by massive haemorrhage, balloon tampon-

ade is carried out immediately until the patient's condition is stabilized, followed by sclerotherapy.

- *Medical control*

  (a) Nitroglycerin.
  (b) Vasopressin (pitressin).
  (c) Somatostatin and its analogues.

- *Surgery.* Operative intervention is reserved for the those patients who are not controlled by sclerotherapy. Oesophageal stapling and portosystemic shunts should be reserved for the 5–10% of patients in whom sclerotherapy fails to control the bleeding. However this procedure carries a high mortality.

Further reading

Birkett DH. Gastrointestinal tract bleeding. Common dilemmas in management. *Surgical Clinics of North America*, 1991; **71**: 1259–68.

Report of a Joint Working Group of the British Society of Gastroenterology, the Research Unit of the Royal College of Physicians of London and the Audit Unit of the Royal College of Surgeons of England. Guidelines for good practice in and audit of the management of upper gastrointestinal haemorrhage. *Journal of the Royal College of Physicians of London*, 1992; **26**: 281–9.

Related topics of interest

Intravenous fluids (p. 180)
Shock (p. 269)

GENITOURINARY TRAUMA

Renal injuries

Ninety per cent of renal injuries are due to blunt abdominal trauma, with associated injuries occurring in 40% of cases. Children are more prone to renal injuries perhaps because of the relative lack of perinephric fat.

Few renal injuries need immediate treatment. The urinary tract is evaluated as part of the secondary survey.

Classification

- *Minor* (85%). Contusions/superficial lacerations with an intact capsular and pelvicalyceal system.
- *Major* (10%). Deep lacerations with associated capsular tear and/or pelvicalyceal system involvement.
- *Critical* (5%). Renal fragmentation or renal pedicle injury.

Clinical signs

Renal injury should be suspected if there is a history of injury to the flank and the patient complains of loin pain.
Clinical signs include:

- Soft-tissue injury to the flank or penetrating injury.
- Loin tenderness.
- Loss of loin contour.
- Loin mass.
- *Haematuria.* This is not an accurate indication of the severity of renal injury, i.e. a renal pedicle injury may present with only microscopic haematuria. Conversely macroscopic haematuria need not be due to severe damage.

Investigations

The stable patient will be assessed first with kidneys, ureters, bladder (KUB). The presence of the following suggests potential renal damage:

- Scoliosis (with concavity towards the side of the injury).
- Loss of psoas shadow.
- Enlarged renal outline.
- Displaced bowel.
- Elevation of the ipsilateral diaphragm.
- Fractured ribs or transverse processes.

2. Intravenous urography (IVU) is indicated in patients with:

- Macroscopic haematuria.
- Microscopic haematuria and systolic blood pressure < 90 mmHg (after completion of the primary survey).

Patients with microscopic haematuria and haemodynamic stability probably have minor renal injuries. The decision to investigate will be based on clinical judgement and discussion with a urologist.
  Abnormal IVU features include:

- Delayed excretion.
- Extravasation.
- Disruption of renal outline.
- Calyceal distortion.
- Filling defect in the collecting system.
- Non-visualization.
- Hydronephrosis.

  Non-visualization or extravasation of contrast necessitates further evaluation by arteriography, but only if the patient remains stable.

Management

- ABCs.
- Stage renal injury radiologically.
- Treat most patients with minor/major renal injuries expectantly.
- Operate on patients with cortical and unstable major injuries.

Complications of renal trauma include:

- Hypertension.
- Arteriovenous fistula.
- Hydronephrosis.
- Pseudocyst and calculus formation.
- Chronic pyelonephritis.
- Loss of renal function.

Bladder injuries

Bladder injuries make up approximately 22% of urological injuries and are due to blunt trauma in 86% of cases. There are often associated injuries in addition to the commonly found pelvic fracture. Types of injuries include:

- Contusion.
- Extraperitoneal rupture.
- Intraperitoneal rupture.
- Both intra- and extraperitoneal rupture.

  Rupture is caused by:

- Penetration of a bone spicule.
- Compression of a distended bladder.

  Suspect a bladder injury when there is:

- Pelvic fracture.
- Lower abdominal trauma (blunt or penetrating).
- Gross haematuria.
- Inability to void.

Investigations	• *KUB*. • *Cystography* if no urethral injury suspected (to include post-micturition film).
Treatment	By a urologist.

Urethral injury

Urethral injury is more common in males. Injuries are usually either:

- *Bulbar*. Usually caused by straddle injuries.
- *Membranous*. Caused by pelvic fracture or penetrating trauma.

  The suspicion of urethral injury is raised by:

- Pelvic fracture or deep perineal laceration with gross haematuria.
- Blood at the meatus.
- Perineal bruising.
- Abnormal voiding or inability to void. High-riding or boggy prostate.
- Vaginal bleeding or laceration.

Investigations	An anterior retrograde urethrogram, followed by a cystogram.
Treatment	An option is to place a suprapubic catheter and withhold further investigation until a urologist is available. A urethral catheter must not be placed as it risks the creation of a false passage or completion of a partial tear.

If no sign of urethral injury exists, attempt to pass a well-lubricated Foley catheter. If any difficulty is encountered, the procedure must be stopped and further investigation undertaken.

Further reading

Talbot-Stern JK. *Critical Decisions in Emergency Medicine*, Lesson 5, Urinary tract injuries. Dallas: American College of Emergency Physicians, 1990: 35–40.
Terry T. ABC of major trauma. Trauma of the upper urinary tract. *British Medical Journal*, 1990; **301:** 485–8.

Related topics of interest

Abdominal trauma (p. 4)

Head injury (p. 146)

Interhospital transfer – trauma (p. 174)

Major injuries – initial management (p. 190)

Major injuries – Royal College of Surgeons of England Report (p. 194)

Maxillofacial injury (p. 198)

Missile injuries (p. 211)

Spine and spinal cord trauma (p. 278)

Thoracic trauma (p. 292)

Trauma scoring and injury scaling (p. 297)

GYNAECOLOGY

Vaginal bleeding

Vaginal bleeding is the most common gynaecological reason for attendance in accident and emergency. Causes include menstruation, spontaneous abortion, pregnancy (including ectopic), infection, tumour, foreign body, endocrine disturbance, bleeding disorders, anticoagulant therapy and trauma. Vaginal bleeding in women is a normal physiological process during the child-bearing years, but any bleeding which the patient considers to be abnormal must be taken seriously and investigated accordingly.

Management

It is essential to take a complete history with particular reference to sexual practice, contraception and last menstrual period and to perform a full physical examination.

- Give oxygen.
- Estimate the volume and rate of bleeding.
- Establish intravenous access and treat shock.
- Investigate with FBC, U & E, β-human chorionic gonadotrophin (β-HCG) pregnancy test and clotting screen.
- Take blood for cross-match and rhesus status.
- Perform an ultrasound scan.
- Early referral to a gynaecologist for treatment of specific conditions is essential.

Pelvic pain

Gynaecological causes

1. Pregnancy related. Ectopic pregnancy, spontaneous abortion, abruptio placentae, pre-eclampsia and labour.

2. Non-pregnancy related

- Infection (pelvic inflammatory disease and tubo-ovarian abscess).
- Ovarian (ruptured cyst, torsion or haemorrhage into cyst or tumour).
- Others including menstruation, ovulation, endometrosis and pelvic tumour.

Non-gynaecological causes

Consider all the surgical causes for lower abdominal pain (especially acute appendicitis).

Ruptured ectopic pregnancy

This is the most common cause of maternal mortality in early pregnancy. Most patients will present with lower abdominal pain, and 80% will also have vaginal bleeding. Although there is often a history compatible with known early pregnancy, this is not always the case: patients can present with sudden collapse from hypovolaemic shock without any prodromal illness or symptoms and the diagnosis must be considered in any woman of reproductive age. Note that in 10% of cases the β-HCG pregnancy test will be negative.

Predisposing factors include a previous ectopic pregnancy, tubal surgery, an intrauterine contraceptive device and pelvic infection.

Management	Even if the patient is haemodynamically stable with normal vital signs, hypovolaemic collapse can occur at any time. Give oxygen, establish venous access, initiate shock resuscitation and arrange transfer to the operating theatre.
	Ultrasound scan in the accident department will confirm the diagnosis in patients who are haemodynamically stable.

Spontaneous abortion

Threatened	The patient presents with mild abdominal cramps associated with transient vaginal bleeding. The uterine size is compatible with the presumed length of pregnancy and the cervix is closed on speculum examination. Most patients can be treated with rest, abstinence from sexual activity and regular gynaecological review.
Inevitable	The patient presents with persistent abdominal cramps and heavy vaginal bleeding. On examination the cervix is open (greater than 0.5 cm) and the products of conception may have been passed or lie in the vagina or cervical os. If this is the case they should be removed gently with forceps, especially if the patient is hypotensive. The symptoms and signs of pregnancy disappear.
Incomplete	The vaginal bleeding and abdominal cramps are persistent and products of conception are passed or lie in the vagina.
Complete	There is bleeding and pain. After the products of conception have been passed the symptoms and signs of pregnancy disappear.
Missed	The products are retained, the symptoms and signs of

pregnancy usually disappear and the vaginal bleeding is replaced by a brownish discharge. Intrauterine fetal death occurs, evidenced by lack of fetal heart sounds and the ultrasound scan fails to demonstrate a live fetus.

Management   Most women will be understandably very emotional and require sympathy, support and privacy. Many women with gynaecological problems prefer to be seen by a female doctor, and if possible this should not be denied.

Toxic shock syndrome

This is rare. Associated with tampon use, the exact mechanism is unknown. The patient presents with fever, rash, hypovolaemic shock, desquamation and organ failure. It is caused by group 1 staphylococcal phage types or group 5 enterotoxin B.

Emergency contraception

Yuzpe regime   Combined oestrogen and progestrogen method of emergency contraception. The first dose must be given within 72 hours of intercourse. The failure rate is 2%. It is contraindicated in established known pregnancy and in patients with thromboembolic disease. Where possible emergency contraception is best performed at a family planning clinic or by the general practitioner so that the patient can be counselled and future contraception plans arranged.

Further reading

Van Look PFA, von Hertzen H. Emergency contraception. *Contraception British Medical Bulletin*, 1993; **49**: 158–70.
Williams GR. The toxic shock syndrome. *British Medical Journal*, 1990; **300**: 960.

Related topics of interest

Abdominal pain (p. 1)
Genitourinary trauma (p. 132)
Obstetric emergencies (p. 223)
Shock (p. 269)
Urological conditions – acute (p. 303)

HAEMATOLOGICAL CONDITIONS

Sickle cell disease

Sickle cell disease is a haemoglobinopathy transmitted by autosomal dominant inheritance which causes a single amino acid substitution (valine for glutamine) at position 6 on the β-chain of haemoglobin A. It occurs in races originating from Africa, the Mediterranean and parts of Asia.

Sickle cell trait occurs in heterozygotes (HbSs). Sickling usually only occurs following extreme hypoxia, for example cardiac arrest, at high altitude and sudden decompression in aircraft. It is associated with a normal lifespan and has a genetic advantage in offering some protection against malaria. The blood film is usually normal. Detection is by sickle testing.

Sickle cell disease occurs in homozygotes (HbSS). Symptoms do not normally appear in the first 6 months of life as fetal haemoglobin tends to prevent sickle crisis from occurring. Clinical features include haemolytic, microvascular occlusive and aplastic crises, splenic sequestration, anaemia and nutritional deficiencies (especially folate). Complications include TIAs, cerebrovascular accidents (CVAs), convulsions, osteomyelitis, gall stones and renal and pulmonary infarction.

Sickle cell crisis

This is precipitated by hypoxia, dehydration, acidosis, infection or cold exposure. When exposed to such insults the HbS molecules inside the erythrocytes polymerize and form strands, which initially reduces the flexibility of the red cell and impairs its passage through the microcirculation, resulting in further tissue hypoxia. Increased polymerization ultimately causes the cells to assume the characteristic sickle shape. This process is reversible providing that the red cell membrane has not become damaged. Haemolysis and microvascular occlusion cause the clinical manifestations of the crisis, typically pleuritic pain and cough, bone pain, muscle tenderness, abdominal pain, priapism and neurological syndromes. Haemolysis results in acute anaemia, aplastic crisis and haemoglobinurea Splenic sequestration may occur.

Management of crisis

- Analgesia – intravenous opiates.
- Rehydrate with intravenous fluids.
- Oxygen.
- Investigations – FBC, ABG, blood cultures and septic screen.
- Consider intravenous broad-spectrum antibiotics if infection is suspected.

Sickle cell screening	The exposure of red cells to an oxidizing agent will cause cells from both homozygotes and heterozygotes to sickle and, although it does not differentiate between them, in practical terms patients who do not have symptoms of sickle cell disease are likely to be heterozygotes. Haemoglobin electrophoresis will differentiate between the two and will also detect the presence of other haemoglobinopathies.

Bleeding disorders

Haemophilia A (factor VIII deficiency)	This is a sex-linked recessive disorder affecting 1:10 000 males and accounts for 85% of haemoglobinopathies. It has a variable penetrance, resulting in a spectrum of severity. It commonly presents with bleeds into joints and muscles, spontaneously or following minor trauma.
Haemophilia B (factor IX deficiency)	Haemophilia B is less common than haemophilia A but the clinical features are identical.
von Willebrand's disease	In this disorder factor VIII deficiency is associated with an abnormality of platelet function. Inheritance is autosomal dominant.
Management	Management of all familial bleeding disorders should follow expert haematological advice. Life-threatening haemorrhage requires resuscitation with whole blood, fresh-frozen plasma and platelet transfusion if the patient is thrombocytopenic. It is important to ascertain the underlying cause of bleeding and, if in doubt, early specialist advice should be sought.

Disseminated intra-vascular coagulation (DIC)

The clinical syndrome comprises bleeding, secondary to loss of platelets and clotting factors, associated with fibrin deposition, which leads to small-vessel obstruction and tissue ischaemia. There are many causes including:

- Infection (especially Gram-negative septicaemia).
- Pregnancy (amniotic fluid embolism, abruptio placentae, toxaemia, retained products).
- Shock, adult respiratory distress syndrome (ARDS), burns, trauma, cardiogenic shock.
- Incompatible blood transfusion.

| **Treatment** | Treatment of DIC is extremely complex and should be undertaken in combination with monitoring platelet count, prothrombin time, fibrinogen levels and fibrin degradation products under the guidance of a haematologist. In general terms management includes: |

- Resuscitation.
- Identification and treatment of the precipitating cause.
- Platelet concentrates.
- Cryoprecipitate (a source of fibrinogen).
- Fresh-frozen plasma.
- Heparin.

Idiopathic thrombocytopenic purpura

The acute form is seen in children aged 2–6 and usually presents with a purpuric rash within about 3 weeks of a viral infection. The platelet count often falls to less than 20000/mm^3. In 90% of patients the disease remits spontaneously, however the patient should be referred to a paediatrician for further assessment, supportive treatment and consideration for steroid therapy.

Haematological malignancy

Patients with haematological malignancy occasionally present to A & E. Consider the diagnosis in patients whose symptoms might be attributable to:

- Marrow failure – anaemia, infection and bleeding.
- Bone pain.
- Lymphadenopathy.

Consider this diagnosis also in patients with non-specific illness, lethargy and malaise.

Further reading

Moore GP, Jordan RC, eds: *Haematologic/Oncologic Emergencies. Emergency Clinics of North America.* Philadelphia: W.B. Saunders, 1993; 11(2).

HEADACHE

Headache is the main complaint of 0.3% of patients presenting to accident and emergency departments. Up to 16% have serious underlying pathology. A detailed history and full examination are the most important aspects in establishing cause.

Causes of headaches presenting to A & E departments (commonest first) are:

- Local scalp and skull lesions.
- Post-traumatic headache.
- Migraine and cluster headache.
- Tension headache.
- Intracranial vasodilatation (e.g. secondary to systemic infection).
- Psychogenic headache (a diagnosis of exclusion).
- Post-ictal headache.
- Referred pain, e.g. from ears, eyes, sinuses, throat, neck, teeth and temporo mandibular joints.
- Intracranial space-occupying lesions, i.e. tumour, haematoma or abscess.
- Meningitis.
- Cranial arteritis.
- Cranial nerve pain – tumour, trigeminal and post-herpetic neuralgia and atypical facial pain.
- Miscellaneous

  (a) Hypertension.
  (b) Exertional and cough headache.
  (c) Hydrocephalus.

Investigations	For most patients, presenting to the A & E department few tests will be helpful but consider: • *Skull radiography.* • *Computerized tomography.* • *Lumbar puncture.* • *ESR.*
Subarachnoid haemorrhage	The majority of patients are aged over 40 years and there is a slight female predominance. Mortality from subarachnoid haemorrhage (SAH) varies from 30 to 45%. The commonest cause is a cerebral aneurysm, but in up to 20% of cases no underlying cause can be determined. It is associated with hypertension, poly-cystic kidneys, coarctation of the aorta and connective tissue disorders. Warning headaches occur in approxi-mately 50% of patients and are thought to be caused by a leak of subarachnoid blood or stretching of the aneurysm.

1. History. The headache of SAH is often referred to as 'a blow to the head', 'a terrible bursting sensation' or 'the worst headache I've ever had'. A sudden severe headache different from any headache previously suffered or a severe pain that may be localized should alert the physician.

A high index of suspicion is needed to differentiate between benign headaches and the warning headaches of SAH.

In 25% of cases extertional activities precede the event. Other symptoms include:

- Nausea and vomiting (20%).
- Syncope or brief loss of consciousness.
- Sudden onset of confusion (28%).
- Epilepsy.

2. Examination

- Focal neurologic signs – nerve palsies of the III, IV and VI cranial nerves.
- Motor or sensory paresis.
- Coma (36%).
- Meningism (30%).
- Hypertension (32%).
- Visual disturbances (15%) and retinal haemorrhages.

3. Treatment. The patient with SAH should be admitted to a neurosurgical intensive care unit. Appropriate sedation, prophylaxis of seizures and further evaluation are essential.

Nimodipine is used for the prevention and treatment of ischaemic neurological deficits following SAH. It is a calcium channel blocker with a smooth muscle relaxant effect and acts preferentially on cerebral arteries.

Early aneurysm surgery is now advocated after appropriate imaging.

Brain tumour and abscess

The headache is caused by inflammation, traction and displacement or distension of the pain-sensitive structures of the cranium. With increased intracranial pressure, headache is usually a prominent symptom.

1. History. Tumour headache is often deep, aching, steady and dull. The headache may worsen owing to enlargement of the mass and associated cerebral oedema. Pain is exacerbated by increases in intracranial pressure (ICP) (such as that occurring during coughing or the Valsalva manoeuvre).

2. Examination. The headache associated with a brain abscess is usually preceded by pain in the adjacent nasal and aural structures from which it originates. Associated signs include fever, papilloedema and focal neurology. Hypertension and bradycardia (the Cushing's reflex) are features of raised ICP. Sinus radiographs and CT scans are required and upon diagnosis referral to the appropriate specialist.

3. Treatment

- Drainage of the abscess.
- Reduce intracranial pressure.
- Antibiotics.

Temporal arteritis

Temporal arteritis is caused by an inflammatory process in the cranial arteries. *Headache* is the commonest presenting complaint and the physician needs to be alert to the potential diagnosis in the previously asymptomatic patient over the age of 50 who has a recent-onset headache.

1. History. The patients are more commonly female and associated symptoms are weight loss, night sweats, low-grade fever and jaw claudication (characteristic of this disorder).

The term *polymyalgia rheumatica* refers to the muscle pains and stiffness in the shoulders and pelvic girdles associated with variable systemic symptoms and an elevated ESR.

2. Examination. The area around the temporal artery is usually tender to palpation, and the skin may appear red. In 50% of untreated cases irreversible blindness may result. If the vertebral and carotid arteries are affected this may present as a transient ischaemic attack or stroke.

The *ESR* (a value over 40 mm/h has good diagnostic value) is the investigation of choice followed by a *temporal artery biopsy* (there may be skip lesions and a normal biopsy does not totally exclude the diagnosis).

3. Treatment. Therapy with high-dose steroids should be initiated as soon as possible, even before the temporal artery biopsy. The patient may have to remain on steroids for several years, with maintenance therapy according to clinical symptoms and ESR.

Further reading

Fontanarosa PB. Recognition of subarachnoid haemorrhage. *Annals of Emergency Medicine*, 1989; **18**: 1199–205.

Freitag FG, Diamond M. Emergency treatment of headache. *Medical Clinics of North America*, 1991; **75**: 749–61.

Related topics of interest

Head injury (p. 146)
Meningitis (p. 204)
Migraine (p. 209)

HEAD INJURY

Approximately 50% of all trauma deaths result from head injuries. Of deaths that occur in patients who reach hospital alive, two-thirds are due to head injury, and head injury is the commonest cause of life-long disability. Approximately eight severe, 18 moderate and 280 minor head injuries occur per year per 100 000 population in England and Wales.

Damage to the brain can occur directly as a result of the original injury (*primary brain damage*) or indirectly as a result of other factors (*secondary brain damage*). *Primary brain damage* is instantaneous, irreversible and results from shearing and pressure forces that cause diffuse axonal injury, microcirculatory disruption, tissue haemorrhage, lacerations and contusions. *Secondary brain damage* is due to increased ICP, reduced cerebral blood flow (CBF) and hypoxia. *Potentially avoidable deaths* are often the result of delayed, inappropriate or inadequate treatment of secondary brain damage.

Causes of secondary brain damage include:

- Hypoxia.
- Hypercapnia.
- Hypotension.
- Cerebral oedema.
- Intracranial haemorrhage.
- Intracranial infection.
- Epilepsy.

Head injury severity   The Glasgow Coma Scale (GCS) can be used to categorize patients. Coma is defined as a GCS of 8 or less.

- Severe   GCS ≤8
- Moderate   GCS 9 – 12
- Minor   GCS 13 – 15

A deterioration in GCS is the most significant sign of the development of increased ICP and a hallmark of secondary brain damage, hence the importance of repeated neurological assessment.

The risks of intracranial haematoma are as follows:

- Fully orientated no skull fracture   1:5983
- Confused with no skull fracture   1:121
- Fully orientated with skull fracture   1:32
- Confused with skull fracture   1:4

Focal signs or fits increase the likelihood of presence of intracranial haematoma.

History	• Accident mechanism and details (road traffic accident, fall, etc.)
	• Clinical condition of the patient.
	• Baseline GCS at accident scene.
	• <u>A</u>llergies
	<u>M</u>edications
	<u>P</u>ast medical history
	<u>L</u>ast meal
	<u>E</u>vents leading up to injury
	• Specifically seek details regarding alcohol ingestion, anticoagulants, epilepsy and diabetes.
	• Symptoms of nausea, vomiting, headache, fits, diplopia, amnesia.

Examination

- AVPU and Glasgow Coma Scale.
  <u>A</u>lert.
  Responds to <u>V</u>ocal stimuli.
  Responds only to <u>P</u>ainful stimuli.
  <u>U</u>nresponsive.
- Pupil size and response to light.
- Examine for basal skull fracture.
- Examine for a compound head injury or depressed skull fracture.
- Lateralized extremity weakness, sensation (include sacral region), deep tendon reflexes and plantar responses.

Basal skull fracture

These fractures are not apparent on skull radiographs but intracranial air or an opaque sphenoid sinus suggests their presence. More important are the following physical findings:

- Racoon eyes (bilateral periorbital haematoma) with cribriform plate fracture.
- Subhyaloid haemorrhage.
- Scleral haemorrhage without a posterior limit.
- Haemotympanum, rhinorrhoea and otorrhoea.
- Battle's sign (bruising over the mastoid process).

Management

The ABCs are followed.

1. The indications for intubation and ventilation after head injury are:

- Coma.
- Loss of protective laryngeal reflexes.
- Inadequate ventilation. *Hypoxaemia* ($PaO_2 < 9$ kPa

on air or <13 kPa on oxygen). *Hypercarbia* ($PaCO_2$ > 6 kPa).
- Spontaneous hyperventilation causing $PaCO_2 < 3.5$ kPa.
- Respiratory arrhythmia.
- Reduction of ICP by inducing hypocarbia.
- Failure to control seizures by conservative methods.

2. Indications for skull radiography include:

- Loss of consciousness or amnesia at any time.
- Neurological symptoms or signs.
- Cerebrospinal fluid or blood from the nose or ear.
- Suspected penetrating injury.
- Scalp bruising or swelling.
- Alcohol intoxication.
- Difficulty in assessing the patient (e.g. the young, patients with epilepsy).

3. Admission criteria include:

- Confusion or any other depression of the level of consciousness at the time of examination.
- Skull fracture.
- Neurological signs of headache or vomiting.
- Difficulty in assessing the patient, e.g. drunks, the young, patients with epilepsy.
- Other medical conditions, e.g. haemophilia.
- The patient's social conditions or lack of responsible adult/relative.

Note:

- Post-traumatic amnesia with full recovery is not an indication for admission.
- Patients sent home should be given written instructions about possible complications and appropriate action.

4. Criteria for consultation with a neurosurgeon include:

- Fractured skull in combination with either confusion or other depression of the level of consciousness, focal neurological signs or fits.
- Confusion or other neurological disturbance persisting for more than 12 hours even if there is no skull fracture.
- Coma continuing after resuscitation.

- Suspected open injury of the vault or base of the skull.
- Depressed fracture of the skull.
- Deterioration in Glasgow Coma Scale.

5. *Indications for immediate CT include:*

- Persistent neurological deficit.
- Depressed or deteriorating mental status.
- Penetrating injury.
- Depressed skull fracture.
- Post-traumatic seizure.
- Signs of basal skull fracture.
- Progressive headache.

6. *Further investigations include*

- *Glucose.* To exclude hypoglycaemia.
- *Arterial blood gases.*
- *Coagulation studies.* There is a risk of disseminated intravascular coagulopathy in patients with severe head injuries.

ICP monitoring

The normal ICP is 15 mmHg or less, and an elevated ICP is associated with increased mortality. If it rises above 20 mmHg active therapy is advised.

The *cerebral perfusion pressure (CPP)* is calculated using the formula:

$$CPP = \text{Mean arterial blood pressure} - ICP$$

This pressure must be above 70 mmHg to provide adequate oxygen to a severely injured brain.

An ICP monitor should be inserted in a patient who remains in coma despite resuscitation and when CT demonstrates cerebral oedema or diffuse axonal injury.

Management techniques in prevention and treatment of raised ICP

1. *Hyperventilation. Hypocapnia*: lowering the $PaCO_2$ to 26–28 mmHg (3.5–3.7 kPa) reduces intracranial blood volume and secondarily lowers ICP. Hyperventilation also reduces intracerebral acidosis and increases cerebral metabolism, both of which are helpful. This procedure requires endotracheal intubation, controlled ventilation and paralysis.

2. *Fluid control*

- *Intravenous fluids* should be administered cautiously to prevent overhydration and should not be hyperosmolar, as this may augment cerebral oedema.

- *Mannitol.* Its use before CT in the emergency management of head injury is controversial. It should only be administered with the consent of a neurosurgeon, or to buy time when neurosurgical intervention will be delayed and the patient is deteriorating. A dose of 0.5–1.0 g/kg is given over a 15–20 minute period and may reduce raised ICP temporarily.

3. *Steroids.* No longer advised.

4. *High-dose barbiturates.* These have no role in the early treatment of raised ICP.

5. Agents that may minimize secondary brain damage, such as *nimodipine* (a calcium channel blocking agent) and drugs that limit the cellular damage caused by the release of free radicals (lipid peroxidase inhibitors and free radical scavengers) are undergoing clinical trials.

Complications

1. *Intracranial haematomas*

(a) *Extradural.* Usually related to bleeding from the middle meningeal artery.
(b) *Intradural*

- *Subdural.* Usually due to bleeding from superficial veins ruptured indirectly by shearing forces or by direct impact.
- *Intracerebral.*

(c) *Subarachnoid.*
(d) *Mixed.*

Rapidly expanding intracranial haematoma, usually extradural, may be life-threatening. In such circumstances *burr holes* can be considered if a surgeon, properly trained in this procedure, is available and only with the advice and consent of a neurosurgeon. Generally in the UK, patients are transferred to a neurosurgical unit for surgical decompression.

2. *Epilepsy.* Prolonged or repeated seizures should be treated aggressively as they increase cerebral hypoxia, cause oedema and raise ICP.

Treatment

- *Diazepam.* Respiratory function must be closely monitored.

- *Phenytoin* (5–10 mg/kg) at a rate of 50 mg/min, with continuous ECG monitoring.
- *Thiopentone* infusion with paralysis and ventilation.

Further reading

American College of Surgeons. Head trauma. In: *Advanced Trauma Life Support Instructor Manual*. Chicago: American College of Surgeons, 1993: 159–60.

Gentleman D, Dearden M, Midgley S, Maclean D. Guidelines for resuscitation and transfer of patients with serious head injury. *British Medical Journal*, 1993; **307**: 547–52.

Suggestions from a group of neurosurgeons. Guidelines for initial management after head injury in adults. *British Medical Journal*, 1984; **288**: 983–5.

White RJ, Likavec MJ. The diagnosis and initial management of head injury. *New England Journal of Medicine*, 1992; **327**: 1507–11.

Related topics of interest

HEALTH OF THE NATION

The Government White Paper *The Health of the Nation: A Strategy for Health in England* (Department of Health, 1992) sets out a strategy for improving the health of the population of England (similar initiatives exist in Wales, Scotland and Northern Ireland). The overall goal is:

> "To secure continuing improvements in the general health of the population of England by adding years to life – increasing life expectancy and reducing premature death – and adding life to years – increasing years lived free from ill-health, reducing or minimising the effects of illness and disability, promoting healthy lifestyles, promoting healthy physical, and social environments, and improving quality of life."

The areas with the greatest need and the greatest scope for cost-effective improvements in the overall health of the nation are:

- Coronary heart disease and stroke.
- Cancers.
- Mental illness.
- Accidents.
- Human immunodeficiency virus/acquired immunodeficiency syndrome and sexual health.

For each key area, objectives and targets are set for improving health and reducing risk factors for disease.

Accidents

Accidents are a major cause of death and disability, being the commonest cause of death in people under 30. Accidents account for approximately 13% of all potential years of life lost under 65 years, and for 7% of NHS expenditure.

The *Health of the Nation* targets are:

- To reduce the death rate from accidents among children aged under 15 years by at least 33% by 2005 (from 6.7 per 100 000 in 1990 to no more than 4.5 per 100 000).
- To reduce the death rate from accidents among young people aged 15–24 years by at least 25% by 2005 (from 23.2 per 100 000 in 1990 to no more than 17.4 per 100 000).
- To reduce the death rate from accidents among people aged 65 years and over by at least 33% by 2005 (from 56.7 per 100 000 in 1990 to no more than 38.0 per 100 000).

This is to be achieved by:

- *Accident prevention.* This requires a multidisciplinary approach from local authorities, the police, health service staff including A & E personnel and voluntary organizations. One individual should coordinate multidisciplinary and multiagency groups to formulate strategy and to manage the implementation of action plans for accident prevention using available epidemiological data. Successful injury prevention requires good data collection; the introduction of the nationally agreed minimum data set in A & E will improve retrieval.
- *Reduce the severity of accidents.* Environmental changes will have as much impact as improving education in preventing death from accidents and includes measures such as cycle helmets, seat belts, child car seats and non-impact-absorbing surfaces in playgrounds, as well as the positioning of fixed objects such as street lights, post-boxes and bus shelters.
- *Improve the treatment of individuals who have suffered an accident to reduce mortality and morbidity.* Improvements in prehospital care with the provision of trained paramedics will continue, supported by the increasing number of doctors in the British Association for Immediate Care (BASICS). By 1997 each front-line ambulance will have one fully trained paramedic aboard. The PHTLS course (prehospital trauma life support course) and the well-established ATLS course (advanced trauma life support course) will continue to improve the quality of prehospital care.
- *Improving the care and support of those with disability resulting from accidents to reduce handicap.* Rehabilitation of accident victims is an essential component of trauma care, especially as many accident victims are young.

Further reading

Department of Health. *The Health of the Nation: A Strategy for Health in England.* London: HMSO, 1992.

Related topics of interest

Major injuries – Royal College of Surgeons of England Report (p. 194)
Prehospital care (p. 248)

HEAT ILLNESS

Heat stroke

Heat stroke describes the syndrome produced by overheating of the body core. It is an uncommon but severe form of heat illness that may be rapidly fatal. The rectal temperature is >40.5°C and sweating may stop. There is often severe metabolic upset with increase metabolic rate and oxygen consumption. The mortality is high (10%) and may result from shock, arrhythmias, myocardial ischaemia, renal failure and neurological dysfunction. Complication and death are more related to the underlying disease than to the actual temperature.

Aetiology

1. Exertional heat stroke. Commonly a young, healthy individual takes excessive exercise. Those in the armed forces and long distance runners are most at risk. Predisposing factors include lack of acclimatization, lack of cardiovascular conditioning, dehydration, the wearing of heavy clothes and excessive exercise.

2. Classic heat stroke is most common in the elderly. The underlying defect may involve impaired heat dissipation. Predisposing causes include cardiovascular disease, neurological disorders, obesity, the use of anticholinergic or diuretic drugs, dehydration and old or young age.

3. Neuroleptic malignant syndrome. This occurs in 0.2% of those on neuroleptics, usually within a month of starting. Haloperidol is the commonest agent. An idiosyncratic reaction with symptoms of muscle rigidity, extrapyramidal abnormalities, and autonomic dysfunction occurs. It tends to develop insidiously over 1–3 days, either after initiation of treatment or when the dose is increased. The mortality is significant and secondary to respiratory complications.

4. Malignant hyperthermia of anaesthesia is a rare autosomal dominant disease. Commonly associated with suxamethonium and halothane.

5. Drug induced. Anticholinergic drugs, alcohol abuse and withdrawal, salicylate overdose and drug abuse (cocaine and amphetamines).

6. Hormonal hyperthermia, e.g. thyrotoxicosis and phaeochromocytoma.

7. *Hypothalamic hyperthermia* is rare, except in association with cerebrovascular accidents.

History and examination

The presentation feature is likely to be of *acute onset*, with a core temperature *above 40.5°C*. Confusion or coma is present. The patient is flushed, dehydrated, with a tachycardia and hypotension. If a young fit patient presents collapsed after exercise it is *vital* that the rectal temperature is taken.

Complications

1. Cardiac

• Myocardial ischaemia.
• Arrhythmias.
• Hypotension.
• Congestive heart failure.

2. Neurological

• Seizures.
• Confusion.
• Delirium.
• Coma.
• Persistent peripheral neuropathies.

3. Metabolic

• Hypoxia.
• Hypoglycaemia.
• Electrolyte disturbances.
• Acid–base disturbances.

4. Haematological

• Leucocytosis and thrombocytosis.
• Disseminated intravascular coagulopathy.

5. Renal failure.

6. Myoglobinuria and rhabdomyolysis.

Treatment

The most important step is to diagnose and treat the underlying disorder. Physical cooling is essential. The rapidity of treatment is more important than the precise method of cooling.

These patients require admission and if unconscious or if the temperature has been raised for some hours admit to an ITU/HDU.

- *High-flow oxygen.*
- *Secure venous access.*
- *Remove all clothing.*
- *Immersion in ice water* is ideal for the true hyperthermic emergency, but is not usually feasible. Other treatments include infusion of cooled intravenous or intraperitoneal fluid, gastric lavage or enemas with ice water, and even extracorporeal circulation.

    Soak sheets in water at 20°C and have fans blow room air over the patient. An alternative is to wrap ice in sheets and place in the axillae, groins and behind the neck.

    Stop cooling when rectal temperature reaches 38°C.
- Check blood glucose, urea and electrolytes, creatine phosphokinase, calcium and phosphate and perform a full blood count and clotting screen. Monitor continuously pulse, blood pressure, respiratory rate, ECG, GCS and rectal temperature.
- Monitor urinary output and check for myoglobinuria.
- *Commence i.v. fluids.* Infuse 1 litre of normal saline (room temperature) over the first 30 minutes and continue as guided by clinical examination, electrolyte disturbance and urinary output.
- Check arterial blood gases.
- *Diazepam* if fits occur.
- Consider *dantrolene* for the treatment of malignant hyperthermia and neuroleptic malignant syndrome.

Heat exhaustion

This is a common but usually benign condition. The rectal temperature is <40.5°C. It is a metabolic/vascular upset owing to water and salt depletion or imbalance.

1. *Water depletion* results from deprivation of water in hot environments. The patient complains of thirst, is clinically dehydrated, with an elevated serum sodium and chloride, but normal haematocrit.

    Treatment consists of oral rehydration with water or intravenous infusion of 5% glucose if the patient is unable to swallow. Death occurs when the weight loss is 15–25% of body weight and is due to excess salt in the body fluids.

2. *Salt depletion* develops gradually over a few hours or days in people working in hot environments, partic-

ularly if unacclimatized. Early features include malaise, headaches and fatigue. There may be sudden collapse with confusion and vomiting. Muscle cramps, which are very painful, develop if there is associated muscular exercise.

There is dehydration associated with a normal serum sodium and chloride but raised haematocrit.

Treatment. Oral treatment with 25 g of sodium chloride in 5 litres of water by mouth is often adequate, and then ensure adequate daily salt intake. In severe cases or if there is associated vomiting intravenous isotonic saline is required. Most patients recover within a few hours.

Further reading

Simon HB. Hyperthermia. *New England Journal of Medicine*, 1993; **329**: 483–7.

Related topic of interest

Hypothermia (p. 168)

HELICOPTER TRANSPORTATION

The role of helicopters includes the *primary evacuation* and *secondary transfer* of seriously ill medical and surgical patients, including those with burns. While the helicopter has a role in the transport of the critically ill or injured patient, it should always be only one component of a thoroughly integrated system for the care of a trauma victim. It should also be used with effective triage guidelines, ensuring that the right patients receive the right treatment at the right time in order to save life.

The evacuation of casualties by helicopter has been used extensively in Germany, the United States and in parts of the UK. Owing to the prohibitive cost of airborne transportation, many authorities continue to question the effectiveness of this mode, and there have been many calls for definitive objective assessment.

Safety

The safety record of ambulance helicopters is poor, with accident rates substantially higher than those of commercial helicopters. The accident rate of 1 per 5000 flying hours is twice the general aviation rate and 100 times the rate experienced by scheduled airlines.

Factors affecting the accident rate include:

- The number of flights made by the helicopter flight programme (the busier programmes having a low accident rate).
- Whether the programme can be operated under instrument flight rules. This reduces the number of accidents.

Training

Any doctor escorting a critically ill patient by air needs to be aware of the differences between the airborne and terrestrial environments. Model curricula in air medical transport are now available for the emergency physician. These provide advice concerning staff training, evaluation and safety criteria. 'Aviation medicine' is now a subspecialty.

Primary transfer

In the USA mortality is significantly reduced if patients are transported to a trauma centre by helicopter. The improved survival is more marked in patients with low trauma scores and may relate more to a shorter interval between injury and the institution of prehospital resuscitative treatment than to more rapid arrival at the trauma centre, since the helicopter transport teams are experienced in many life-saving techniques.

The presence of an in-flight physician reduces mortality by up to 50% when compared with teams led by non-physicians. The physicians' psychomotor skills and judgement are the two factors most instrumental in lowering mortality; aggressive life-saving procedures are performed more frequently by the physicians, particularly in head-injured patients.

The reduction in mortality brought about by the use of helicopters in rural areas has been proven, but no survival advantage has been shown for helicopter-transported patients in an urban area with a sophisticated prehospital care system.

It appears that aeromedical transport systems using fix-wing or helicopter transport can extend the clinical benefit of the regional trauma service up to 800 miles without increasing trauma-related mortality.

Secondary transfer   The success of interhospital transfer of the patients of the Careflight Project was assessed by pre-transfer and post-transfer sickness scores and it was found that there was no deterioration in patients' health during transfer.

A helicopter transfer system using suitable equipment and appropriate staff is a practical and safe method of interhospital transfer and is probably preferable to land transfers for distances in excess of 25 miles.

Further reading

Cusack SC, Robertson CE. The value of helicopter transportation for trauma patients. *Injury*, 1991; **22**: 54–6.
Kee SS, Ramage CMH, Mendel P, Bristow ASC. Interhospital transfers by helicopter: the first 50 patients of the Careflight Project. *Journal of the Royal Society of Medicine*, 1992; **85**: 29–31.
Ramage C, Kee S, Bristow A. Interhospital transfer of the critically ill patient by helicopter. *British Journal of Hospital Medicine*, 1990; **43**; 147–8
Ridley SA, Wright IH, Rogers PN. Secondary transport of critically ill patients. *Hospital Update*, 1990; **April**: 289–98.

Related topics of interest

HEPATITIS B

Hepatitis B virus (HBV) is a DNA virus, and in the UK is present in about 1 in 1000 of the population. Infection with HBV causes liver damage, which may lead to acute fulminant hepatitis (<1%), chronic carrier state [Hepatitis B surface antigen-positive (HBsAg) in 5–10%], chronic active hepatitis, cirrhosis or primary hepatocellular carcinoma. The incubation period ranges from 2 to 6 months. Transmission is by person to person, by saliva, semen and other body fluids, or by the parental route, contaminated syringes, needles and dialysis and other equipment serving as vectors.

A UK Advisory Panel can be consulted when specific occupational advice is needed regarding HBV or human immunodeficiency virus (HIV) infection.

Groups at high risk of HBV infection include:

- Those living in endemic areas, e.g. South-east Asia, the Middle East and Africa.
- Homosexual men.
- Prostitutes.
- Intravenous drug abusers.
- Sexual contacts of carriers.
- Health care workers.

Methods of control include:

- Universal precautions.
- Vaccination against HBV.
- Active and passive immunization of exposed individuals.
- Sterilization of all equipment.
- Isolation of infected persons.

Treatment

Acute viral hepatitis is usually self-limiting and management is largely supportive.

Most patients can be managed as out-patients, however those patients with signs and symptoms of acute liver failure or in whom there are doubts over diagnosis or social factors require admission. In cases of sexually transmitted hepatitis contact tracing is essential, and contacts should be offered passive immunization. Additionally, counselling of the HBsAg-positive carrier is necessary.

- Immunoglobulin (IG).
- Hyperimmune gamma-globulin (HBIG).
- Antiviral chemotherapy.

Hepatitis B vaccination

All health care workers who are at risk of acquiring hepatitis B occupationally should be immunized against hepatitis B, unless immunity to hepatitis B as a result of natural immunity or previous immunization has been documented.

The vaccine is genetically engineered and is given in three doses. Response to the vaccine should be checked 2–4 months after completion of the primary course. An anti-HBs level of 100 miu/ml is considered to reflect an adequate response and to confer immunity.

- *Poor responders.* Blood level between 10 and 100 miu/ml. This level may not confer long-lasting immunity and may require a booster dose.
- *Non-responders.* Below 10 miu/ml. Approximately 10% of individuals are non-responders to a primary course (commoner with increasing age and in immunocompromised individuals) and should be given a repeat course. Some non-responders are carriers of the hepatitis B virus.

  Staff who fail to respond to the vaccine are able to continue to perform invasive procedures provided they are not e antigen (HBeAg)-positive carriers of the virus.

Universal precautions

All patients are considered to be potentially infected with HIV, HBV and other blood-borne pathogens. For this reason 'universal precautions' have been recommended by the Centers for Disease Control (CDC) to prevent transmission. Hepatitis B transmission is more likely than HIV. Of primary concern is contact with the patient's blood or mucosal surfaces or penetration of the skin, i.e. needlestick injury.

Universal precautions include:

- Hands should always be washed before and after contact with patients. Hands should be washed even when gloves are used. If hands come in contact with blood, body fluids, or human tissue, they should be washed with soap and water.
- Gloves should be worn when contact with blood, body fluids or contaminated surfaces is anticipated.
- Gowns are indicated if blood splattering is likely. Masks and protective goggles should be worn if aerosolization or splattering is likely.
- The need for emergency mouth-to-mouth resuscitation and mouth pieces should be minimized by strategically locating resuscitation bags or other ventilation devices in areas where they may be needed.
- Sharps should be handled cautiously to prevent acci-

dental cuts or punctures. Used needles should not be bent, broken, reinserted into the original sheath or unnecessarily handled. They should be discarded immediately after use into an easily accessible, impervious needle disposal container. All needle-stick accidents, mucosal splashes or contamination of open wounds with blood or body fluids should be reported immediately.

- Blood spills should be cleaned up promptly with a disinfectant solution, such as 1:10 dilution of chlorine bleach.
- All patients' blood specimens should be considered biohazards.

Universal precautions apply to blood and other body fluids containing visible blood, and to fluids such as semen and vaginal secretions, cerebrospinal fluid, synovial fluid, pleural fluid, peritoneal fluid, pericardial fluid and amniotic fluid. Universal precautions do not apply to faeces, nasal secretions, sputum, sweat, tears, urine, vomiting and saliva unless they contain visible blood. All health care workers should routinely follow general infection control guidelines and adopt safer working practices to prevent transmission of HIV and HBV.

The infection control measures to prevent transmission of blood-borne viruses in the health care setting include:

- Apply good basic hygiene practices with regular hand washing.
- Cover existing wounds or skin lesions with waterproof dressings.
- Avoid invasive procedures if suffering from chronic skin lesions on hands.
- Avoid contamination of person and clothing by appropriate use of protective clothing.
- Protect mucous membranes of eyes, mouth and nose from blood splashes.
- Prevent puncture wounds, cuts and abrasions in the presence of blood.
- Avoid using sharps wherever possible.
- Institute safe procedures for handling and disposal of needles and other sharps.
- Institute approved procedures for sterilization and disinfection of instruments and equipment.
- Clear up spillages of blood and other body fluids promptly and disinfect surfaces.

- Ensure safe disposal of contaminated waste.

More specific measures to surgical technique are given below:

1. Invasive procedures in all patients

- Have vaccination against hepatitis B.
- Cover all cuts and abrasions with waterproof dressings.
- Do not pass sharps hand to hand.
- Do not use hand needles.
- Do not guide needles with fingers.
- Do not resheathe needles.
- Dispose of all sharps safely into approved containers.
- Put disposable waste into yellow clinical waste gags for incineration.

2. Additional precautions when caring for known HIV- and hepatitis B-positive and high-risk patients

- Consider non-operative management.
- Remove unnecessary equipment from theatre.
- Use double gloves, high-efficiency masks, eye protection, boots, impervious gowns, closed wound drainage.
- Disinfect theatre floor with hypochlorite.
- Observe highest level of theatre discipline.
- Have only experienced personnel workers in theatre.
- Use disposable anaesthetic circuitry or an appropriate method of decontamination.

Further reading

British Medical Association. *A Code of Practice for The Safe Use and Disposal of Sharps*. London: BMA, 1990

Joint Working Party of the Hospital Infection Society and the Surgical Infection Study Group. Risks to surgeons and patients from HIV and hepatitis: guidelines and management of exposure to blood or body fluids. *British Medical Journal*, 1992; **305**: 1337–43.

Recommendations of the Advisory Group on Hepatitis. UK Health Departments. *Protecting Health Care Workers and Patients from Hepatitis B*. London: HMSO, 1993.

Related topics of interest

HUMAN IMMUNODEFICIENCY VIRUS

Human immunodeficiency virus (HIV), the cause of the acquired immunodeficiency syndrome (AIDS), was first isolated in 1983. It consists of an RNA core and an enzyme – *reverse transcriptase*.

HIV is probably present in 1 in 2000 people (about 0.05% of the general population). In the minority of cases, patients experience the *seroconversion syndrome* 1–3 weeks after exposure. This is like glandular fever, with lymphadenopathy, a maculopapular rash, fever and occasionally a peripheral neuropathy or meningoencephalitis. After seroconversion there is a long asymptomatic phase, with a median duration of 10 years.

HIV destroys T-helper lymphocytes, causing immunosuppression. Patients with moderate immune deficiency, associated with symptoms such as fever, fatigue, diarrhoea, weight loss, enlarged lymph nodes and oral candidiasis, are said to have *AIDS-related complex (ARC)*.

Secondary infections caused by opportunistic organisms (e.g. *Pneumocystis* pneumonia, cerebral toxoplasmosis, *Cryptosporidium* diarrhoea, cytomegalovirus, herpes, myobacteria and *Candida* infections) and the development of tumours such as Kaposi's sarcoma and lymphoma characterize the full-blown syndrome known as AIDS.

Transmission	Transmission occurs via direct sexual contact either homosexual or heterosexual, via contaminated needles and syringes, blood transfusions with contaminated blood and blood products, transplacental and mother-to-child transfer.
Control	Avoid contact and take universal precautions when handling blood and body fluids.
Risk factors	*1. High-risk groups*

* Homosexual or bisexual males.
* Intravenous drug abusers.
* Persons who have had penetrative sexual contact with others from areas of high HIV prevalence.
* Persons who have received unscreened blood transfusions.
* Haemophilic patients who have received untreated blood and blood products.
* Known HIV-positive patients.
* Sexual contacts of any of the above.
* Children born to seropositive mothers.

2. High-risk areas

- Local – where the prevalence of HIV infection is known to be high.
- International, e.g. sub-Saharan Africa; other countries with known high prevalence of HIV.

Tumours

- *Kaposi's sarcoma* is commoner in homosexual men, and is widespread, commonly affecting the mucous membranes, viscera and lymph nodes.
- *Non-Hodgkin's lymphoma* commonly affects the CNS, bone marrow and gastrointestinal tract and heralds a poor prognosis.

Opportunistic infection

Most relates to reactivation of latent organisms, and treatment often suppresses rather than eradicates the organisms. Relapses are common.

1. Pulmonary

- *Pneumocystis carinii*. This is the commonest infection in HIV patients. Symptoms include increasing dyspnoea, cough and weight loss. Hypoxia and bilateral infiltrates on chest radiographs support the diagnosis. Cytological confirmation of sputum or bronchial aspirates is necessary.
- *Mycobacterium tuberculosis.*
- *Cytomegalovirus* (CMV).
- Bacterial pneumonia.

2. Gastrointestinal

- Oral and oesophageal candidiasis, CMV and herpes simplex virus (HSV).
- Diarrhoea, weight loss, cryptosporidiosis, infection with *Isospora belli*, CMV, HSV and atypical mycobacteria.
- Hepatitis and cholestasis.
- Perianal ulceration.
- Neoplasia – Kaposi's sarcoma, lymphoma, hairy leucoplakia and anorectal warts.

3. Neurological

- AIDS-related dementia.
- Meningitis (cryptococcal meningitis) and meningoencephalitis.
- CMV retinitis.

- Intracranial mass – cerebral toxoplasmosis, lymphoma.
- Peripheral neuropathy.

The evidence available indicates that the risk of transmission of HIV from infected patients to health care workers is far higher than the risk of transmission from workers to patients. Up to December 1992, there have been 148 reported cases worldwide of health care workers infected with HIV though contact with their patients.

Recently, guidelines on the management of infected health care workers were revised after it was revealed in the press that some A & E personnel have been HIV positive. The Centers for Disease Control, Atlanta, have reported transmission of HIV to patients during invasive dental procedures performed by a dentist with AIDS. There have been no other cases of an HIV-infected health care worker transmitting HIV to a patient.

Although the risk of transmission from health care worker to patient during an exposure-prone invasive procedure is considered remote, such procedures should not be undertaken by an HIV-infected health care worker as injury to the worker could result in blood contaminating a patient's open tissues. Exposure-prone invasive procedures are defined as surgical entry into tissues, cavities or organs or repair of major traumatic injuries; cardiac catherization; vaginal or caesarean deliveries or other obstetric procedures during which sharp instruments are used; the manipulation, cutting or removal of any oral or perioral tissues, including tooth structures, during which bleeding may occur.

Health care workers found to be infected must seek appropriate medical and occupational advice, and those who continue to work with patients must remain under close medical supervision.

Health care workers who believe they may have been exposed to infection with HIV, in whatever circumstances, must seek medical advice and, if appropriate, diagnostic HIV antibody testing.

Workers who are found to be HIV positive and who have performed exposure-prone invasive procedures while infected must cease these activities immediately and inform the relevant designated senior medical/dental staff. Patients who may have been exposed to this risk should, as far as practicably possible, be notified and offered counselling and an HIV antibody test if they so wish.

Physicians who are aware that infected health care workers under their supervision have not sought or followed advice to modify their practice must inform the employing authority and appropriate regulatory body.

Employers must make every effort to arrange suitable alternative work and retraining or, where appropriate, early retirement for HIV-infected health care workers.

Employers have a duty to keep information on the health, including HIV status, of employees confidential and are not legally entitled to reveal that an employee has HIV infection without the employee's consent, unless to do so would be in the public interest.

Further reading

Adler MW. *ABC of AIDS*, 2nd edn. London: BMJ Publishing Group, 1991.

Related topics of interest

Hepatitis B (p. 160)
Needlestick injuries (p. 220)

HYPOTHERMIA

Hypothermia, defined as a core temperature below 35°C, is confirmed by a low-reading thermometer, and is classified as:

Mild   32 – 35°C
Moderate   30 – 32°C
Severe   < 30°C

Full recovery is possible after prolonged resuscitation and the prognosis is usually determined by the underlying illness.

Aetiology

1. Increased heat loss

- Cold immersion.
- Vasodilatation, e.g. alcohol, drugs, infection and skin disease.

2. Decreased heat production

- Unconsciousness.
- Hypothyroidism.
- Hypopituitarism.
- Hypoadrenalism.
- Old age.
- Children.

3. Underlying disease

- Pneumonia.
- Pancreatitis.

Clinical features

1. Mild

- Shivering.
- Tachycardia.
- Hypertension.
- Tachypnoea.

2. Moderate

- No shivering.
- Bradycardia.
- Hypotension.
- Bradypnoea.
- Confusion.

3. Severe

- No shivering.
- Bradycardia.
- Hypotension.
- Hypoventilation.
- Stupor/coma.
- Arrhythmias.

Cardiac effects

- *Arrhythmias.* With progressive hypothermia, brady-cardia is followed by atrial fibrillation, then ventricular fibrillation and finally asystole.
- *Ventricular fibrillation* may not respond to cardioversion if the core temperature is below 30°C. Active rewarming is advised.
- Other arrhythmias tend to revert spontaneously as the core temperature rises, and thus do not require immediate treatment.
- The *ECG* features of hypothermia (all of these features are reversible with rewarming) include:

  (a) Prolongation of the PR, QRS and QT intervals.
  (b) Muscle tremor artefact may be present even in the absence of clinical shivering.
  (c) *J-waves* – a characteristic secondary deflection on the terminal portion of the QRS complex.
  (e) Low-voltage complexes.

Investigations

- Electrolytes.
- Blood glucose.
- Alcohol and drug screen.
- Amylase.
- Thyroid function.
- Blood cultures.
- Arterial blood gases (correct for temperature).
- ECG.
- Chest radiographs.
- CT scan (for cerebral haemorrhage).

Basic life support

- Further core heat loss should be prevented by removing wet garments and insulating the victim.
- Handle the victim carefully as inadvertent movement can precipitate ventricular fibrillation.
- A minimum of 1 minute is suggested when performing a pulse check. Only if no pulse is detected should external cardiac massage be started.

Advanced life support

In hypothermic cardiac arrest, cerebral metabolism slows and the brain's requirement for oxygen is greatly reduced. The time between cessation of heart beat and brain damage is increased to as much as 30 minutes at a body temperature of 25°C.

The aphorism *'no one is dead until warm and dead'* still applies. Prolonged resuscitation may be required as death should not be confirmed until the casualty has warmed to at least 32°C or until attempts to raise the core temperature have failed.

A central vein is cannulated as drug pooling in the periphery may occur if a more peripheral vein is used.

Treatment

1. Mild hypothermia. By passive rewarming in a warm room using warm blankets with the aim of increasing the temperature by 0.5°C per hour.

2. Moderate hypothermia. May be treated with a cautious *infusion of warm saline.*

3. Severe hypothermia. May require *active core rewarming with:*

(a) Heated humidified oxygen.
(b) Centrally administered warm intravenous fluids (40°C).
(c) Invasive surgical rewarming techniques until extracorporeal rewarming can be accomplished. Techniques used include:

- Gastric lavage (40°C).
- Thoracic/pleural lavage (40°C).
- Peritoneal lavage (40°C).
- Haemodialysis.
- In cases of accidental hypothermia with cardiac arrest, rapid institution of *full cardiopulmonary bypass* provides excellent circulatory support and rapid rewarming. This avoids the complications of prolonged inadequate circulation that occur when closed cardiac massage and external warming are used. There is a case report of a successful outcome of prolonged arrest in a patient suffering from acute deep hypothermia who required continuous external cardiac massage for 6.5 hours. Continuous arterio-venous rewarming reverses hypothermia more rapidly than standard rewarming techniques and is associated with an improved survival and a significant reduction in organ failure and length of ICU stay.

Complications
- Pneumonia.
- Pulmonary oedema.
- Cardiac arrhythmias.
- Myoglobinuria.
- Disseminated intravascular thrombosis.
- Seizures.

Further reading

Advanced Life Support Group. *Advanced Cardiac Life Support. The Practical Approach.* London: Chapman and Hall, 1993.
Bolgiano E *et al.* Accidental hypothermia with cardiac arrest: recovery following rewarming by cardiopulmonary bypass. *Journal of Emergency Medicine.* 1992; **10**: 427–33.
Weinberg AD. Hypothermia. *Annals of Emergency Medicine*, 1993; **22**: 370–7.

Related topics of interest

INHALATION INJURIES

Historically the major causes of death following thermal injury were shock and wound sepsis, however now that these can be vigorously treated respiratory complications are the leading cause of mortality. Up to 55% of victims are dead at the scene. In those that survive to hospital pulmonary complications are caused by direct thermal injury to the airways and inhalation of smoke. The degree of thermal injury depends on the temperature, duration of exposure and most importantly the moisture content of the inspired gases: the higher this is, the greater the heat capacity. Smoke may contain carbon dioxide, carbon monoxide, ammonia, hydrogen cyanide, the oxides of sulphur, nitrogen and chlorine, hydrochloric acid, polyvinyl chloride and other hydrocarbon compounds. Like particles of carbon (soot), these substances can adhere to the mucosa of the respiratory tract, causing damage to the ciliary mechanism and obstruction of the small airways. In the presence of water they dissolve to form acids and alkalis that may cause pulmonary oedema by local corrosion. Absorption can result in systemic toxicity.

Clinical diagnosis

The presence of three or more of the following features suggests pulmonary damage:

- Fire in an enclosed space.
- Production of carbonaceous sputum.
- Oropharyngeal burns.
- Confusion or altered consciousness level.
- Hoarseness or loss of voice.
- Respiratory symptoms.
- Respiratory signs.

Investigations

- Arterial blood gases (ABG). Although helpful in monitoring progress, ABG studies do not correlate well with inhalational injury. A low PaO_2 may be seen, but must be interpreted in relation to the inspired oxygen concentration.
- Chest radiographs are usually normal initially.
- Carbon monoxide blood level. A high level suggests that smoke inhalation may have occurred; a low level does not exclude it.
- Fibreoptic bronchoscopy. This technique allows direct inspection of the major airways. It should be performed by someone skilled in the technique and can be performed under general or local anaesthesia. It will not reveal injury to the small airways or alveoli.
- Xenon lung scan. Intravenous xenon will at first perfuse the whole lung because the pulmonary circulation is initially intact. As the gas is expired it will be

trapped in the areas of damage and show up as high density levels. It is not a routine tool and has been used primarily in research.

Management
Administer 100% humidified oxygen to all patients in whom the diagnosis is suspected. If oedema of the upper airways is evident, early endotracheal intubation should be performed before laryngeal swelling makes this procedure impossible, in which case a needle or surgical cricothyroidotomy will have to be undertaken. When pulmonary oedema or respiratory acidosis is present or when PaO_2 is falling then assisted ventilation using positive end-expiratory pressure or mechanical intermittent positive-pressure ventilation can be started.

Further reading

Settle JAD. *Burns: the First Five Days.* London: Smith & Nephew, 1986.
Shapiro BA, Cane RD. Respiratory care. In: Millar RD, ed. *Anaesthesia.* New York: Churchill Livingstone, 1990: 2204–9.

Related topics of interest

Airway (p. 7)
Burns (p. 46)
Carbon monoxide poisoning (p. 53)

INTERHOSPITAL TRANSFER – TRAUMA

Ideally, all patients will be sent to the hospital appropriate to their needs. Realistically, however, patients may need definitive care at another hospital and thus require secondary transfer.

In 1988, a survey by the Clinical Shock Study Group in Glasgow estimated that 10 000 patients with life-threatening illness are transferred between hospitals annually in the UK.

Life-threatening injuries that can be stabilized, operatively or non-operatively, at the initial hospital must be treated prior to transfer as inadequate resuscitation (untreated hypoxia, hypotension, etc.) prior to transfer will jeopardize the patient's outcome.

The *referring physician* should complete the primary and secondary surveys, and institute appropriate resuscitation to *stabilize* the patient. The referring and *receiving physicians* should communicate directly to decide:

- The method of transportation.
- The transfer personnel, who must be adequately skilled, appropriately equipped to monitor the patient and able to administer treatment *en route* as required.

Transfer protocol

The American College of Surgeons guidelines are:

1. The *referring physician* should speak directly to the receiving physician and provide the following details:

- The patient's identity.
- A brief history, including prehospital details.
- Details of the clinical finding in the department and the treatment administered.

2. The *transferring personnel* should have knowledge of the patient's condition and requirements during transfer including:

- Airway control.
- Fluid replacement.
- Special procedures that may be necessary.
- Revised trauma score.
- Resuscitation procedures.
- Potential complications to be anticipated *en route*.

3. Documentation. A written record of events should accompany the patient and should include:

- Patient's details.
- History of injury/illness.

- Prehospital and hospital vital signs.
- Treatment record.
- Fluids given by type and volume.
- Investigations performed with results.
- Diagnosis.
- Time of transfer.
- Details of referring and receiving physicians.

4. Priorities pretransfer are resuscitation and stabilization of the patient based on this suggested outline.

(a) *Respiratory*
- Insert an airway or endotracheal tube as necessary.
- Determine the rate and method of administration of oxygen.
- Provide suction.
- Provide mechanical ventilation when needed.
- Insert a chest tube as needed.
- Insert a nasogastric tube to prevent aspiration.

(b) *Cardiovascular*
- Control external haemorrhage.
- Establish two large-bore i.v. lines and infuse appropriate fluids.
- Restore blood volume loss and continue replacement during transfer.
- Insert an indwelling catheter to monitor urinary output.
- ECG monitoring.

(c) *Central nervous system*
- Controlled hyperventilation for head-injured patients.
- Administer mannitol after neurosurgical consultation.
- Immobilize the spine.

(d) *Investigations*
- Radiographs of the cervical spine, chest and pelvis. Others as indicated.
- Haemoglobin, haematocrit, blood type and cross-match and arterial blood gases.
- ECG.
- Urinalysis.
- Blood alcohol and/or drugs as indicated.

(e) *Wounds*
- Clean and dress.
- Tetanus prophylaxis as necessary.

- Antibiotics as necessary.

(f) *Fractures* – splintage and traction.

5. *Management*

- Continued monitoring of vital signs.
- Continued support of the cardiorespiratory system.
- Appropriate medication to maintain the patient's clinical state.
- Communication with the receiving hospital.
- Continuing written record of events during transfer.

Further reading

American College of Surgeons. *Advanced Trauma Life Support Instructor Manual.* Chicago: American College of Surgeons, 1993: 293–304.

Andrews PJD, Piper IR, Dearden NM, Miller JD. Secondary insults during intrahospital transport of head-injured patients. *Lancet*, 1990; **335**: 327–30.

Hope A, Runcie CJ. Inter-hospital transport in the critically ill adult. *Intensive Care*, 1993; **5**: 187–92.

Related topics of interest

INTRAOSSEOUS INFUSION

Intraosseous infusion is recommended for children 6 years of age or younger (it has also been used in adults) who require vascular access that cannot be achieved in a timely manner via another route. It is a reliable, safe procedure with a less than 1% complication rate. It is useful in emergencies when rapid vascular accesses by other methods are unsuccessful in conditions such as:

- Cardiopulmonary arrest.
- Shock.
- Major trauma.
- Extensive burns.
- Status epilepticus.
- Overwhelming sepsis.

Anatomy

Fluid or drugs infused via the intraosseous route diffuse a short distance before entering the network of venous sinusoids within the medullary cavity. These sinusoids drain into central venous channels and exit bone via nutrient or emissary veins to enter the circulation.

The use of bone marrow of long bones as a route for infusion is generally limited to young children. Red marrow is gradually replaced by less vascular yellow marrow after about the fifth year of life. This change begins in the distal part of the limbs and progresses proximally.

Physiology

Animal studies have demonstrated the successful rapid infusion of crystalloid and blood in a fluid bolus of 20 ml/kg in less than 10 minutes.

Comparisons after injection of adrenaline have demonstrated that intraosseous and central venous injection result in similar blood levels during cardiopulmonary resuscitation.

Method

The technique of intraosseous infusion is suitable for use in and out of hospital, paramedics having demonstrated success rates of 80–94% in correct siting of intraosseous needles.

Needle insertion can be practised on a variety of models, from chicken legs to mannikins.

Various needles have been used, including spinal needles (gauge 18–20) and bone marrow biopsy needles (gauge 12–18), but specifically designed intraosseous needles are available. They vary in gauge

(14–18), length and trocar tip and have a positioning mark to indicate probable depth for ideal placement into the bone marrow. The trocar includes a handle to allow controlled pressure during insertion. The newer needles have a threaded screw-tip design to allow atraumatic stabilization at the access site to help prevent leakage.

Site of insertion

The anteromedial surface of the *proximal tibia* is the preferred site of insertion. The tibial tuberosity is palpated and the needle inserted on the subcutaneous surface, 1–3 cm distal to the tuberosity, thus avoiding damage to the epiphyseal growth plate. This is an ideal site since it is easily located with only a layer of skin covering bone and is free from any significant neurovascular structures or major muscle groups.

The needle can be inserted in the *distal tibia* proximal to the medial malleolus where it will not endanger the epiphyseal plate or saphenous vein. The cortex of the bone and the overlying tissues are thin.

The *distal femur* is an alternative site (although bony landmarks are often difficult to palpate).

Contraindications

This procedure is only recommended in life-threatening conditions when vascular access is vital and thus there are few contraindications.

- Needle placement through an area of cellulitis or burn increases the risk of *infection* and should be avoided if possible.
- Ipsilateral *fractures, vascular injuries* and *multiple unsuccessful attempts* preclude reliable venous outflow.
- *Osteogenesis imperfecta* and *osteopetrosis* increase the risk of iatrogenic fractures.

Drug administration

- Emergency drugs (adrenaline, atropine, bicarbonate, calcium, glucose, lignocaine, naloxone) and fluids (crystalloids and colloids including blood) can be administered intraosseously at essentially the same dosage and rate as when given intravenously.
- Strong alkaline and hypertonic solutions should be diluted.
- Saline boluses administered after each drug will hasten delivery to the systemic circulation.
- When rapid fluid replacement is required fluid should be infused under pressure and bilateral infusions may be necessary.

Complications

Major complications are infrequent and the majority of difficulties are technical.

To minimize complications it is recommended that correct placement be verified prior to infusion and signs of extravasation checked for.

The intraosseous needle should be removed promptly once venous access is obtained.

- Failure to enter the marrow cavity or incorrect placements have been reported in 0–18% of attempts. This may lead to extravasation of fluid or subperiosteal infiltration.
- *Osteomyelitis* is a rare complication (0.66%). Increased incidence is associated with prolonged needle placement, pre-existing bacteraemia and the use of hypertonic fluid infusions.
- Localized cellulitis, abscess formation and skin necrosis have been reported.
- Pain.
- Compartment syndrome.
- Fractures.
- Fat and bone marrow microemboli.
- Though the epiphyseal growth plate could be at risk from incorrect needle placement no cases of damage have been reported.

Further reading

Fisher DH. Intraosseous infusion. *New England Journal of Medicine*, 1990; **322**: 1579–81.

INTRAVENOUS FLUIDS

Intravenous (i.v.) fluids are indicated to provide normal maintenance requirements or to replace fluid losses when these cannot be absorbed orally.

Blood products

Blood is used in the resuscitation of patients with haemorrhage. In the presence of exsanguinating haemorrhage group O rhesus-negative blood should be immediately available. Full grouping, antibody screening and cross-matching may take up to 1 hour, but type-specific or saline cross-matched blood should be available in about 15 minutes. The donor blood is of the same ABO and rhesus type as the recipient but has only had a rudimentary cross-match of donor red cells in saline against recipient serum. Significant transfusion reactions using these techniques are rare and usually due to errors in sample labelling and patient identification.

Laboratories usually supply blood as packed red cells, which may be used in combination with crystalloid or colloid as whole-blood replacement.

Rapid transfusion of large volumes of blood which has been stored at 4°C will cause hypothermia unless it is given through a blood warmer.

Fresh-frozen plasma is separated and frozen immediately after donation, thus preserving coagulation factors. It is used for correction of coagulation defects.

Plasma protein fraction (PPF) is an isotonic solution of protein obtained from plasma and largely consisting of albumin. Classically used in burns resuscitation, it has been replaced by synthetic colloids because of its expense and the transmission of infections.

Human albumin solution is similar to PPF but contains over 95% albumin as an isotonic or hypertonic solution. It has a shelf-life of approximately 2 years.

Platelet concentrates may be used to correct thrombocytopenia as a result of massive transfusion.

Colloids

These are synthetic macromolecular solutions which are used to produce intravascular volume expansion in patients with hypovolaemia resulting from haemorrhage or plasma loss.

1. Gelatins. Polygeline (Haemaccel) and succinylated gelatin (Gelofusine) are modified gelatin solutions. They have a shelf-life of 5 years.

2. Starches. Hetastarch (Hespan) is a solution of hydrolysed starch. In comparison with the gelatins it has a prolonged half-life in the circulation and improves haemodynamic status for up to 24 hours.

3. Dextrans. These are solutions of polymers of glucose. Dextran 70 is hypertonic and produces greater volume expansion than other colloids. It interferes with haemostasis and cross-matching and is now less commonly used.

Crystalloids

Isotonic electrolyte solutions are used for correction of water and electrolyte imbalance. The choice of specific fluid depends on the biochemical disturbance present and may be a combination of the fluids listed here.

Normal (0.9%) saline is used in any condition in which there is sodium depletion, such as diabetic ketoacidosis, gastroenteritis and ileus. Potassium can be added as required. Normal saline is also used in the initial resuscitation of haemorrhage.

Hartmann's solution or compound sodium lactate solution or Ringer–lactate solution contains sodium chloride in more nearly physiological concentrations than normal saline. It also contains potassium, calcium and lactate. Its more complex contents appear to offer no additional benefit.

Ringer's solution is similar to Hartmann's but contains no lactate.

Glucose solutions

Isotonic glucose solutions (5%) are indicated when water depletion occurs without electrolyte loss. This is rare in clinical practice but may occur when oral intake is insufficient or in water-losing states such as diabetes insipidus. Hypoglycaemia requires hypertonic glucose solutions (50%) to provide sufficient glucose.

Crystalloids versus colloids

There is long-standing and unresolved controversy as to whether crystalloids or colloids are preferable in hypovolaemic shock following trauma.

1. Crystalloids

- Three times the volume of crystalloid is required to replace blood loss.
- May increase adult respiratory distress syndrome by reducing intravascular osmotic pressure.
- Replenish extracellular fluid deficit as well as intravascular deficit.

- Large volumes of fluid may increase interstitial fluid.
- No anaphylaxis.
- Cheaper.

2. *Colloids*

- Replace blood on an equal volume basis.
- May increase adult respiratory distress syndrome if increased capillary permeability is present.
- Risk of anaphylaxis.
- Greater cost.
- May inhibit reticuloendothelial function.

Further reading

Trentz O, Friedl HP. Fluid resuscitation in acute trauma and multiple injuries. *Current Opinion in Anaesthesiology*, 1992; **5**: 255–7.
Velanovich V. Crystalloid versus colloid fluid resuscitation. *Surgery*, 1990; **105**: 65–71.

Related topic of interest

Shock (p. 269)

IONIZING RADIATION EXPOSURE

Ionization involves the forcible ejection of an electron from an atom, hence creating an ion, and may lead to biological damage. Ionizing radiations include X-rays, γ-rays and particle radiation.

All accident and emergency departments must be prepared to treat patients contaminated by ionizing radiation, as those seriously ill or injured will be taken to the nearest major accident and emergency department. Other patients will be taken to the nominated regional hospital.

The first priority should be to treat life-threatening emergencies, while removing contamination, and at all times *avoid any spread of contamination*.

Patients exposed to high doses of ionizing radiation may later develop *radiation sickness*. This is different from the more common contamination by low-level radioactive substance, but neither presents an immediate hazard to hospital staff. Correct management requires advance preparation and appropriate major incident planning.

Effects of total body irradiation

The radiation effects depend on the magnitude of the accumulation dose.

1. Acute exposure

- *CNS.* Nausea, vomiting, anxiety, disorientation, coma and death, within hours of exposure to doses between 30 and 100 sieverts (Sv) owing to direct damage to CNS conduction and cerebral oedema.
- *Gastrointestinal effects.* Exposures of the order of 10 Sv result in severe acute radiation sickness, severe nausea and vomiting (starting 1–2 hours after exposure, but remitting in 4–6 hours). Death results in 4–14 days because of GI tract damage, resulting in diarrhoea and infection.
- *Haemopoietic syndrome.* At doses between 1 and 10 Sv, transient nausea and vomiting may be seen. Within 24–48 hours the peripheral lymphocyte count falls. As the haemopoietic stem cells are damaged there is a decrease in the white blood cells and platelets at 2–3 weeks with resultant overwhelming sepsis and haemorrhage.

2. Chronic effects. The risk increases with the total radiation dose.

- *Leukaemogenesis.* May occur 3–10 years after acute exposure, especially acute myeloid leukaemia.
- *Carcinogenesis.* Occurs after 40 or more years, especially skin, lung, breast and bone cancers and lymphomas.

Protocol for contaminated patient

- Contact the local *radiation protection advisor*, who will be responsible for measurement of the level of radioactive contamination and advice.
- A predetermined *separate entrance and treatment area* where the patient can be isolated and decontaminated should be demarcated. An area equipped with a shower and irrigation facility will be necessary. Disposable paper towels should be taped along the floor and along all transit areas. Portable equipment should be removed from the area and non-disposable items covered with polythene sheeting. Air conditioning should be switched off.
- Patients and staff must not eat, drink or smoke within the designated area.
- An area should be demarcated where ambulances and crews can be examined after arrival and decontaminated if required.
- A nominated controller should record details of all personnel in contact with the designated area(s). The number of personnel must be kept to the minimum. All patients and staff must be checked for contamination before leaving the designated area(s).
- Seriously ill patients should be taken to an appropriate resuscitation area. Again only essential equipment should be taken into the contaminated area.

Emergency decontamination

- If possible, levels of contamination should be measured before and after the decontamination procedure. This is accomplished by using a meter or by taking dry cotton wool swabs from exposed areas and storing them in labelled containers.
- Undress patients carefully to reduce contamination. If the patient is in a bag, open the bag, turning the contaminated inner surface inwards. Remove headgear, footwear, gloves and clothes by gently cutting with scissors and folding the cut material outward and under to provide a clean surface.
- Collect all clothing, swabs and fluids in plastic bags marked with a radioactive warning label and seal for examination by the *radiation protection advisor*.
- Cover wounds prior to decontamination. Avoid splashing. Exposed skin has priority. Wash contaminated hands with soap under warm running water. Clean the nails with a brush for 4 minutes. If monitoring reveals residual contamination, repeat the procedure with Hibiscrub, abrasive detergent or potassium permanganate, followed by application of sodium

bisulphite. If contamination remains, overnight skin occlusion using adhesive tape can be used.
- Advice regarding the use of other decontamination solutions should be sought.
- To decontaminate the face, close eyes and plug ears. Swab the face with Hibiscrub. Irrigate ears and eyes with saline or clean with pledgets. Blow the nose with tissue and irrigate if necessary. Wash out the mouth and clean teeth or dentures. Wash hair with Hibiscrub.
- Apply paper drapes to demarcate areas and wounds. Wipe these areas clean using swabs moistened with saline or Hibiscrub.
- Irrigate open wounds with saline. Encourage to bleed. Debride, when appropriate, to reduce contamination.
- *The irradiated patient.* Radiation sickness develops as a delayed phenomenon, and such patients should be referred to the nearest oncology unit after discussion with the local radiation protection advisor.

Further reading

Berry RJ. Radiation. In Weatherall DJ, Ledingham JGG, Warrell DA, eds. *Oxford Textbook of Medicine*, Vol. 1, 2nd edn. Oxford: Oxford University Press, 1987: 6.130–6.135.

Related topic of interest

Disaster planning (p. 93)

LIMPING CHILD

Children commonly present to the accident and emergency department with a limp or reluctance to bear weight on one limb. This may have developed suddenly or insidiously. As children fall over frequently there is often a history of trauma which may or may not be relevant. Small children are especially difficult to assess as they are often unable to localize pain to one specific bone, joint or even side.

Clinical approach

Always take a history from both parent and child and include prodromal or intercurrent illnesses. Carefully observe the gait and note which leg the child is reluctant to move or to stand on.

Examine all bones and all joints of both lower limbs. Start with the good leg and demonstrate to the child that you are not going to inflict pain. Work towards the site most likely to be the root of the problem and examine this last. If necessary distract the child by asking questions while palpating and moving the limb. Always watch the face of the child rather than ask when it hurts.

Differential diagnosis

1. Any age

- Trauma from an unrecognized fracture of any bone in the lower limb to local bruising (children will often limp or refuse to bear weight with soft-tissue injuries alone).
- Foreign bodies in foot – typically needles.
- Septic arthritis.
- Osteomyelitis.
- Malignant disease including leukaemia.
- Juvenile rheumatoid arthritis.
- Sickle crisis.
- Referred pain from inguinal lymphadenopathy, groin herniae, testicular torsion or epididymo-orchitis and acute appendicitis.
- Non-accidental injury.

2. Aged 0 – 3 years

- Congenital dislocation of the hip (CDH).

3. Aged $1^1/_2$ – 12 years

- Irritable hip.

4. Aged 3 – 8 years

• Perthes' disease.

5. Aged 10 – 16 years

• Slipped upper femoral epiphysis.

Irritable hip (transient synovitis)

This is the most common cause of a painful hip in children. It is, however, a diagnosis of exclusion. The peak incidence occurs at 5–6 years. There is often an antecedent illness, usually an upper respiratory tract infection. Investigations are not diagnostic.

• FBC the white cell count is often raised.
• The ESR is often but not always raised.
• A radiograph is usually normal, although an effusion may be seen.
• Ultrasound scanning is very useful and will often demonstrate an effusion.

Management depends on clinical status. When infection is considered the child must be admitted, and if there is evidence of CDH, Perthes' disease or slipped upper femoral epiphysis then refer the child for an orthopaedic opinion. If the child is well, symptoms are minimal, investigations normal and the parents are sensible, then it is reasonable to prescribe simple analgesia and allow the child home with advice to rest and return for review the following day. The parents should be instructed to return if there is any deterioration. Otherwise the child should be admitted for bed rest and possibly traction if severe. Transient synovitis usually settles spontaneously in 48 – 72 hours.

Congenital dislocation of the hip

With the development of neonatal screening the incidence of late presentation of CDH is much reduced.
The clinical features are:

• Limp, waddling or Trendelenburg gait.
• Painful hip.
• Asymmetric leg length.

On radiography:

• With abduction to 45° the femoral shaft should point towards the acetabulum.

- The acetabular roof should be at about 20°. An angle greater than this suggests CDH.

For treatment, refer to an orthopaedic surgeon.

Perthes' disease

Avascular necrosis of the femoral head is uncommon, affecting 1:10 000 of the population. Males are four times more commonly affected than females. It usually presents between the ages of 3 and 8 years with a painful limp which may be progressive or intermittent.

There is often painful restriction of movement of the hip, especially abduction and internal rotation.

The radiograph is usually normal at first, progressing to fragmentation and collapse of the femoral head as the disease progresses.

The disease requires expert follow-up by an orthopaedic surgeon.

Slipped upper femoral epiphysis

This occurs at or around the pubertal growth spurt. Males are more commonly affected than females and the left side more often than right, though it may occur bilaterally. Clinical features may or may not follow an injury (often minor). It is more common in the obese, hypogonadal male. Symptoms and signs vary with the degree of slip from a painful limp to shortening and external rotation.

Anteroposterior radiographs show:

- Widening of the epiphyseal plate.
- Trethowan's lines – the line of the upper border of the femoral neck should pass through the femoral head.

On lateral radiography the line bisecting the base of the upper femoral epiphyseal plate and the middle of the femoral neck should be at 90°. Any angle less than this suggests slip.

Refer for orthopaedic admission and internal fixation.

Further reading

Jolly H, Levine MI. *Diseases of Children*. Oxford: Blackwell, 1985: 623–9.

Related topics of interest

MAJOR INJURIES – INITIAL MANAGEMENT

Patients with multiple or major injuries present complex management problems and should be treated by clinicians who are trained and experienced in this field. Where possible a multidisciplinary team approach should be applied with a clearly defined team leader. Resuscitation of patients with life-threatening injuries starts on the basis of history and clinical findings before confirmation of diagnosis by investigation. The processes of assessment and resuscitation are performed simultaneously. The resuscitation must be systematic and thorough with frequent re-evaluation. A full history should be obtained as soon as possible, including time and mechanism of injury, entrapment, prehospital treatment, any change of condition, associated factors, previous medical history, drug history, allergies, last oral intake and other casualties at the scene.

Assessment and treatment

1. Airway with cervical spine control

(a) Simple airway manoeuvres: 90 – 95% oxygen (at 12 – 15 l/min) via reservoir mask, clear upper airway, suction, jaw thrust, oro- or nasopharyngeal airway. It this is not sufficient then proceed to:

(b) Advanced airway manoeuvres. The precise route and method to secure an airway will depend on the urgency of the situation, the skill of the operator and the likelihood of an associated cervical spine injury.

- Orotracheal intubation.
- Nasotracheal intubation.

(c) Surgical airway. This is indicated if there is failure to intubate for whatever reason.

- Needle cricothyroidotomy with jet insufflation is indicated for children under 12 and as a temporary measure in adults. The duration of the technique is limited to 30 – 40 minutes by carbon dioxide retention, which also limits its use in patients with head injury.
- Surgical cricothyroidotomy through the cricothyroid membrane can be performed in adults and children over 12 years.

Note: Tracheostomy is a time-consuming and difficult procedure which should not be performed by accident and emergency staff.

The cervical spine must be protected at all times by inline immobilization or with a semirigid collar, wide tape and sandbags until injury has been excluded.

2. Breathing. Expose the chest, and look, listen, palpate, percuss and auscultate; examine the neck for tracheal deviation and venous distension. Assess the rate and quality of respiration. Life-threatening conditions to treat are tension pneumothorax, large flail chest, sucking chest wounds, massive haemothorax and cardiac tamponade.

3. Circulation. Assess pulse rate and quality, skin colour and capillary return and measure blood pressure non-invasively.

Treatment:

(a) Insert two 14-G peripheral intravenous lines. If this is not possible establish venous access via:

- Percutaneous venous cutdown.
- Saphenous or femoral vein cannulation at groin.
- Seldinger replacement on existing small-gauge cannulae.
- Intraosseous access (for children).

Note: CVP lines are for monitoring not resuscitation.

(b) Stop exsanguinating haemorrhage by direct pressure.
(c) Cross-match.

Resuscitation fluids. Crystalloid or colloid may be used initially. If crystalloid is used then 2–3 times the blood volume will be required. If the patient does not respond or remains unstable despite adequate volume resuscitation then continue with blood products. Full cross-match is preferable but if unavailable type specific may be used. When immediate transfusion is required then use O negative blood. All intravenous fluids should be warmed.

4. Minineurological examination. Conscious level, pupil size and reaction.

5. Complete exposure.

Head to toe examination	After completing the initial assessment and resuscitation, external monitoring systems should be applied and urinary catheters and nasogastric tubes can be inserted unless contraindicated. The patient should be systematically examined from top to toe including internal examinations and log roll. After completion and dependent upon clinical status the definitive management plan can be made.
Routine investigations	• Blood – FBC, U & E, glucose, pregnancy test. • ECG. • ABG. • Radiographs – lateral cervical spine, chest and pelvis.
Monitoring	• ECG. • Non-invasive automated blood pressure. • Pulse oximetry. • Urine output. • CVP. • End-tidal carbon dioxide.
Special investigations	Dependent on clinical indications and local availability. • Radiographs. • Ultrasound scan. • CT scan. • Contrast studies. • Diagnostic peritoneal lavage.

Further reading

Driscoll PA, Vincent CA. Organizing an efficient trauma team. *Injury,* 1992; **23**: 107–10.
Skinner D, Driscoll P, Earlam R, eds. *ABC of Major Trauma.* London, BMJ Publishing Group, 1991.

Related topics of interest

MAJOR INJURIES – ROYAL COLLEGE OF SURGEONS OF ENGLAND REPORT

Trauma causes 40 deaths per day or 14 500 a year in the UK. In addition 620 000 patients are admitted to hospital following injury and some 7–8 million attend accident and emergency departments for treatment.

The Medical Commission on Accident Prevention estimated that the total cost to the British economy of road traffic accidents alone was £2.8 billion in 1985. Yet the survivors from trauma are young and achieve a good quality of life, returning to their previous work and enjoying a similar life expectancy to those of the same age.

The Royal College of Surgeons report on the management of patients with major injuries was published in 1988. It is divided into three sections. The first sets the scene regarding trauma management, and includes the development of A & E services in the UK, and reviews the systems in the United States, West Germany and France. The second section concerns the current management of major trauma in the UK and the final section makes recommendations regarding the future management of major trauma.

Retrospective study

This was carried out on 1000 trauma deaths in 11 districts in England and Wales and excluded deaths following fractured neck of femur in patients over the age of 65. Four assessors were asked to answer yes or no to the question: 'If this patient had been admitted to a fully staffed and equipped American-style trauma centre might death have been prevented?'.

The important findings were:

(a) Forty nine per cent of victims died at the scene or were certified dead on arrival (DOA) at hospital. There was a considerable interdistrict variation in the DOA rate (23 – 74%).

(b) CNS injury was the cause of death in 65% of admitted patients.

(c) Twenty per cent of the hospital deaths were judged by all four assessors to be potentially preventable (43% of all non-CNS deaths and 7% of all CNS deaths).

(d) A further 13% of hospital deaths were judged by three out of four assessors to be potentially preventable.

(e) The following were causes for the preventable deaths:

- Haemorrhage – spleen, lung, and liver.
- Hypoxia.

- Subdural haemorrhage.
- Pulmonary embolism.
- Misdiagnosis and inappropriate treatment.

Prospective studies

1. Comparison of a district general hospital versus a teaching hospital. Using Trauma and Injury Severity Scoring (TRISS) methodology, there were unexpected survivors in the teaching hospital, demonstrating the positive benefit of the provision of a coordinated trauma service.

The essential characteristics of such survivors appeared to include:

- Rapid transport from the scene of the accident.
- Resuscitation performed by senior medical personnel and rapid definitive surgery if necessary.
- Continuing care on the ITU was based on measurements of oxygen transport and delivery.

2. A detailed investigation of 150 patients admitted following traumatic injury.

- Seventy-one per cent of initial consultations were made at senior house officer level. Only 11% were being treated by either the senior registrar or consultant.
- Consultant surgeon was present in only four cases.
- Of the 32 patients who died, 10 had a probability of survival of greater than 50%.

Recommendations

1. Prehospital care

- Improve the basic first aid skills of bystanders.
- Increase the number of paramedics, particularly those with extended skills.
- Increase the numbers of BASIC doctors (particularly in rural areas) and the number with the Immediate Medicine Diploma.
- Greater medical involvement in the training of ambulance personnel.
- Improvements in the transportation of seriously injured patients from the scene of the accident and secondary transfers to more centralized units. Helicopters have a role to play.
- Prehospital triage of patients.
- Improved radio communication between the prehospital carers and the hospital to allow preparations for receiving the injured patient.

- Doctors should play a more active role in the prehospital management of the trapped trauma victim.

2. Hospital. Institute a system in which the multiply injured patient is managed by an experienced surgical and anaesthetic team capable of performing definitive surgery within the thorax, abdomen and the head.

Proposals

The scheme proposed by the Royal College of Surgeons is a two-tiered system:

(a) The *first level* of care would be provided by a designated district general hospital in each district, which with an accident and emergency department and intensive care unit would be expected to receive all injured patients with an injury severity score (ISS) of 20 or less. Each hospital would also have a *trauma team* to deal with such patients.
(b) The *second level* of trauma care would be provided by the *trauma centre*. Patients with major damage to the head, chest, abdomen and complex orthopaedic injuries would be secondarily transferred from the district hospital or transferred directly from the scene. It is estimated that one centre is required per 2 million population.

Characteristics of a trauma centre

- *The emergency department* staff should ensure immediate and appropriate care for the injured patient.
- The *trauma team* should be organized and directed by a consultant who is expert in and committed to care of the injured, supported by the accident and emergency staff and other relevant specialties. All patients with multiple system or major injury must initially be evaluated by the trauma team, and the surgeon who will be responsible for the overall care of the patient (the team leader) must be identified.
- The hospital must include 24 hour a day availability of surgical specialties and operating theatres.

The North Staffordshire trauma system

The Department of Health has funded a 3-year project to compare the North Staffordshire Trauma Centre with the Hull Royal Infirmary and the Royal Preston Hospital. Independent evaluation of the outcome of severely injured patients, using TRISS methodology, will provide information on the effectiveness of the trauma centre model in the UK.

Further reading

Redmond AD. The North Staffordshire trauma system. *Journal of the Royal College of Surgeons of Edinburgh*, 1993; **38**: 248–50.

Royal College of Surgeons of England. Commission on the Provision of Surgical Services. *Report of the Working Party on The Management of Patients with Major Injuries*, November 1988. London: RCOS.

Related topics of interest

Health of the Nation (p. 152)

Helicopter transportation (p. 158)

Interhospital transfer – trauma (p. 174)

Prehospital care (p. 248)

Trauma scoring and injury scaling (p. 297)

MAXILLOFACIAL INJURY

Mandibular fracture

This may occur either in isolation or associated with other facial injuries. Fracture may occur at a site remote from the point of impact. Forty per cent involve the condyle, 20% the angle and 20% the body. Multiple fractures occur in over half of all cases.

1. Clinical features. Pain, swelling, tenderness and malocclusion. Numbness over the lower lip indicates injury to the inferior dental nerve.

2. Radiography. Orthopantomography will show most fractures. However, condylar injuries and temporo-mandibular joint dislocations are best shown by condylar views with mouth open and closed or by CT scan.

3. Treatment. Simple stable fractures may be treated with analgesia, and out-patient orofacial follow-up. Comminuted, displaced or unstable fractures require surgical fixation. Many fractures are compound into the mouth and should be treated with prophylactic antibiotics.

Temporomandibular dislocation

This may occur either following trauma or sponta-neously while opening the mouth wide (e.g. yawning). There is an inability to close the mouth. In the differ-ential diagnosis consider oculogyric crisis. Reduction can be achieved without anaesthesia in many cases, although sedation or general anaesthesia may be required.

Zygomatic fracture

The zygoma comprises body and arch. Tripod fracture may occur through the.

- Zygomaticotemporal suture.
- Zygomaticofrontal suture.
- Infraorbital foramen.

This causes flattening of the cheek, especially when viewed from above, numbness in the distribution of the infraorbital nerve and diplopia. Subconjuctival haem-orrhage occurs, especially following fracture through the zygomaticofrontal suture.

Alternatively zygomatic arch fracture may occur in isolation.

Radiography. In addition to posteroanterior and lateral skull views a 10–15° occipitomental view is required to show vertical displacement of the zygoma and 30° occipitomental projections to show horizontal displacement. These fractures usually require elevation.

Orbital blow-out fractures

These are caused by a blow to the globe of the eye, causing the orbital contents to prolapse downwards through the orbital floor into the maxillary antrum. Clinical features include diplopia and enophthalmos. On the anteroposterior radiograph look for the teardrop sign (localized opacity in the roof of the maxillary antrum). Refer the patient for specialist advice as these fractures require surgical reconstruction.

Maxillary fractures

Classically described by LeFort, these may be unilateral or bilateral and can occur in combination (e.g. LeFort III on one side and LeFort II on the other).

LeFort I (Guérin type) involves the tooth-bearing portion of the maxilla. The hard palate may be split. Always examine for movement between the two sides of the hard palate. Examine for haematoma of the soft palate and malocclusion.

LeFort II involves maxilla, nasal bones and medial aspects of the orbits. Clinical features include a dish face appearance due to posterior displacement of the maxilla, numbness over the cheek and upper teeth and cerebrospinal fluid rhinorrhoea. The maxilla may be floating, and if the upper incisor teeth are grasped they may be felt to move relative to the skull.

LeFort III involves maxilla, zygoma, nasal bones, ethmoid and all the small bones of the base of the skull, the entire mid-face being fractured away from the base of the skull (craniofacial dysfunction).

Management. The airway is at risk following these fractures and should be the priority. Treatment of the fractures is complex and all patients should be referred for specialist opinion. CT scanning is often required to clarify diagnosis and plan surgical treatment.

Further reading

Cantrill SV. Facial trauma. In: Rosen P, Barking RM, eds. *Emergency Medicine*. St Louis: Moseby Yearbook, 1992: 355–70.

Related topics of interest

Airway (p. 7)
Ear, nose and throat (p. 107)
Fractures – principals of treatment (p. 125)

MEDICOLEGAL PROBLEMS

Confidentiality

The facts of a patient's visit to an accident and emergency department and details of the consultation are confidential and except in rare circumstances must not be revealed to the police or anyone else without the patient's consent. (If a written statement is required, this consent should usually be in writing.) Exceptions include:

- For the purposes of medical teaching, research or audit.
- To satisfy a specific statutory requirement, e.g. the notification of infectious disease or of drug addicts (see below).
- When ordered to by a judge (or similar) in a court of law.
- In rare cases when the consequences are so serious that a doctor's duty to society overrides that to the patient, e.g. possibly an epileptic car driver.

The police have a duty to investigate road traffic accidents (RTAs) involving personal injury and so on request should be given the names, addresses and ages of patients involved in RTAs. They can also, in general terms, be informed of the nature of the injury (e.g. leg injury), the severity (e.g. minor, severe, critical) and whether the patient is being admitted.

Drivers who have consumed alcohol

Following an RTA the police may require a driver to provide a specimen of breath or blood to measure the alcohol level. They must ask consent from the doctor looking after the patient. This consent can (and should) be refused if:

- The patient is unable to give consent.
- Provision of the specimen would be detrimental to the patient's health (e.g. facial injuries might preclude giving a specimen of breath and limb fractures causing limited venous access might preclude giving blood).
- Giving the statutory warning would be detrimental to the patient's health.

Venepuncture in these cases must be done by the police surgeon and not the doctor looking after the patient.

Drug addicts

By law all doctors should notify the Chief Medical Officer of the Home Office of any patient they treat who they know or suspect is addicted to controlled drugs.

Consent

It is a patient's fundamental right to withhold consent to examination or treatment, and procedures done without the patient's (or parents') consent constitute an assault. Consent is usually implied (e.g. the patient climbs onto the theatre table to be sutured), but if the procedure carries any risk then written consent must be obtained. If a patient is unconscious or otherwise unable to give a consent then in an emergency a doctor can undertake whatever treatment is necessary without consent. In these circumstances it is sensible (if possible) to seek the agreement of the patient's next of kin, but this carries no legal validity.

Children under 16 can give consent to treatment if they fully understand its nature, purpose and hazards. This will vary with the age of the child and with the complexity of the procedure i.e. a 12-year-old child may be able to consent to having a minor wound sutured. Usually one should have the consent of both the child and parent. In the absence of a parent one should consult another relative or person *in loco parentis* if possible, but essential treatment should not be delayed by the inability obtain such consent.

Similarly, a patient who is unable to given consent because of a mental disorder may be treated for a medical condition without consent if, in the opinion of the doctor, the treatment is in the patient's best interests.

Patients may give restricted consent only (e.g. a Jehovah's Witness may give consent to all treatment except a blood transfusion). The reason for the clinical recommendation should be explained to the patient and if the patient still refuses then a note should be made to that effect and the patient asked to sign the note.

If parents refuse essential treatment for a child despite explanations, the doctor must act in the child's best interests. The child may be old enough to understand and give consent, but if not the doctor must make a note of the parents' refusal of consent and a second medical opinion from a consultant should be sought. If time permits a court order may be obtained, but this is not essential and doctors must act on their clinical judgment.

Sexual assaults	Patients who attend accident and emergency following a sexual assault must be treated for any injuries they have sustained. However, it may be necessary to prove the assault in court, and so in the absence of significant injury the genital examination and collection of samples for evidence should be left to a trained police surgeon. Victims will need counselling and advice on sexually transmitted diseases, and female victims may need advice on pregnancy.

Further reading

General Medical Council. *Professional Conduct and Discipline: Fitness to Practice.* London: GMC, 1992: 26–9.
Medical Defence Union. *Consent to Treatment.* London: Medical Defence Union, 1992.

Related topics of interest

Deliberate self harm (p. 83)
Drug overdose and accidental poisoning (p. 99)

MENINGITIS

In 1990 there were 2572 notifications of meningitis is England and Wales. The majority of cases were *meningococcal* (1138), *Haemophilus influenzae* (431), *viral* (353) and *pneumococcal* (156).

Bacterial meningitis can be a fulminant, rapidly fatal illness requiring immediate recognition, diagnosis and therapy. Meningitis may occur in acute and chronic forms, but presentation of the chronic form is rare.

The key to preventing morbidity of these patients is early diagnosis and treatment with the appropriate antibiotic. The causes of death include septic shock, cerebral oedema and brain coning.

Susceptibility is determined by predisposing factors such as:

- Immunocompromise.
- Post-splenectomy.
- Sickle cell disease.
- Alcoholism.
- Hypogammaglobulinaemia.
- Cirrhosis.
- Diabetes.

The mortality varies with the organism: *Neisseria meningitidis*, 7–14%; *H. influenzae*, 3–10%; *Streptococcus pneumoniae*, 15–60%; and *Listeria monocytogenes*, 20%. Mortality is highest in the very young and old and those patients with underlying disease.

Permanent neurological sequelae include:

- Mental retardation.
- Deafness.
- Cranial nerve palsies.
- Hydrocephalus.
- Subdural effusion.
- Cerebral venous thrombosis.
- Epilepsy.

Organisms

1. Bacterial. Haemophilus influenzae, Neisseria meningitidis and *Streptococcus pneumoniae* cause approximately 90% of all cases of proven bacterial meningitis. Less common pathogens include Gram-negative bacilli, *Listeria* and *Staphylococcus aureus*. Age is the most important variable in considering which organism is most likely to be the pathogen.

Birth to 3 months Group B streptococci
Escherichia coli
L. monocytogenes

4 months to 5 years	*H. influenzae* *N. meningitidis*
6 – 65 years	*N. meningitidis* *S. pneumoniae*
Over 65 years	*S. pneumoniae* Gram-negative bacilli *L. monocytogenes*

2. *Viral* infection is probably three to four times more common and most often occurs in the summer in patients under the age of 40. The most common virus is the enterovirus, followed by flavivirus, mumps virus and herpes simplex.

Pathophysiology

Colonization by the pathogen, usually in the naso-pharynx, is followed by systemic invasion and intravascular replication. Systemic invasion is more likely in the predisposed, which includes those with cellular and immunological deficiency. Additionally, there is a HLA B12 association with *Haemophilus* infection in children. The next step is blood brain penetration. Once this occurs replication within the cerebrospinal fluid (CSF) is facilitated by the lack of adequate immune defence systems in the CSF. Pathogens are usually limited to the subarachnoid space. Altered membrane permeability at the blood–brain barrier is one of the possible mechanisms for the cerebral oedema and the subsequent risk from herniation and death.

Clinical features

Unfortunately, the classic signs and symptoms – headaches, lethargy, vomiting and meningism – occur in only 80% of cases. The remainder present with flu-like illness.
    Patients *present* with either:

- The *acute form* (10%), in which symptoms develop within 24 hours and progress rapidly to altered states of consciousness. The mortality is 50% in bacterial disease.
- The *subacute form* with symptoms developing over 1–7 days accounts for the other 90%. A precedent viral-type illness is followed by a relatively rapid onset of fever, vomiting and stiff neck.

    Only 20% of patients with bacterial meningitis present in a completely alert and orientated manner, and

10% are in coma. A deteriorating level of consciousness correlates with worsening prognosis.

Rash can be identified in 50% of patients with meningococcal infection but often begins as a maculopapular rash before the characteristic petechial rash develops.

Twenty per cent of patients present with *seizures*, while 15% have *focal neurology*. Papilloedema takes 24–48 hours to develop.

Other associated findings include *otitis media*, *sinusitis* and *pneumonia*. These are most common with *S. pneumoniae* but can occur with *H. influenzae*.

Paediatric

1. Children under 3 years. Bacterial meningitis is most common in this age group, but the diagnosis is more difficult. The classical signs of neck rigidity, photophobia, headache and vomiting are often absent. The signs and symptoms in this age group are mainly related to the raised intracranial pressure that is usual in children with bacterial meningitis:

- Drowsiness.
- Irritability.
- Poor feeding.
- Unexplained pyrexia.
- Convulsions with fever.
- Apnoea or cyanotic attacks.
- Purpuric rash.

2. Children aged 4 and over are more likely to present with the more classical signs of headache, vomiting, pyrexia, neck stiffness and photophobia. In an ill child a purpuric rash is almost pathognomonic of meningococcal infection and warrants immediate treatment.

Since raised ICP is the rule in the child with bacterial meningitis the concern is the development of coning, which is the direct cause of as many as 30% of deaths. If contraindications to lumbar puncture exist then *blood and throat cultures* should be taken before prompt treatment with intravenous antibiotics.

Blood cultures will identify the organism in 90% of cases within 24–48 hours with *Haemophilus* or pneumococcal meningitis but in only 50% of cases of meningococcal meningitis.

There is no place for routine computerized tomography before or after lumbar puncture in the child with clinically uncomplicated acute bacterial meningitis.

Relative contraindications to lumbar puncture include:

- Papilloedema.
- Coma.
- Hypertension.
- Bradycardia.
- Bradypnoea or irregular respirations.
- Fixed dilated or irregular pupils.
- Impaired doll's eye movements.
- Recent or prolonged convulsive seizures.
- Focal seizures.
- Decerebrate or decorticate posture.
- Focal neurological signs.
- Septic shock.
- Coagulation disorder.

Treatment

Pay attention to the ABCs and specifically:

- *Antibiotics* as appropriate to the clinical setting, e.g. an ill child with a purpuric rash should receive immediate intravenous penicillin 50 mg/kg and cefotaxime 50 mg/kg, given slowly over 10–15 minutes.
- *Raised ICP* and cerebral oedema may require treatment with mannitol, dexamethasone and hyperventilation.
- *Septic shock and adult respiratory distress syndrome* may necessitate ventilation and intensive care support.
- *Convulsions.* Treat with intravenous diazepam or phenytoin.
- *Hyperpyrexia.* Treat with paracetamol in the first instance.
- *Headache* may require treatment with codeine phosphate.
- *Inappropriate antidiuretic hormone secretion.* Restrict fluids and monitor the serum sodium.

Differential diagnosis

- Posterior fossa tumours.
- Acute hydrocephalus.
- Cerebral abscess.
- Subdural haematoma.
- Bleeding from an arteriovenous malformation.
- Meningoencephalitis.
- Herpes simplex encephalitis.
- Reye's syndrome.
- Intracerebral haemorrhage.

Further reading

Juel-Jensen BE, Phuapradit P, Warrell DA. Infections of the nervous system. In: Weatherall DJ, Ledingham JGG, Warrell DA, eds. *The Oxford Textbook of Medicine*, 2nd edn. Oxford: Oxford Medical Publications, 1987: 21.129–21.152.

Mellor DH. The place of computed tomography and lumbar puncture in suspected bacterial meningitis. *Archives of Disease in Childhood*, 1992; **67:** 1417–19.

Related topics of interest

Coma (p. 73)
Convulsions (p. 81)
Headache (p. 142)

MIGRAINE

Migraine is an episodic disorder with a lifetime prevalence of 8% for men and 25% for women. Typically neurological examination is normal and diagnosis rests solely on the history.

Features

- A migraine attack may be preceded by *prodromal symptoms* such as subtle changes in mood or behaviour, e.g. lethargy, yawning.
- An *aura,* typically visual or sensory, lasting up to an hour precedes about 10% of migraine headaches.
- The severe throbbing *headache* of classical migraine is unilateral, associated with nausea, vomiting and photophobia.
- *Status migraine* may make the patient dehydrated secondary to prolonged vomiting and may necessitate hospitalization.
- *Complicated migraine* is characterized by neurological symptoms that accompany the acute attack and may persist after resolution of the headache. *Hemiplegic migraine*, manifest by hemiparesis, and *ophthalmoplegic migraine*, with defects of the III and V cranial nerves, are examples.

Treatment

Prevention is by avoidance of trigger factors. Prophylactic drug therapy should be considered if the attacks occur more than twice a month . *Beta-blockers and pizotifen* are the principal drugs used for prophylaxis.

Treatment of the acute attack:

1. First-line-treatment. Simple analgesics such as aspirin, ibuprofen, paracetamol or over-the-counter proprietary preparations for migraine, containing analgesics plus cyclizine, buclizine, doxylamine, or isometheptene mucate.

2. Second-line treatment (oral). Analgesics plus metoclopramide or domperidone or domperidone plus indomethacin or diclofenac.

3. Third-line treatment. Ergotamine by oral, sublingual, rectal or inhalation route or sumatriptan given orally or subcutaneously.

Cluster headaches　　This uncommon headache has a characteristic presentation, mostly in men aged between 30 and 50 years.

1. History. Typically an episodic, severe unilateral headache that is localized behind the eye, typically described as stabbing. The acute headache lasts 20 minutes to 2 hours and occurs several times a day. The headaches last for periods from 3 weeks to 3 months followed by spontaneous resolution. A previous history of cluster headaches will help the physician establish the diagnosis.

2. Examination reveals ipsilateral lacrimation, rhinorrhea and a partial Horner's syndrome.

3. Treatment. Cluster headaches are usually short-lived but approximately 75% of patients will respond to oxygen therapy, administered at 10 litres/min for 10–15 minutes. Ergot derivatives may also prove effective.

Further reading

MacGregor EA. Prescribing for migraine. *Prescribers' Journal*, 1993; **33**: 50–8.

Related topic of interest

Headache (p. 142)

MISSILE INJURIES

Gunshot wounds are relatively rare in the UK. Doctors unfamiliar with missile injuries must remember lessons learned elsewhere. Gas gangrene is a consequence of mismanagement and should not be seen.

Ballistics

The severity of the wound depends on the energy released in the tissues, which in turn depends on initial energy and degree of retardation in the tissues. Low-velocity missiles (LVMs) tend to be heavy bullets and cause laceration and crushing directly in their path. High-velocity missiles (HVMs) – rifle bullets and some bomb fragments – cause severe effects at a distance from their track.

Behaviour in flight is important: instability reduces velocity but may lead to tumbling end over end in tissue, causing wider destruction. Dense tissues (e.g. bone) retard more than others, releasing more energy. Secondary missiles may be produced (e.g. bone fragments).

Pathology

1. *Laceration and crushing*. LVMs cause injury only in the track with no hidden damage.

2. *Shock waves*. HVMs produce spherical shock waves which last only milliseconds but produce extensive damage at a distance from the track. The shock waves are transmitted along blood vessels. Solid organs are very vulnerable.

3. *Temporary cavitation* is distinctive of HVM injuries. A highly destructive cavity up to 40 times the diameter of track may be formed. Negative pressure draws in debris. The injury may be explosive in effect, rupturing the bowel or blowing the skull apart. The resulting cavity may be grossly necrotic and contaminated.

Management

1. *Triage*. Prioritizing victims may become essential if facilities are overwhelmed.

2. *Resuscitation* follows advanced trauma life support principles.

3. *Initial wound treatment*. Excise the wound and remove all contaminated necrotic and non-viable tissue. Leave only tissue with a good blood supply. Skin

is resistant to damage and may be trimmed lightly. The track must be carefully explored and all foreign bodies removed. Avoid the temptation to limit excision. Lightly pack with gauze and bulky padded dressing. Do not plug the wound but allow to drain.

4. Limitation of closure

- Face and neck wounds may be closed.
- Close muscle only over sucking chest wounds.
- Close dura and rotate flaps to cover with skin.
- Cover exposed tendon, nerve, repaired vessels and synovium of joints. If the capsule cannot be closed, the joint is probably irretrievable. Splint in position of function.

5. Delayed primary closure by grafting or suture at 3–5 days should be used in all HVM injuries. About 95% of wounds are suitable. Ninety per cent will heal without complication.

6. Pitfalls

- Failure to appreciate the extent of damage.
- Inadequate excision of damaged muscle.
- Primary closure.
- Antibiotics do not replace exploration/excision.

Further reading

Owen-Smith MS. *High Velocity Missile Wounds.* London: Edward Arnold, 1992.

Related topics of interest

Antibiotics (p. 32)
Major injuries – initial management (p. 190)
Tetanus (p. 289)
Wound management (p. 307)

MONITORING – PULSE OXIMETRY AND END-TIDAL CARBON DIOXIDE

While there is no substitute for good clinical observation, monitoring devices are essential to A & E management. Monitoring in the prehospital setting is simple and non-invasive, but in the accident and emergency department more complex monitoring is available.

The traditional indices include temperature, pulse rate, blood pressure, electrocardiogram (ECG), respiratory rate and forced expiratory volume (FEV_1). Additional non-invasive monitoring includes non-invasive automated blood pressure (NIBP), pulse oximetry, capnography, transcutaneous oxygen and carbon dioxide detection, and conjunctival oxygen and carbon dioxide detection. Invasive monitoring includes arterial, central venous, Swan Ganz and intracranial pressure monitors.

Pulse oximetry

The *early* detection of hypoxia clinically is difficult. Pulse oximetry allows for a continuous, reliable, non-invasive estimation of the PaO_2 and has been heralded as 'a fifth vital sign'. The value of pulse oximetry in the prehospital setting requires further evaluation, although its use as a non-invasive monitor in the A & E department is well established.

The potential errors of pulse oximetry must be understood by those interpreting the oxygen saturation. Pulse oximetry is based upon differences in the optical transmission spectrum of oxygenated and deoxygenated haemoglobin measuring the absorbance of light at two wavelengths, 660 nm (where there is a maximum difference in absorbance between oxygenated and deoxygenated blood) and the control wavelength of 940 nm. The probe is fixed to a finger, toe, nose, earlobe or forehead and contains an emitter and a detector for light at the two wavelengths. The relative amount of haemoglobin present in solution and its degree of oxygenation can be determined.

Studies have shown a close correlation between pulse oximeter saturation and arterial haemoglobin saturation in conscious volunteers during anaesthesia and in critically ill patients.

Uses

- To aid in detection of hypoxaemia.
- During apparent tonic–clonic seizures it may help to identify patients with low arterial oxygen tension who need immediate intervention.

- In the prehospital setting pulse oximetry has been found to be of benefit in detecting and monitoring hypoxia in patients with airway obstruction, depressed respiration due to head injury, or closed chest injuries.
- The monitoring of procedures carried out under sedation, such as the manipulation of fractures and dislocations.
- For accurate monitoring of the systolic blood pressure.
- As a non-invasive assessment of peripheral arterial occlusive disease.
- For assessment of collateral blood flow to the hand.
- To monitor pregnant patients and their infants at delivery and on the neonatal intensive care unit and to monitor the fetus before and during labour.

Limitations of use

- It will not reveal the patient with hypoventilation when being delivered high-flow oxygen.
- Poor perfusion – shock, hypothermia.
- Movement artefact.
- Severe anaemia.
- Methaemoglobin, carboxyhaemoglobin.
- Electrical interference.
- Optical interference, e.g. nail polish.

Complications are rare, but burns and skin necrosis have been reported.

End-tidal carbon dioxide detection

Capnography is a valuable tool to assess ventilatory failure. In conditions of cardiovascular stability, the end-tidal carbon dioxide concentration bears a constant relationship to $PaCO_2$. If the alveoli from all areas of the lung are emptying synchronously, end-tidal carbon dioxide will be synonymous with alveolar PCO_2.

Uses

- End-tidal monitoring identifies inadvertent misplacement of an endotracheal tube in the oesophagus.
- To detect sudden changes in the breathing circuit (disconnection, leaks, obstruction, twisting of tubes or ventilator or valve malfunction).
- To aid blind nasal intubation.
- To monitor cardiopulmonary resuscitation (return of spontaneous circulation precedes a palpable pulse).

The measurement of end-tidal carbon dioxide as a guide to the probability of survival needs further evaluation.

The *FEF*™ *end-tidal carbon dioxide detector.* This small, disposable monitor uses a colorimetrically controlled reaction to allow estimation of the end-tidal carbon dioxide.

In the non-arrested patient it allows verification of tracheal location of the endotracheal tube, although careful attention to ensure the correct placement is still appropriate.

In the arrested patient interpretation requires caution. It may indicate an absence of cellular metabolism, inadequate CPR or incorrect tube placement.

Further reading

Phillips GD, Runciman WB, Ilsley H. Monitoring in emergency medicine. *Resuscitation*, 1989; **18**: S21–35.
Tremper KK, Barker SJ. Pulse oximetry. *Anaesthesiology*, 1989; **70**: 98–108.
Zorab JSM. Who needs pulse oximetry? *British Medical Journal*, 1988; **296**: 658–9.

Related topic of interest

Interhospital transfer – trauma (p. 174)

MYOCARDIAL INFARCTION

Acute myocardial infarction (MI) most commonly results from thrombosis within an epicardial coronary artery, triggered by fissuring or rupture of an atheromatous plaque. Platetet aggregation and fibrin deposit on the plaque lead to clot formation and occlusion of the artery.

Approximately 50% of deaths occur within 1 hour of onset of symptoms, usually due to an arrhythmia. The in-hospital mortality is age dependent, with an overall mortality of 8% in men and 14% in women.

The diagnosis is based on two out of three findings:

- A classical history.
- Typical ECG changes (including evolving Q waves, ST elevation).
- A diagnostic rise in serum cardiac enzymes (e.g. creatine phosphokinase, the MB isoenzyme of creatine phosphokinase (MB-CPK), myoglobin, troponin T).

Symptoms

The commonest presentation is central chest pain with characteristic features:

- Characteristically a constriction, compression or pressure.
- Radiation to the neck, jaw, arms and back.
- Precipitation by exercise, emotion and after meals.
- Associated with sweating, shortness of breath, nausea and vomiting.

The patient presents typically with pain that lasts longer than 30 minutes unrelieved by glyceryl trinitrate. However, the presentation may be atypical or detected incidentally.

Management

Physical examination is rarely helpful, but complications such as heart failure, heart valve lesions, arrhythmias and risk factors such as hypertension, evidence of peripheral vascular disease, diabetes and hypercholesterolaemia may be detected. This should not delay prompt treatment.

- *Oxygen.* Via a mask or nasal cannula at a flow rate of 4–6 l/min.
- *Intravenous access.* A large-bore i.v. line should be sited and blood taken for serum potassium, cardiac enzymes and glucose.
- *ECG monitoring* is required because of the high incidence of arrhythmias, especially ventricular fibrilla-

tion and ventricular tachycardia, during the early hours of infarction.

- *Twelve-lead ECG.* Repeat every 15–30 minutes if not diagnostic of acute MI.
- *Analgesia.* This is a high priority as the release of catecholamines potentiates arrhythmias and may extend the infarct.

    (a) Make the patient comfortable.
    (b) Entonox is useful in the prehospital setting and nalbuphine has been used.
    (c) Give sublingual nitrate initially, unless the patient is hypotensive (systolic BP < 90 mmHg).
    (d) If unsuccessful or pain is severe, small (1 mg/min) intravenous doses of diamorphine should be titrated to the patient's needs. This should be accompanied by an antiemetic such as metoclopromide (10 mg).

- *Beta-blockers.* The ISIS-1 trial showed that intravenous atenolol (15 mg in aliquots of 5 mg) followed by oral atenolol limits infarct size and reduces the incidence of ventricular rupture. Contraindications include heart failure, hypotension and asthma (ISIS-1).
- *Aspirin.* All patients should receive aspirin (300 mg chewed) as soon as possible because it reduces mortality and reinfarction rates (ISIS-2).
- *Heparin.* Administer as per local protocol.

    Consider subcutaneous heparin if there is a high risk of deep vein thrombosis or cardiac thrombus.

- *Magnesium sulphate.* Additional trials are needed to determine the benefits of early magnesium, to optimize the dose, and to determine the subgroup of patients to whom magnesium may be especially helpful. Patients with subnormal magnesium concentrations need magnesium.
- *Angiotensin-converting enzyme inhibitors.* Long-term survival and quality of life are improved if angiotensin-converting enzymes inhibitors are administered to patients with significantly impaired left ventricular function.

Thrombolytic therapy   The early administration of thrombolytic therapy reduces morbidity (left ventricular function, coronary patency) and mortality in patients with a transmural

MI. If administered within 6 hours of onset of continuous symptoms in patients with ECG-proven MI its benefit is unequivocal. Its value in patients with non-Q-wave MI or after 12 hours remains in dispute.

Maximum benefit is attained if thrombolysis is given as soon as possible after onset of symptoms *(minutes = muscle)*.

Streptokinase is the cheapest drug but is antigenic and therefore patients should not be re-exposed during a period from 5 days to 12 months. It may cause a pseudoallergic reaction.

Anistreplase (APSAC) is the most easily administered drug and is preferred for prehospital thrombolysis. It is antigenic and may cause hypotension.

Alteplase (rt-PA-tissue-type plasminogen activator) is the drug of choice in patients with systolic blood pressure < 90 mmHg and in those in whom possible urgent surgical intervention is required (e.g. pacing, angioplasty, coronary artery by-pass surgery). It is non-antigenic and can be used in patients previously exposed to streptokinase or anistreplase and in those with a history of allergy.

The inclusion criteria for thrombolysis are:

- History of > 30 minutes to 6 hours of chest pain, unrelieved by sublingual nitrate.
- Diagnostic changes on ECG.

    (a) 2 mm ST elevation in two standard precordial leads.
    (b) 1 mm ST elevation in two standard limb leads.
    (c) A true posterior MI.

Contraindications to thrombolysis include:

- Bleeding diathesis including thrombocytopenia and warfarin.
- Severe renal or liver failure.
- Recent gastrointestinal bleeding.
- Visceral carcinoma.
- Hypertension: systolic BP>200 mmHg or diastolic BP>100 mmHg.
- Diabetic retinopathy grade III or IV.
- Cerebrovascular accident or subarachnoid haemorrhage less than 6 months ago.
- Major trauma or surgery 2 weeks ago.
- Pregnancy or recent parturition (caution during menstruation).

- Known allergy to streptococcal protein.
- Prolonged or traumatic CPR.
- Severe bronchitis, active tuberculosis and pneumothorax.
- Potential for cardiac thromboemboli (e.g. active or recent infective endocarditis).

Adverse reactions include:

- Pyrexia, allergic reactions.
- Rarely anaphylaxis.
- Transient hypotension.
- Reperfusion arrhythmias, especially idioventricular rhythm.
- Haemorrhage.
- Emboli (of intracardiac thrombus).

Reversal of thrombolysis

- Give tranexamic acid (10 mg/kg by slow i.v. injection) and aprotinin.
- Give fresh-frozen plasma.

Further reading

Casscells W. Magnesium and myocardial infarction. *Lancet*, 1994; **343:** 807–9.

ISIS-1 (First International Study of Infarct Survival) Collaborative Group. A randomised trial of intravenous atenolol among 16,027 cases of suspected acute myocardial infarction. *Lancet*, 1986; **ii:** 57–65.

ISIS-2 (Second International Study of Infarct Survival) Collaborative Group. Randomised trial of intravenous streptokinase, oral aspirin, both, or neither among 17,187 cases of suspected acute myocardial infarction. *Lancet*, 1988; **ii:** 349–60.

ISIS-3 (Third International Study of Infarct Survival) Collaborative Group. A randomised comparison of streptokinase vs. tissue plasminogen activator vs. anistreplase and of aspirin plus heparin vs. aspirin alone among 41 299 cases of suspected acute myocardial infarction. *Lancet*, 1992; **339:** 753–70.

Weston CFM, Penny WJ, Julian DG (on behalf of the British Heart Foundation Working Group). Guidelines for the early management of patients with myocardial infarction. *British Medical Journal*, 1994; **308:** 767–71.

Related topics of interest

NEEDLESTICK INJURY

Sharps injuries are a major concern to health care workers. Twenty-two pathogens have been transmitted by sharps injuries. These include hepatitis B virus, HIV, hepatitis C virus and the causative agents of malaria and syphilis. The risk of sero-conversion following a needlestick injury with HIV-infected blood is low (1 in 200). Since the prevalence of HIV infection in the general population is 1 in 2000, the probability of acquiring HIV infection from a random needlestick injury is 1 in 400 000. The risk of infection with HBV is much higher (1 in 5), and since approximately 1 in 1000 people in the UK is a carrier the probability of becoming infected with HBV from a random needlestick injury is 1 in 5000.

The majority of needlestick injuries are of low risk to the recipient. The injuries with the greatest risk are those that involve an injection of blood into the tissues. Solid needles or needles with very little contamination are much less likely to cause any problems. 'Splash' injuries are extremely unlikely to cause transmission, even if they are into an open wound or mucous membrane. Needles found at the beach pose little risk because of the effects of the sea and sun. Needles found lying in parks and bins are less hazardous than those immediately discarded by drug addicts.

Basic precautions should be adopted universally, and certain additional measures may be adopted with high-risk patients. It is recommended that departments draw up a local policy on the safe handling and disposal of sharps and a policy of action in cases of accidental exposure.

Sharps procedure

1. General. After a needlestick injury, bleeding should be encouraged and the area washed with free-running water and soap. Do not forget tetanus immunization. The incident should be immediately reported to a superior and then referred to the occupational health department, and out of hours to the accident and emergency department. The incident should be logged in the accident report book and the health and safety officer should investigate if appropriate. Record the following details:

- Time of incident.
- Type of incident.
- Source of needle or sharps instrument.
- Whether the 'donor' can be identified.
- Whether the 'donor' is in an identified high-risk group.
- Whether the 'recipient' has received hepatitis B immunization.

It is recommended that a blood specimen is taken, after informed consent, and stored for possible future testing.

When possible blood from the source patient should be taken (after informed consent) to ascertain the HBV and HIV antibody status. Ideally the source patient should be retested after 6 months.

2. Management of exposure to HBV

If the source patient is HBsAg antigen negative then no further action is required. The injured person should be encouraged to be immunized against hepatitis B.

- If the source patient is HBsAg antigen positive, then the antibody status of the injured person is checked.

  (a) If the antibody response is less than 10 miu/ml, then hepatitis B immunoglobulin should be given as soon as possible after the incident (preferably administered within 48 hours) along with a course of hepatitis B vaccination.

  (b) If the antibody response is between 10 and 100 miu/ml then a booster dose of hepatitis B vaccine is required.

  (c) If the antibody response is over 100 miu/ml, no further action is necessary.

3. Management of exposure to HIV. If the source patient is HIV negative and not a high-risk individual no further action is necessary.

If the source patient is antibody positive the injured person must be counselled regarding the risk of HIV transmission.

In cases of massive exposure or definite parenteral exposure the injured person should also be advised regarding prophylactic zidovudine. Additionally, measures to prevent transmission of infection such as protection during sexual intercourse and refraining from blood donation are advised. An HIV test, even if negative, will usually have to be declared on any future insurance form.

Zidovudine prophylaxis is advised in massive (>1 ml) and definite parenteral (intramuscular or deep needle-sticks) exposure to known HIV-infected blood. The role of zidovudine in prophylaxis is not fully known and it causes side-effects such as headaches, nausea, diarrhoea, fever and insomnia. The initial dose should be started as soon as possible and monitored appropriately. Exposure to known HIV-infected patients should be discussed with a virologist and reported to the surveillance scheme at the Communicable Disease Surveillance Centre or the CD(S)U in Scotland.

Further reading

British Medical Association. *A Code of Practice for The Safe Use and Disposal of Sharps.* London: BMA, 1990.
Department of Health, Welsh Office, Scottish Home and Health Department, DHSS (Northern Ireland). Hepatitis B. In: *Immunisation Against Infectious Disease.* London: HMSO, 1990: 110–19.

Related topics of interest

Hepatitis B (p. 160)
Human immunodeficiency virus (p. 164)
Tetanus (p. 289)

OBSTETRIC EMERGENCIES

Vaginal bleeding

Vaginal bleeding occurs in about 4% of all pregnancies.

Abruptio placentae

Abruptio placentae, in which the placenta separates from the uterine wall, accounts for approximately one-third of cases. It is more common in smokers and in multiparous and older women. Small separations may go undetected until the placenta is examined after delivery. However with large separations fetal and maternal death can occur.

Grade I (40%)	Slight vaginal bleeding, no uterine irritability and no signs of fetal distress.
Grade II (45%)	Vaginal bleeding or hidden bleeding into the decidua basalis associated with maternal tachycardia, uterine irritability and fetal distress.
Grade III (15%)	Significant vaginal bleeding or maternal hypotension from concealed interuterine blood loss. There are painful uterine contractions with signs of fetal distress or intrauterine death. Consumption of maternal clotting factors results in reduced fibrinogen levels.

Complications
- Maternal or fetal death.
- Disseminated intravascular coagulation.
- Amniotic fluid embolism.

Placenta praevia

Implantation of the placenta over the cervix occurs more frequently following caesarean section and in multiparous women and usually presents with painless vaginal bleeding.

Complications
- Hypovolaemic shock.
- Fetal distress and intrauterine death.

Other causes	• Cervical erosions.
	• Cervical polyps.
	• Infection.
	• Labour.

Management	• Oxygen via a face mask.
	• Place the patient in the left lateral position to prevent inferior vena cava obstruction. Alternatively, raise the right hip and manually displace the uterus to the left side.
	• Establish intravenous access with two 14-gauge cannulae. Take blood for baseline investigations including clotting screen and cross-match 4 units of blood. Start shock therapy.
	• Early referral to an obstetrician.

Investigations

- Monitor maternal vital signs.
- Fetal monitoring.
- Ultrasound scan.

Do not perform speculum vaginal examination as this can precipitate catastrophic haemorrhage.

Hypertension in pregnancy

Hypertension complicates approximately 7% of all pregnancies. It is defined as diastolic blood pressure greater than 105 mmHg or a rise of 15 mmHg over known pre-pregnancy levels or a blood pressure greater than 140/90 mmHg.

Pre-eclampsia   Hypertension, oedema and proteinuria are present. Most patients are otherwise asymptomatic, although headache, nausea, vomiting and visual disturbance may herald the onset of eclampsia. Most patients can be treated with rest, reassurance and regular obstetric follow-up.

Eclampsia   Seizures are associated with hypertension, oedema and proteinuria.

Differential diagnosis

- Epilepsy.
- Intracranial bleeding.
- Intracranial tumour.

Treatment

- Oxygen.
- Diazemuls 5–10 mg intravenously to control fits.
- Hydralazine or labetolol intravenously to control hypertension (alternatively oral nifedipine if the patient is able to take oral medication).
- Early obstetric referral. Emergency caesarean section may be required.

Amniotic fluid embolism The release of amniotic fluid into the maternal circulation usually presents with sudden unexpected cardiovascular collapse.

Causes

- Labour.
- Spontaneous.
- Amniocentesis.
- Trauma.
- Abruptio placentae.

Complications

- Maternal death occurs in up to 90% of cases.
- Fetal death.
- Disseminated intravascular coagulation.
- Adult respiratory distress syndrome.

Differential diagnosis

- Pulmonary embolism.
- Myocardial infarction.
- Abruptio placentae.

Treatment

- Oxygen.
- Cardiorespiratory support.
- Emergency lower segment caesarean section.

Resuscitation in pregnancy Follow the same protocol as for the non-pregnant patient. However, treat the mother, not the fetus. Always nurse the patient in the left lateral position or manually displace the uterus to the left to prevent inferior vena caval obstruction and involve obstetricians early in management, especially if the delivery suite is not on the same site as the accident and emergency department.

Further reading

Walker JJ. The management of hypertensive disease in pregnancy. *Current Obstetrics and Gynaecology.* 1993; **3**: 82–7.

Related topics of interest

Abdominal pain (p. 1)
Gynaecology (p. 136)

OPHTHALMIC EMERGENCIES

The great majority of urgent eye problems can be diagnosed with careful history taking and with basic examination. A slit-lamp microscope is invaluable, providing illumination and magnification, especially for small superficial foreign bodies, penetrating wounds, the track of intraocular foreign bodies, flare in the anterior chamber and small abnormalities of the iris. Local anaesthetic and mydriatric drops aid complete examination.

Examination

- Check the *visual acuity* of each eye separately (completely occlude the other eye with a card or palm of the hand). Use a *Snellen chart* at 6 metres. If this fails then test vision at 3 metres, then 1 metre. If there is still no response, test whether the patient can count fingers, detect hand movement or perceive light. Patients should use their own distance glasses or a pinhole to correct any refractive error.

- Check the *pupil reactions*, including the afferent pupillary reflex. Only test *accommodation* if the pupils or light reactions are abnormal.

- Test the *visual fields* to confrontation of each eye. Central defects can be detected using the *Amsler grid test* (white grid on a dark background).

- *Inspect the conjunctiva and sclera.* Look for evidence of inflammation, a laceration or haemorrhage.

- *Evert the upper eyelid.* Ask the patient to look down, pull the lashes down and press a cotton bud at the upper border of the tarsal plate to evert the lid. Examine with a bright light and remove a subtarsal foreign body with a cotton bud.

- Measure the *intraocular pressure.* This is measured using aplanatic tonometry or pneumotonometry. The normal intraocular pressure is 10–21 mmHg above atmospheric pressure. An estimate of intraocular pressure may be gauged by palpating the eye with two fingers above the upper eyelid when the patient is looking down.

- *Inspect the cornea.* Stain with *fluorescein* and use a cobalt blue light to reveal areas of denuded corneal epithelium. Remove contact lenses as they will stain.

If small scratches are seen in the upper cornea, evert the upper eyelid as a subtarsal foreign body may be present. Fluorescein will reveal an abrasion, epithelial defect or dendritic ulcer.

- *Examine the anterior chamber.* Is blood present (hyphaema)? Inflammatory cells and increased protein make the fluid cloudy.

- *Look within the pupil and inspect the iris.* Look for evidence of an iris prolapse. Is the lens damaged, or displaced?

- *Ophthalmoscopic examination.* A normal red reflex may be impaired by a corneal opacity, aqueous turbidity, pupillary exudate, cataract or vitreous haemorrhage.

- *Retinal examination.* Consider dilatation of the pupil with a short-acting mydriatic, e.g. tropicamide 0.5%, but beware of the older patient in whom acute glaucoma may be precipitated. Pupil dilatation is advisable except when:

    (a) The anterior chamber is so shallow that a light shone from the side in the plane of the iris throws the nasal part of the iris into shadow (the patient is at risk of angle closure glaucoma).
    (b) The patient is under neurological observation.
    (c) There is a square pupil with an iris-supported lens implant following cataract surgery.

- *Check the ocular movements.*

Perforating eye injury Maintain a high index of suspicion. High-risk injuries include hammering and chiselling injuries and those involving glass. Most involve the anterior chamber and therefore are visible on anterior examination. Important signs include:

- A protruding or retained foreign body.
- Prolapse of intraocular contents.
- Pupil distortion (the pupil points towards the perforation).
- An iris hole or track in the lens.

A retained steel fragment will result in blindness because ferric ions are toxic and destroy the retina. Radiographs are important to aid exclusion of a radio-opaque foreign body but are not a substitute for thorough examination.

Any patient with a suspected or proven intraocular foreign body should be immediately referred to the ophthalmologist. Take care in patients with suspected perforation as increased pressure may result in further bleeding or prolapse of intraocular contents.

Retinal detachment

The history of blurred vision preceded by floaters (vitreous disturbance) and peripheral flashes of light (retinal traction) in a patient, especially a myopic one, makes one suspect retinal detachment.

The red eye

Never use topical steroids for an undiagnosed red eye without specialist advice. After exclusion of a foreign body and corneal abrasion consider the following:

- *Conjunctivitis.* May be allergic, viral or bacterial. Symptoms include grittiness and a watery or purulent discharge. The visual acuity, cornea, pupil and anterior chamber are all normal.

- *Keratitis.* May be viral, bacterial or allergic.

- *Acute glaucoma.* A painful red eye is associated with profound visual loss, and there may be associated systemic symptoms such as nausea and vomiting. The cornea is cloudy and oedematous with circumoral injection. The pupil is fixed, mid-dilated and oval and the anterior chamber shallow. Treat with miotics and acetazolamide and refer immediately to a specialist.

- *Acute iritis.* The eye is painful and red with impaired visual acuity, photophobia, circumoral injection, anterior chamber cells and flare, keratitic precipitates, pupil constriction and adhesions between the pupil and the lens (posterior synechiae). Associated conditions include Reiter's syndrome, AIDS, spondylitis and gonorrhoea. Urgent referral to an ophthalmologist for pupil dilatation and local steroids is warranted.

- *Episcleritis.*

- *Herpes simplex and herpes zoster ophthalmicus.* Both require referral to an ophthalmologist.

Chemical injury   *Alkali burns* are the most serious as they penetrate rapidly and deeply. *Acid burns* rarely penetrate the eye itself.

    Treatment. First aid includes immediate irrigation with copious amounts of water. In hospital measure the pH and irrigate with copious amounts of normal saline using a giving set until neutral. Assess damage and refer to an ophthalmologist.

Further reading

Eagling EM, Roper-Hall MJ. *Eye Injuries – an Illustrated Guide.* London: Butterworths, 1986.

Elkington AR, Khaw PT. *ABC of Eyes.* London: BMJ Publishing Group, 1990.

Related topics of interest

Headache (temporal arteritis) (p. 142)

Maxillofacial injury (p. 198)

Organ donation (p. 231)

ORGAN DONATION

Over the last 20 years kidneys and corneas have been the most commonly transplanted organs. Advances in surgical techniques and transplant immunology have made transplantation of the following possible:

- Cornea.
- Kidney.
- Liver.
- Heart.
- Heart/lung.
- Heart valves.
- Pancreas and bowel.
- Bone.

Exclusion criteria for donation include:

- Age more than 70 years. There is no lower age limit.
- Malignant disease except primary brain tumour.
- Major systemic sepsis.
- Positive hepatitis B surface antigen test.
- Positive HIV antibody test.

Most organs come from patients who have been declared dead after brain-stem function tests, referred to as the *heart-beating cadaver donor*. Another potential source is the patient who is declared dead, referred to as the *non-heart-beating cadaver donor*.

Transplant coordinator   The functions of a transplant coordinator are:

- To organize the retrieval operation and liaise between the donating unit and other transplant teams in the case of multiple organ donation.
- To maintain organ function.
- To approach the next of kin.
- To approach the coroner or, in Scotland, the procurator fiscal, if required.
- To provide follow-up information to staff in the donating hospital and relatives where appropriate.

Corneal transplantation   Corneal grafting was pioneered in the UK in the 1930s by Tudor Thomas, and today corneal grafts have a very high success rate of 85%. The vast majority of people who die can be considered for corneal donation. The need for glasses does not in most cases affect suitability for corneal donation. There is no age limit to corneal donation.

Enucleation, which does not cause disfigurement to the donor, can be carried out up to 12 hours after death. The cornea is not directly dependent on the blood supply for nutrition and does not deteriorate as quickly as other organs. After death the cornea should not be exposed or allowed to dry.

Contraindications are few, however there must be no:

- Scarring of the cornea or deterioration of tissue.
- Infectious disease residing in the eye tissue.
- Rare invasive brain tumours which may infiltrate eye tissue.

Heart valve transplant The first human valve transplant was performed in 1962. Because of the absence of rejection they are very successful.

The donor may have died at home or in hospital, including in the A & E department. Ideally donors should be aged between 3 months and 60 years. Donation must take place within 72 hours of death. The valves are removed during a post-mortem or multiorgan retrieval.

Contraindications are few. Cardiac arrest or myocardial infarction and malignancy are not contraindications to donation but there must be no:

- Congenital valve defect.
- Major systemic infection.
- Hepatitis B or C positivity.
- HIV positivity.
- Viral disease.

Brain-stem death Irreversibility of the loss of brain-stem function is determined by the passage of time and failure of attempts to reverse the condition. Brain-stem death should be diagnosed by two doctors as recommended at the Conference of Royal Colleges and set out in the current Code of Practice. The doctors may carry out the tests together or separately, and even if they confirm brain-stem death it is recommended that the tests are repeated. The interval between tests is a medical decision and will depend on the primary diagnosis. The time of death is the time at which the tests were carried out for the final time. These doctors act on behalf of the donor, not the recipient.

Preconditions

- That the patient is unresponsive and on a ventilator.
- That the cause of the coma has been properly ascertained and is irremediable structural brain damage due to a disorder that can lead to brain-stem death.

Common pathologies resulting in brain-stem death

- Cerebral trauma.
- Intracranial haemorrhage.
- Anoxic brain damage, e.g. following cardiac or respiratory arrest.
- Primary brain tumour.

Exclusions

- Drug depressants or relaxants.
- Very recent circulatory arrest, persisting shock and hypotension.
- Primary hypothermia (<35°C).
- Acid–base abnormality.
- Metabolic or endocrine disturbance, e.g. uncontrolled diabetes mellitus, uraemia, hyponatraemia, Addison's disease, hepatic encephalopathy, thyrotoxicosis.

Brain-stem function tests

- *No pupillary response to light.* There is absence of both direct and consensual reactions, which tests the II cranial nerve and the parasympathetic outflow.
- *No corneal reflex.* Tests the V and VII cranial nerves.
- *No vestibulo-ocular reflex.* After visualizing both ear drums, 30 ml of ice cold water is injected into each external auditory canal. No response is seen if the VIII nerve and brain stem are dead. Nystagmus occurs if the vestibular reflexes are intact
- *No motor responses* within the cranial nerve distribution in response to adequate stimulation of any somatic area. A painful stimulus to the face tests the V and VII cranial nerves.
- *No gag reflex* in response to tracheal stimulation. This tests the IX and X cranial nerves.

- *Doll's eye movement.* The head is moved rapidly from side to side. If the brain stem is dead the eyes remain in a fixed position within the orbit. This is the *oculocephalic reflex* and tests the VIII cranial nerve. If the cortex is dead but the brain stem is intact, the eyes appear to move to the opposite side and then realign with the head.
- *Apnoea test.* After proper preoxygenation the patient is disconnected from the ventilator while diffusion oxygenation is maintained by catheter down the trachea. The patient is then carefully observed to establish that no respiratory movements occur in response to a $PaCO_2$ that should reach 6.65 kPa – a level sufficient to stimulate the respiratory centre if it is still functional.

Further reading

Cadaveric Organs for Transplantation: A Code of Practice. London: HMSO, 1983.

OVERUSE INJURY

The term is applied to a variety of conditions not usually attributable to any one injury or event. Pain may develop insidiously, and there may be no obvious precipitating factors. It is therefore essential to include a complete occupational/recreational history during the initial assessment.

Pathology

- Inflammation, usually of the tendon sheaths, which may become thickened and fibrosed (tenosynovitis).
- Failure of repetitive minor injury to heal.
- Ischaemia, particularly of muscles occupying tight fascial compartments.
- Stress fracture.
- Tendon rupture.

Syndromes

1. Stress fractures. These are caused by repetitive overloading or muscle traction on bone, causing osteoblastic resorption to predominate over osteoblastic new bone formation, resulting in weakness of the trabecular bone structure. They may occur at any age after puberty and are more common in females. Stress fractures are also commonly seen in athletes and servicemen (march fractures), but may occur after any repetitive, unusual activities such as charity walks or runs, especially if there is a lack of preparation in training, in which case a lack of muscle bulk may contribute to its causation.

Sites

- Tibia 50%.
- Tarsus 25%.
- Metatarsus 10%.
- Also femur, fibula, pelvis, lumbar spine and sesamoid bones.

The presenting symptom is usually pain localized at the site of fracture. This is worse on load bearing or jarring. There is often local tenderness, swelling and occasionally redness. Radiographs are usually normal in the early stages, but up to 90% of fractures will become visible in 2–12 weeks. A technetium-99 bone scan will be positive in the majority of cases within 72 hours of symptoms appearing.

Treatment is rest of the affected part until the pain has subsided. In the case of tibial stress fractures this may take 2–6 months.

2. *Shin splints.* There is pain in the middle and lower thirds of the tibia as a result of inflammation, usually at the insertion of tibialis posterior and occasionally at the insertion of tibialis anterior.

The differential diagnosis includes stress fracture and anterior or posterior compartment syndrome.

Treatment is rest, non-jarring exercises and careful attention to footwear and sporting technique.

3. *Tennis/golfer's elbow.* There is pain and tenderness of the common flexor origin (golfer's elbow) or common extensor origin (tennis elbow).

The differential diagnosis includes posterior interosseous nerve entrapment and referred pain from the neck.

Treatment is with rest, NSAIDs and local steroid injection. Surgery may be required in a small proportion of patients who are resistant to treatment.

4. *Repetitive strain injury (RSI).* This is a painful condition of the forearm with tenderness, swelling, redness and crepitus. At present RSI is not recognized as a disease by the courts. The term tenosynovitis should be avoided as it has medicolegal implications and can only be diagnosed when there is a tendon sheath and probably only really occurs in rheumatoid arthritis. Classical peritendinitis crepitans (de Quervain's disease) may arise spontaneously or as a result of repetitive activity.

5. *Others*

- Rotator cuff syndrome.
- Chondromalacia patellae.
- Patella tendinitis.
- Trochanteric bursitis.

Further reading

Barton NJ, Hooper G, Noble J, Steele WM. Occupational causes of disorders in the upper limb. *British Medical Journal*, 1992; **304**: 309–11.
Brooks P. Repetitive strain injury. *British Medical Journal*, 1993; **307**: 1298.

Related topics of interest

PARACETAMOL POISONING

Paracetamol was the probable cause of death from hepatic failure in 150 patients in England and Wales in 1990, and in combination with other drugs was probably the cause of many more. Paracetamol overdose is increasing, and accounts for approximately one-third of all attempted suicides.

In overdose the drug causes liver damage, once glutathione is depleted, through the formation of metabolites that bind to sulphydryl groups in cell membrane enzymes.

Toxicity is dose related and amounts of paracetamol over 150 mg/kg are potentially lethal. Patients who are fortunate enough to recover from the hepatic necrosis make a complete recovery.

Symptoms and signs
- Early nausea and vomiting.
- Localized, right upper quadrant abdominal pain.
- Progressive deepening of consciousness level, secondary to encephalopathy.
- Hypoglycaemia or hyperglycaemia.
- Progressive prolongation of the prothrombin time, jaundice and liver enzyme elevation.
- Progression to grade 4 encephalopathy and brainstem coning, from cerebral oedema.
- May be complicated by renal tubular necrosis.

Antidote

The antidote of choice is *intravenous acetylcysteine* administered in 5% dextrose.

A *pseudoallergic reaction* of wheeze, flushing and hypotension may occur. If this is the case, stop the infusion, give chlorpheniramine and hydrocortisone, and restart at a lower rate.

Acetylcysteine is safe in pregnancy.

The antidote is given according to a treatment line of log concentration against time, joining 200 mg/l at 4 hours and 50 mg/l at 12 hours. If the plasma paracetamol concentration is above, on or even slightly below the line, antidote treatment should be given. The treatment line is not infallible since the response of individuals to the same amount of paracetamol is variable and its validity beyond 15 hours after ingestion is less certain because there are insufficient data from untreated patients.

Patients who are *chronic alcoholics* or taking *enzyme-inducing drugs* such as phenytoin, carbamazepine, barbiturates, primidone, phenobarbitone and rifampicin should be treated at plasma paracetamol concentrations half as great as those indicated by the standard treatment line.

Previously it was thought that *N*-acetylcysteine was harmful if given after 15 hours post ingestion. Now it has been shown to reduce morbidity and mortality when given up to 36 hours and even in patients with hepatic encephalopathy.

Alternatively, *oral methionine* may be given in those patients who present within 4 hours whilst waiting for the 4 hour plasma paracetamol concentration. The dose is 2.5 g orally every 4 hours until four doses have been given. However, the effect is unreliable in patients who are vomiting and those given activated charcoal. Methionine has no significant side-effects.

Treatment

Treatment is based on three principles:

(a) Reducing the amount of drug absorbed.
(b) Preventing liver damage by providing sulphydryl groups to facilitate the synthesis of glutathione.
(c) Mitigating the effects of liver damage.

1. Presentation within 4 hours of ingestion

- Consider emptying the stomach in adults who have taken > 12 g or > 150 mg/kg, and children > 150 mg/kg.
- Record a 4-hour plasma paracetamol level.
- Give antidote as required.

2. Presentation 4–8 hours after ingestion

- Measure the plasma paracetamol level immediately.
- Give antidote as necessary.

3. Presentation 8–15 hours after ingestion. If a potential toxic dose of paracetamol is taken, *antidote is given immediately*, and this may be stopped if the paracetamol level is below the treatment line. This is because the efficacy of antidote treatment falls with time after 8 hours.

4. Presentation 15–24 hours after ingestion. Antidote should be initiated immediately and continued until the patient has clearly escaped significant hepatic and renal damage.

5. *Presentation more than 24 hours after ingestion.* Discuss urgently with the regional poisons centre.

Specialist liver or poison treatment centre advice should be sought if any of the following is recorded:

- The INR is above 3.0.
- A raised serum creatinine concentration.
- Blood pH below 7.3.
- Evidence of encephalopathy.
- Hypotension (mean arterial pressure < 60 mmHg).
- Those patients with pre-existing liver disease.

In all patients who have presented within 8 hours of overdose, the INR and serum creatinine should be measured about 24 hours after the overdose, or after antidote treatment is complete. Patients can be discharged if the results are normal.

In patients who have presented after 8 hours the INR and creatinine should be measured after completion of treatment and at 48 hours after overdose.

In patients who present after 16 hours, monitor for signs of liver failure. Look for signs of encephalopathy, exclude hypoglycaemia and treat haemorrhage with fresh-frozen plasma. Refer the patient to a liver unit for further treatment and consideration for possible liver transplantation. Patients who recover from liver damage suffer no long-term sequelae.

Further reading

Ferner R. Paracetamol poisoning – an update. *Prescribers' Journal*, 1993; **33**: 45–50.
Proudfoot AT. *Acute Poisoning. Diagnosis and Management*, 2nd edn. London: Butterworth-Heinemann, 1993.

Related topic of interest

Drug overdose and accidental poisoning (p. 99)

PERIPHERAL NERVE INJURY

Peripheral nerves consist of fascicles of nerve fibres containing both myelinated and unmyelinated axons. Each fasicle has its own fibrous sheath (perineurium). Fasicles are bound together by the epineurium, which forms the outer layer of the nerve. After a nerve has been divided, Wallerian degeneration occurs throughout the entire nerve distal to the injury and also for a few millimetres proximally. The axons and myelin sheaths degenerate and fragment. As healing occurs axons from the proximal stump grow outwards and if the nerve remains in apposition or the nerve sheath is intact the new axons will enter into the distal stump growing distally at a rate of 1–3 mm per day.

Types of injury

- *Ischaemia.* Often occurs following application of a pneumatic tourniquet or local acute compression and results in a transient loss of function with full recovery usually within 30 minutes. Traction, compression and laceration also result in nerve injury, the degree of which was described by Seddon.
- *Neuropraxia.* Trauma leading to nerve conduction block in the anatomically intact nerve. Recovery recurs spontaneously but may take several months.
- *Axonotemesis.* Commonly caused by a crush injury leading to a disruption of the nerve fibres in the intact nerve sheath. Spontaneous recovery can occur but is not predictable.
- *Neuronotemesis.* The anatomical disruption or division of a nerve. All functions are absent unless the nerve is repaired.

Clinical features

A high index of suspicion is required whenever there is a laceration or injury to an area known to contain a nerve. If the patient is conscious always enquire about numbness, paraesthesia and loss of function. Examination must be thorough and careful.

1. Motor function. Including range of active movement, tone and power. Power is graded as follows:

0 Complete paralysis.
1 Detectable contracture.
2 Power but not against gravity.
3 Power against gravity.
4 Power reduced from normal.
5 Normal power.

2. *Sensory function*. Chart the area of reduced or absent sensation to pinprick and light touch. For digital nerves the loss of two-point discrimination is a reliable sign of nerve injury.

3. *Appearance*. Look and feel the skin. Following acute injury there is loss of sweating and in established injury the skin appears shiny and thin.

Management

Closed injuries usually recover spontaneously and can be treated expectantly, surgical exploration being reserved for patients in whom predicted recovery does not occur. When there is nerve dysfunction associated with an injury likely to have divided or injured a nerve such as laceration or stab wound then wound exploration is mandatory.

Note: It is possible to have some sensation in a nerve which has been completely divided if the ends are in close proximity.

Nerve repair is best performed as a primary procedure if possible. However, delayed primary or secondary repair may be performed following missed injuries and when the patient's general condition dictates. Repair must always be performed by a surgeon trained to undertake epineural or group fascicular repair. The results of repair depend on the age of the patient, the proximity of the lesion, the type of nerve injury and the time elapsed between injury and repair.

Brachial plexus injury

The brachial plexus is formed by the anterior primary rami of C5 to T1 nerve roots. They pass between scalenius anterior and medius into the anterior triangle of the neck, exiting into the upper limb as lateral, medial and posterior trunks which surround the axillary artery. Injury usually follows major trauma, often falling from a motorcycle or horse onto the neck or shoulder, causing traction on the brachial plexus. Exact localization of the level of injury is often difficult clinically, but it is important to differentiate preganglionic lesions with avulsion of the nerve root, which is an irreparable condition, from peripheral lesions, which may benefit from exploration and surgical repair. Horner's sign suggests nerve root avulsion. CT myelography will demonstration leakage of contrast, indicating nerve root avulsion.

Further reading

Noble J. Nerves and tendons. In: Dudley HAF, ed. *Emergency Surgery*. Bristol: Wright, 1986: 627–39.

Related topics of interest

Fractures – principals of treatment (p. 125)
Spine and spinal cord trauma (p. 278)

PNEUMOTHORAX – SPONTANEOUS

A district general hospital with a catchment population of 200 000 may expect to treat 25 patients with spontaneous pneumothorax a year. Presentation is commonly in the healthy young adult, who tolerates a large air leak well, and in the older patient with emphysema, in whom even a small pneumothorax may cause respiratory failure.

The *British Thoracic Society* has issued guidelines for the management of spontaneous pneumothorax, which stress the advantage of *simple aspiration* over *intercostal tube drainage* and the importance of involving the respiratory physician in those cases that are not managed by simple aspiration alone.

Management

In patients with *chronic lung disease*, e.g. emphysema or cystic fibrosis, respiratory compromise is commoner, drainage procedures are less successful and referral to a respiratory specialist is more likely. This group of patients must be admitted, whether or not they have had aspiration.

The degree of collapse is defined as:

- *Small.* Small rim of air around the lung.
- *Moderate.* Lung collapsed halfway towards heart border.
- *Complete.* Airless lung, separate from diaphragm.
- *Tension.* pneumothorax with cardiorespiratory collapse. It requires immediate treatment.

Significant dyspnoea refers to an obvious deterioration in usual exercise tolerance and necessitates aspiration, whatever the size of pneumothorax.

1. Simple aspiration. Infiltrate local anaesthetic down to the pleura in the second intercostal space in the midclavicular line (alternatively use the axillary approach). Using a cannula (French gauge 16 or larger), enter the pleural cavity and withdraw the needle. Connect both the cannula and a 50-ml syringe to a three-way tap, so that aspirated air can be voided.

Discontinue aspiration if resistance is felt or the patient coughs excessively, or if more than 2.5 litres is aspirated.

Perform a repeat chest radiograph in inspiration. If only a small pneumothorax remains, the procedure has been successful.

If the cannula is accidentally withdrawn from the

pleural cavity, or becomes kinked, another attempt at aspiration should be considered.

Observe the patient overnight. If the patient is stable both clinically and radiographically, discharge and arrange for a follow-up chest clinic appointment in 7–10 days. The patient must be given a discharge letter and told to attend immediately if there is any deterioration. Air travel and diving are contraindicated until there is radiographic resolution.

2. Intercostal tube drainage. Explanation of the procedure to the patient is essential. In the anxious patient premedication with a small dose of midazolam may be necessary. The site of insertion is the fourth, fifth or sixth intercostal space in the mid-axillary line on the ipsilateral side (which should be double checked with the chest radiograph). Use a 20–24 French gauge (adult) drain and avoid using the trocar. Blunt dissection down to and through the parietal pleura is essential. Attempt to site the drain apically and connect to an underwater seal. Check the position and effect of the drain with a plain chest radiograph.

Further reading

Miller AC, Harvey JE on behalf of Standards of Care Committee, British Thoracic Society. Guidelines for the Management of Spontaneous pneumothorax. *British Medical Journal*, 1993; **307**: 114–16.

Related topics of interest

Chest pain (p. 66)
Respiratory distress in children (p. 257)

POST-TRAUMATIC STRESS DISORDER

Post-traumatic stress disorder (PTSD) is the emotional and behavioural disturbance that follows a recognized trauma, either psychological or physical. The point prevalence of PTSD in the general population is about 1%, although the disorder is commoner in high-risk groups, e.g. victims of personal attack, those involved in terrorist bombings, those involved in wars, victims of torture, those involved in other disasters and health professionals.

PTSD is chronic or recurring in a high proportion of patients and is associated with increased mortality, subsequent psychiatric illness, accidental and non-accidental death.

The medical profession and other emergency care staff involved in accident and emergency work are now more fully aware of the psychological aspects of trauma.

Definition

The diagnostic criteria for PTSD initially outlined by the American Psychiatric Association in 1980 and later revised in 1987 are summarized below:

(a) The person has experienced an event that is outside the range of usual human expcrience and which would be markedly distressing to almost anyone, e.g. serious threat to one's life or physical integrity; serious threat or harm to one's children, spouse or other close relatives and friends; sudden destruction of onc's home or community; or seeing another person who has recently been or is being seriously injured or killed as the result of an accident or physical violence.

(b) The traumatic event is persistently re-experienced in at least one of the following ways.

- Recurrent and intrusive distressing recollections of the event (in young children, repetitive play in which themes or aspects of the trauma are expressed).
- Recurrent distressing dreams of the event.
- Suddenly acting or feeling as if the traumatic events were recurring [includes a sense of reliving the experience, illusions, hallucinations, and dissociative (flashback) episodes, even those that occur upon awakening or when intoxicated].
- Intense psychological distress at exposure to events that symbolize or resemble an aspect of the traumatic event including anniversaries of the trauma.

(c) Persistent avoidance of stimuli associated with the trauma or numbing of general responsiveness (not present before the trauma) as indicated by at least three of the following:

- Efforts to avoid thoughts or feelings associated with the trauma.
- Efforts to avoid activities or situations that arouse recollections of the trauma.
- Inability to recall an important aspect of the trauma (psychogenic amnesia).
- Markedly diminished interest in significant activities (in young children, loss of recently acquired developmental skills such as toilet training or language skills).
- Feeling of detachment or estrangement from others.
- Restricted range of affect, e.g. unable to have loving feelings.
- Sense of a foreshortened future, e.g. does not expect to have a career, marriage, or children, or a long life.

(d) Persistent symptoms of increased arousal (not present before the trauma) as indicated by at least two of the following:

- Difficulty falling or staying asleep.
- Irritability or outbursts of anger.
- Difficulty concentrating.
- Hypervigilance.
- Exaggerated startle response.
- Physiological reactivity upon exposure to events that symbolize or resemble an aspect of the traumatic event (e.g. a woman who was raped in an elevator breaks out in a sweat when entering any elevator).

(e) Duration of the disturbance (symptoms in b, c and d) of at least 1 month.

Management

This is currently being evaluated but presently includes:

- *Debriefing.*
- *Reassurance* and *support* as the individual strives to incorporate the experience.
- For more extreme reactions *psychotherapeutic tech-*

niques ranging from dynamic therapies to strict behaviour modifications may be helpful.

- *Anxiolytics* may palliate symptoms of anxiety.
- *Antidepressants* reduce depressive and intrusive recollection phenomena.
- The development of programmes such as *critical incident or stress debriefing,* which are usually provided in groups by mental health professionals and peer support workers, is to be encouraged in accident and emergency departments. Planning for this should be incorporated into major accident planning.

Further reading

The Disasters Working Party. *Disasters: Planning for a caring response,* Part 1: Main report. Part 2: Guidelines for an action plan. London: HMSO. 1991.

Jackson G. The rise of post-traumatic stress disorders. *British Medical Journal,* 1991; **303**: 533–4.

Turner SW. Post-traumatic stress disorder. *Hospital Update,* 1991; **17**: 644–9.

Related topic of interest

Disaster planning (p. 93)

PREHOSPITAL CARE

The aims of paramedic training are to save life and reduce morbidity and mortality, and this is achieved by applying paramedic techniques in the prehospital care of the patient, namely:

- Intravenous cannulation.
- Endotracheal intubation.
- Fluid administration – crystalloid and colloid.
- ECG monitoring.
- Defibrillation.

Drug therapy includes:

- Oxygen.
- Diazepam.
- Glucogen.
- Dextrose 50%.
- Nebulized bronchodilator therapy.
- Adrenaline.
- Glyceryl trinitrate.
- Entonox.
- Aspirin.
- Atropine.
- Ergometrine.
- Lignocaine.
- Nalbuphine.
- Naloxone.

Cardiac arrest

Out of hospital defibrillation with an automated external defibrillator has been evaluated by 'Heartstart Scotland'. Discharge alive rates of 12.5% were recorded in those with ventricular fibrillation.

Advanced cardiac life support instituted for a prehospital cardiac or respiratory arrest, if not successful prior to arrival at the emergency department, is associated with a poor prognosis.

Acute myocardial infarction

The responsibilities of the ambulance services include:

- Ambulance services should continue to improve training for control staff (ambulance despatchers) and improve prioritization of emergency and urgent calls using 'criteria based response'.
- All patients with chest pain require an emergency response with a vehicle containing a defibrillator and staff trained in its use.

- By 1996 all emergency ambulances must be staffed by at least one paramedic fully capable of advanced cardiac life support.
- Once an ambulance has been despatched, the patient's general practitioner should (when feasible) be informed; this is particularly important in areas where general practitioners are responsible for initiating thrombolytic treatment.

  The role of pre-hospital thrombolysis is still under evaluation. Time savings of 40–60 minutes have been demonstrated but the impact on mortality and morbidity has not been proven.
- Cardiac monitoring must be instituted as soon as possible.
- Protocols should be developed to allow the appropriate administration of oxygen, nitrates and aspirin.
- Direct communication between the ambulance and the admitting hospital departments should be developed.

Trauma

Death within the first hours after injury can be prevented by high-quality prehospital care. The goal of prehospital care of the critically injured patient should be to reduce the time from injury to definitive surgical care, yet provide resuscitation that will increase the chances of the patient arriving at the hospital alive and in a reasonable condition.

Prehospital trauma life support has been shown to be beneficial in:

- A rural setting.
- In urban patients with blunt trauma.
- In patients with penetrating thoracic trauma when immediate transportation without stabilization in the field seems to be the optimal prehospital management.

The major controversies regarding prehospital care include:

- What procedures are useful in the field?
- What is the trade-off between the time spent in the field versus benefit of the procedure?
- Medical control of the team in the field.

Pneumatic antishock garment (PASG) The application of the PASG has the consequence of increasing systemic vascular resistance and afterload, which may raise the arterial pressure. The PASG provides the urban prehospital victim with no significant benefit and its use in the rural setting is controversial.

Intravenous fluids

Computer models reveal that intravenous infusions are of little benefit except:

- Where there is a significant rate of blood loss.
- The prehospital time exceeds 30 minutes.
- The infusion rate is approximately equivalent to the bleeding rate.

This is supported in clinical practice. Prehospital intravenous fluid administration has been found not to influence mortality rates following trauma.

Intravenous catheter placement and initiation of fluid therapy at the scene delay transfer to hospital, but intravenous cannulation *en route*, while the ambulance is moving, prevents delay.

Field triage

Assessment of injury severity requires examination of:

1. *Abnormal physiology.* Revised trauma score.

2. *Anatomical injury*

- Severe penetrating wounds to chest, abdomen, head, neck or groin.
- Two or more proximal long bone fractures.
- More than 15% burns of face or airway.

3. *Mechanism of injury*

- Falls of 20 ft or more.
- Patient ejected from vehicle.
- Death of same vehicle occupant.
- Pedestrian hit at estimated speed of >20 m.p.h.
- Prolonged extrication > 20 min.
- Substantial damage to vehicle.
- Auto impact velocity > 25 m.p.h. without restraints or >30 m.p.h. with restraints.

4. *Concurrent disease.* The triage decision scheme helps to select patients with an injury severity score of greater than 16. Such patients have at least a 10% risk of dying from their injuries. It is estimated that a 35–50% overtriage rate may be required to maintain a minimum level of undertriage.

Stabilization should consist of:

(a) *Assessment.*

(b) *Extrication.*

(c) *Initial resuscitation.* The initial resuscitation should be limited to:

- Airway control with high-flow oxygen.
- Cervical spine stabilization.
- Haemorrhage control.
- Stabilization of fractures.
- While *en route*, insertion of large-bore i.v. catheters and infusion of crystalloid/colloid.

(d) Rapid transport to the closest appropriate hospital.

On-scene time must be brief, and communication to the nearest appropriate hospital for admission should be clear and concise, so that appropriate staff may receive the patient on arrival. This may mean bypassing those facilities not dedicated and committed to the immediate management of the trauma victim, even if they are the closest to the accident. If distances are great, or where such direct transport is not feasible, patients should be taken to the closest facility where adequate stabilization can be achieved. The patient can then be transferred according to previously established protocols.

Further reading

Ambulance Service Paramedic Training. Bristol: The National Health Service Training Directorate, 1991

Cobbe SM, Redmond MJ, Watson JM, Hollingworth J, Carrington DJ. 'Heartstart Scotland' – initial experience of a national scheme for out of hospital defibrillation. *British Medical Journal*, 1991; **302**: 1517–20.

Gray WA, Capone RJ, Most AS. Unsuccessful emergency medical resuscitation – are continued efforts in the emergency department justified? *New England Journal of Medicine*, 1991; **325**: 1393–8.

Weston C, Fox KAA. Prehospital thrombolysis: current status and future prospects. *Journal of the Royal College of Physicians of London*, 1991; **25**: 312–20.

Related topics of interest

PULMONARY OEDEMA – ACUTE

Acute severe pulmonary oedema is a life-threatening condition frequently seen in the accident and emergency department, the patient practically drowning in fluid-filled lungs. Less severe forms, presenting with breathlessness, are more common.

Pulmonary oedema may be considered as a diffuse increase in lung water involving either the interstitium, alveoli or both. Its genesis may involve a disruption in Starling's forces. The following four factors may lead to oedema:

Causes

1. Increased hydrostatic pressure

(a) *Venous hypertension*

- Left ventricular failure.
- Mitral stenosis.
- Cardiomyopathy.

(b) *Pulmonary capillary hypertension*

- Hypoxia.
- Increased plasma volume.
- Altitude.

(c) *Acute pulmonary arterial hypertension*

- Hyperkinetic states.
- Secondary to release of catecholamines.
- Drugs (e.g. aminorex).

2. Decreased oncotic pressure

- Overhydration.
- Nephrotic syndrome.
- Hepatic failure.
- Protein-losing states.

3. Increased capillary permeability

- Catecholamines, histamine, etc.
- Following septicaemia, hypovolaemic shock, etc.
- Hypoxia, oxygen poisoning, smoke, chemical, etc.
- Neurogenic, e.g. post-ictal, post-head injury.

4. Decreased lymphatic clearance.

Pathophysiology

In cardiogenic pulmonary oedema, increasing capillary interstitial pressure results in increased fluid movement across the capillary membrane. Compensatory mechanisms, such as increased lymphatic uptake and lowering of the interstitial oncotic pressure by transudation of fluid into the interstitium, are eventually overcome, resulting in accumulation of interstitial fluid. The subsequent interstitial swelling and dilution of surfactant promotes alveolar collapse, leading to reduced functional residual capacity and lung compliance. Small airways obstruction and even larger airway obstruction may occur as a result of mucosal oedema and/or reflex bronchoconstriction. The effects are to increase the work of breathing and impair gas exchange, resulting in hypoxaemia and in severe cases carbon dioxide retention. Severe pulmonary oedema is associated with circulatory failure, resulting in reduced tissue perfusion due to impaired cardiac performance, elevated peripheral vascular resistance and often hypovolaemia. The presence of hypoxia and hypoperfusion leads to anaerobic metabolism and lactic acidosis.

History and examination

Rapid assessment is required.
A brief *history* for details regarding cardiac history and a drug history are sought.

The e*xamination* in the acutely ill is of limited value as most patients are severely distressed and anxious. A tachycardic, tachypnoeic and hypertensive patient is usual. *Auscultation* of the chest frequently detects transmitted upper airway noises or the presence of wheezing, which may lead to misinterpretation of airways disease. A heart murmur, triple rhythm and pulsus alternans are listened for but are often impossible to hear.

Investigations

1. Chest radiography. The pattern of radiographic changes in acute pulmonary oedema includes:

- Cardiomegaly.
- Upper lobe redistribution.
- Early perihilar congestion.
- Interstitial markings – Kerley's A, B and C lines.
- Later fluid enters the alveoli, which is seen as diffuse clouding – the 'butterfly' or 'bat's wing' pattern.

The so-called 'lag' in radiographic assessment occurs during the resolution phase as haemodynamic improvement precedes radiographic improvement.

2. ECG. Look for evidence of acute myocardial infarction, arrhythmias, pulmonary or systemic hypertension or right and left heart strain.

3. Arterial blood gases. Hypoxia, acidosis and hypocarbia or hypercarbia.

Treatment

1. General. Place the patient in the sitting position with the legs dependent, which increases lung volume and vital capacity, diminishes the work of respiration and decreases the venous return to the heart.

2. Oxygen. Hypoxia is best relieved with high-flow oxygen, via face mask or nasal prongs, aiming to elevate the PaO_2 to 100 mmHg. Ventilation may be required in those patients in whom, despite 100% oxygen delivery:

(a) The oxygen saturation cannot be maintained above 90%.
(b) The PaO_2 cannot be maintained above 60 mmHg.
(c) Signs of cerebral hypoxia are apparent.
(d) There is a progressive rise in $PaCO_2$ or increasing acidosis.

3. Intravenous access.

4. ECG monitoring.

5. Loop diuretics. Intravenous loop diuretics (e.g. frusemide) have long been the mainstay of treatment of acute pulmonary oedema. A venodilating effect occurs, but diuretics chiefly act to promote water and electrolyte excretion. Those patients who respond well to diuretics in terms of urine output have a better prognosis.

The dose is 0.5–2 mg/kg, commensurate with the degree of illness. If the patient is already taking an oral prescription, administer an initial dose twice the daily dose. If no effect occurs after 20 minutes, the initial dose should be doubled. Higher doses may be required in patients with massive fluid retention or renal insufficiency.

6. Morphine in a dose of 1–3 mg intravenously (if the systolic BP is greater than 100 mgHg), despite causing respiratory depression, is widely used. It acts through venodilatation, which reduces venous filling pressure to the heart and reduces sympathetic outflow. Give with an antiemetic such as metochlopramide (10 mg) intravenously.

7. *Venodilators*

(a) *Nitroglycerin* acts rapidly to venodilate and can be administered sublingually, buccally or intravenously. Sublingual therapy (0.4 mg) prior to intravenous therapy should be given every 5–10 minutes, while the systolic BP is greater than 100 mmHg.

(b) *Nitroprusside* reduces pulmonary capillary pressure, left ventricular afterload and systemic arteriolar resistance and increases venous capacitance. It requires intravenous administration and intensive monitoring. Coexistent systemic hypertension strengthens the argument for its use.

8. *Bronchodilator therapy.* 'Cardiac asthma' is a variant of acute left ventricular failure (LVF) in which audible wheeze is prominent. It is due to either small airway oedema or mucosal oedema in larger airways and bronchodilators are unhelpful.

9. *Aminophylline.* In patients with cardiogenic LVF without coexisting chronic obstructive airways disease, and in whom the distinction between the two illnesses cannot be made, it cannot be recommended because of its chronotropic effects.

10. *Inotropes*

(a) *Dopamine.* If the initial BP is less than 90–100 mmHg, a dopamine infusion should be initiated at 2.5 – 20 μg/kg/min.

(b) *Dobutamine* is more potent and may be reserved for the hypotensive patient with LVF.

(c) *Noradrenaline.*

(d) *Digoxin*'s weakly inotropic and atrioventricular nodal blocking actions are not usually required in the acute setting and thus it is rarely prescribed.

11. *Advanced airway management.* When ventilatory function is required, endotracheal intubation and positive-pressure ventilation may be necessary, but the advantages must be weighed against the potential cardiovascular and respiratory complications.

Continuous positive airway pressure (CPAP) using

a specially designed tight-fitting face mask that avoids the need for endotracheal intubation is useful. CPAP results in a dramatic improvement in arterial oxygenation, a decrease in respiratory work and a decrease in left ventricular afterload. Positive end-expiratory pressure increases end-expiratory lung volume with recruitment of alveoli and redistribution of fluid. In patients with severe LVF mask CPAP can result in early physiological improvement and reduce the need for ventilation.

12. *Other options include:*

(a) Angioplasty.
(b) Intra-aortic balloon pump.
(c) Acute surgery.
   • CABG.
   • Mitral valve repair.
   • Cardiac transplant.

Further reading

Prichard JS, Lee G de J. Pulmonary oedema. In: Weatherall DJ, Ledingham JGG, Warrell DA, eds. *The Oxford Textbook of Medicine*, 2nd edn. Oxford: Oxford University Press, 1987: 13.334 – 13.342.

Related topics of interest

Drowning and near-drowning (p. 96)
Myocardial infarction (p. 216)

RESPIRATORY DISTRESS IN CHILDREN

Respiratory conditions in children are the *most common cause of life-threatening disease* and result in over 450 deaths in children in England and Wales annually. Of these deaths over 70% are of children under 1 year.

Initial management includes the ABCs to avoid unnecessary morbidity and mortality.

The causes of respiratory distress can be divided into two categories:

(a) Primary causes (upper, lower or mixed airway).
(b) Secondary causes.

Primary

Upper airway

- Croup.
- Epiglottitis.
- Bacterial tracheitis.
- Retropharyngeal and peritonsillar abscesses.
- Laryngomalacia, tracheomalacia.

Lower airway

- Asthma.
- Bronchiolitis.
- Pneumonia.

Mixed airway

- Foreign body/aspiration.
- Anaphylaxis.
- Burns.
- Near-drowning.
- Trauma.
- Extrinsic compression.

Secondary

- Cardiac.
- Sepsis.
- Head injury/raised ICP.
- Epilepsy.
- Toxins.
- Other causes of metabolic acidosis (methanol, aspirin, uraemia, diabetic ketoacidosis).
- Congenital (diaphragmatic hernia, tracheo-oesophageal fistula).

History

Obtain a brief history from the parents and the child, if possible. Information regarding the progression of symptoms, preceding or concurrent respiratory symptoms, apnoea or cyanotic spells, fever, stridor, character of cough, wheeze, ingestions, trauma, drooling, hoarseness or inability to drink should be sought. A history of previous episodes or respiratory illness may be helpful.

Examination

Clinical assessment of respiratory distress is by observation for:

1. Work of breathing

(a) *Respiratory rate* – according to age.
(b) *Recession* – sternal, subcostal or intercostal.
(c) *Added noises*
  • *Stridor.*
  • *Wheeze.*
  • *Grunting* – attempting to maintain an open airway by expiration against a closed glottis.
(d) *Flare of alae nasi* – in those under 6 months.
(e) *Accessory muscle use.* In infants this may result in head bobbing, which is a preterminal sign.

2. Effectiveness of breathing. Auscultation may indicate added sounds or a silent chest, which is a preterminal sign. The degree of *respiratory distress is measured objectively* by pulse oximetry and capillary or arterial blood gases.

3. Secondary signs. These are due to respiratory insufficiency.

(a) *Heart rate.* Initial tachycardia, or preterminal bradycardia.
(b) *Skin colour.* Hypoxia results in skin pallor; central cyanosis is a preterminal sign.
(c) *Mental state.* Agitation or a reduced level of consciousness with fatigue or exhaustion (preterminal).

Epiglottitis (supraglottitis)

Epiglottitis is most common in children aged 1–6 years, but can occur at any age. Epiglottitis is most frequently due to *Haemophilus influenzae* type B and causes oedema of the epiglottis and surrounding tissues.

The onset is rapid, over 3–6 hours, with high fever, painful stridor, severe dysphagia and a toxic appearance. The child sits immobile, with open mouth, drooling saliva.

Management	• Avoid agitation.

Management

- Avoid agitation.
- Provide oxygen if there are signs of respiratory distress.
- Allow the patient to assume a position of comfort.
- Provide constant senior medical supervision.
- Ensure that the patient is located in an emergency area with full resuscitation equipment.
- Crash call senior anaesthetic and ENT staff.
- Admit the patient to the operating room for visualization of the epiglottis. This is achieved by careful gaseous induction of anaesthesia. If epiglottitis is found, intubate to secure the airway.
- Once the airway is secured, take blood cultures and commence intravenous antibiotics.
- If the patient suffers a respiratory arrest prior to getting to theatre:

   (a) Open the airway with basic life support techniques.
   (b) Attempt to ventilate by bag and valve mask.
   (c) If unable to ventilate, attempt to intubate.
   (d) If unable to intubate, perform needle cricothyoidotomy or mintracheostomy.

- Most children can be extubated within 36 hours and recover within 5 days.

Acute laryngotracheobronchitis (croup)

Croup usually occurs in children aged between 6 months and 5 years. It is seasonal, and its onset is more gradual than that of epiglottitis, occurring over days. Croup is associated with low-grade fever, minimal pain, a barking cough, and is usually preceded by fever and coryza for 1–3 days. Viral croup accounts for over 95% of infections and is most commonly caused by the parainfluenzal virus.

   Recurrent or spasmodic croup takes the form of repeated episodes without fever or coryza and occurs in atopic children. The episodes often occur at night and persist for a few hours. They can be severe but are commonly self-limiting.

Management

Accurate diagnosis, gentle handling and careful observation are important. In most patients the disease resolves spontaneously within 2–4 days, but in others it is more severe, requiring hospital admission.

   The following protocol is recommended:

- Avoid excessive agitation.
- Give oxygen.

- Allow the patient to assume a position of comfort.
- Keep the surrounding air cool and moist.
- Children who are more severely affected can be given nebulized adrenaline (2–5 ml of 1:1000) with oxygen through a face mask and transferred to an intensive care unit, as they may require endotracheal intubation. The nebulized adrenaline produces a transient improvement for 30–60 minutes. Significant rebound can occur and a tachycardia is usually produced.
- The role of *steroids* is controversial but they are occasionally used empirically.

Bacterial tracheitis (pseudomembranous croup)

This may occur in children aged 1–5 years and is rapidly progressive. Infection is usually with *Staphylococcus aureus* or *H. influenzae* and results in copious, purulent secretions and mucosal necrosis. The child is toxic and has stridor. Consider the diagnosis in the seriously ill 'croup' patient Prompt airway support and antibiotic therapy (a combination of ampicillin and flucloxacillin, or ceftazidine) is necessary, with over 80% of children requiring intubation and ventilatory support.

Bronchiolitis

Bronchiolitis is the most common serious respiratory infection of childhood, with 3% of all infants being admitted to hospital each year. The peak incidence is around 3–6 months of age and it tends to occur in seasonal outbreaks, the highest incidence being in the winter months. It is caused most commonly by the respiratory syncytial virus (RSV), and babies present with a history of upper respiratory tract infection for about 2 days followed by increasing respiratory distress, cough and wheeze. The disease may present from mild bronchospasm to respiratory failure.

Feeding difficulties often necessitate admission. Recurrent apnoea is a potentially fatal complication and is seen particularly in premature infants. Respiratory failure is more common in children with pre-existing lung and heart disease.

Diagnosis is clinical, but confirmation of the RSV with a fluorescent antibody technique on nasopharyngeal aspirate is possible. Chest radiographs reveal hyperinflation and collapse or consolidation, especially in the upper lobes, and should be taken only if the diagnosis is not clear or there are focal signs in the chest.

Treatment
Pulse oximetry is used to aid assessment of clinical severity and an apnoea alarm is advised. Oxygen is delivered via a head box if required. Regular review is required, and in infants with severe respiratory distress

or in whom the oxygen requirement is increasing above 40% consider the need for ventilation.

The use of nebulized bronchodilators such as ipratropium bromide is empirical. Antibiotics are rarely required and only if there is evidence of bacterial involvement. Pyrexia is treated with paracetamol. Feeding may be a problem, and either nasogastric feeds or intravenous fluids may be required.

Ribavirin is only used in those who have positive immunofluorescence for RSV and fall into the following categories:

- Those with pre-existing lung disease such as cystic fibrosis or bronchopulmonary dysplasia.
- Those with cardiovascular disease.
- Ventilated patients.
- Premature babies.

Mechanical ventilation is required in 2% of infants admitted to hospital. Most children recover within 2 weeks, but up to half will suffer recurrent episodes of cough and wheeze over the next 5 years. Rarely severe permanent damage to the airways (bronchiolitis obliterans) complicates the disease.

Upper airway foreign bodies

Food (peanuts, sweets, meat), toys, coins and batteries are commonly inhaled. Presenting signs and symptoms include a sudden onset of:

- Stridor.
- Dysphagia.
- Chest pain.
- Coughing.
- Wheezing.
- Respiratory arrest.

Management   This depends on whether *partial* or *complete airway obstruction* exists.

1. Partial airway obstruction. Observe for signs of respiratory distress, position of comfort and effectiveness of cough. Auscultate the chest to identify any areas of abnormal breath sounds. Avoid agitation, supply supplemental oxygen and summon senior help, which should include a team skilled in the use of a ventilating bronchoscope. The team should perform removal as soon as possible as there is a risk of dislodgement, which may result in more severe obstruction.

2. Complete airway obstruction. This occurs if an inhaled foreign body lodges in the larynx or trachea causing complete obstruction. Perform back blows and chest thrusts or the Heimlich manoeuvre according to the European Resuscitation Council guidelines. If these fail then perform direct laryngoscopy with removal of the foreign body if visible with Magill forceps. If these measures fail a surgical airway is necessary.

Lower airway foreign bodies

The child with recurrent pneumonia or pneumonia that does not resolve should be suspected of having a retained foreign body. A child with recurrent cough or wheeze which is localized should be considered as having a retained foreign body.

Inspiratory and *expiratory chest radiographs* are required for evidence of air trapping. Chest screening or high kV views may be needed in very young children. The history of inhalation is very often unclear. Lateral decubitus films may be helpful and bronchoscopy may be required if in doubt.

Further reading

Advanced Life Support Group. Respiratory emergencies. In: *Advanced Paediatric Life Support. The Practical Approach.* London: BMJ Publishing Group, 1993: 61–72.

Related topics of interest

SCAPHOID FRACTURE

Despite increasing awareness, this is still a fracture which can be missed in accident and emergency departments, giving rise to non-union, avascular necrosis, long-term pain, disability and litigation.

Mechanism The cause is usually falling onto the outstretched wrist, but any forced dorsiflexion may result in fracture (historically backfire from car starting handles).

Physical signs There is no single physical sign which is diagnostic, but all patients who present with pain in the wrist following a forced dorsiflexion injury must be examined carefully for:

- Specific tenderness of the scaphoid tubercle.
- Specific tenderness in the anatomical snuffbox.
- Pain on telescoping the thumb.
- Pain on forced dorsiflexion of the wrist.
- Weak grip, particularly between index finger and thumb, and swelling of the anatomical snuffbox, although these are less specific for scaphoid fracture.

  When the mechanism of action is appropriate and one or more of the above signs are present then the diagnosis of fractured scaphoid must be presumed on clinical grounds.

Differential diagnosis The most common conditions that may cause confusion are:

- Fracture of radial styloid process.
- Fracture of base of first metacarpal.
- Wrist sprain.
- Carpal instability.

More complicated carpal fractures and dislocations must be considered, especially if there is excessive swelling or deformity of the wrist.

Radiography Four-plane examination is mandatory (anteroposterior, lateral, pronation oblique and supination oblique). There is disagreement among authors about the incidence of fractures which are not visible at first presentation but which become apparent later.

Classification

- Distal third (20%) including fractures of the tubercle distal pole and distal third proper.
- Middle third (70%).
- Proximal third (10%).

Also look for bone cysts, old fractures and other bone or joint injury.

Management

Local protocols must be followed:

- *Clinical fracture without radiological signs*: Immobilize in plaster of Paris and refer for review by a senior clinician or orthopaedic surgeon (often at 10–14 days, when the plaster of Paris will be removed, further clinical examination performed and further radiographs obtained if indicated).
- *New fracture seen radiologically.* Apply plaster of Paris to the scaphoid and refer the patient to the fracture clinic. Internal fixation is increasingly recommended.
- *Established non-union.* Occasionally this will present as a new injury; immobilize in plaster and refer for senior opinion.

Complications

Non-union occurs in about 10% of distal third fractures and 15–20% of proximal third fractures. Avascular necrosis of the proximal fragment occurs in about 15–40% of proximal third fractures.

Further reading

Fisk GR. Injuries of the wrist. In: Wilson JN, ed. *Watson-Jones Fractures and Joint Injuries.* Edinburgh: Churchill Livingstone, 1982: 716–26.

Related topics of interest

Fractures – principles of treatment (p. 125)
Wrist injury (p. 311)

SEDATION

Sedative drugs are commonly used in accident and emergency departments to reduce the distress caused to patients by diagnostic and therapeutic procedures. Sedation should not be used as a substitute for adequate analgesia or anaesthesia. The dosages of sedative drugs used should be carefully titrated to produce the desired effect while maintaining the patient's ability to respond to command.

Assessment

There are significant risks related to the use of sedation. Patients at risk include the elderly, the obese and those with significant concomitant medical illness. An assessment of the patient's condition prior to sedation should be made and recorded in the notes. Appropriate modifications to the techniques and drug dosage used should be based on these findings.

Equipment

The patient should be on a trolley which has a head-down tilt facility. An oxygen supply and suction apparatus must be provided with full resuscitation equipment nearby.

Agents

1. *Midazolam.* A water-soluble, short-acting benzodiazepine with no active metabolites. Diazepam is not suitable for use on an out-patient basis because of the long half-life of the drug and its active metabolite.

2. *Opiates* may be used intravenously in combination with midazolam, but there may be a synergistic action with increased risk of cardiac and respiratory depression. The opiate should be given first in reduced dose followed by careful titration of midazolam.

3. *Flumazemil.* A specific benzodiazepine antagonist. It has a short half-life and the effects of the agonist may recur.

4. *Naloxone.* A specific opiate antagonist. Again a short half-life may lead to recurrence of the effects of the opiate.

5. *Oxygen.* Supplemental oxygen must be administered to all sedated patients at a rate of 2–4 l/min.

Monitoring

Basic clinical monitoring of pulse, blood pressure, respiration rate and level of consciousness should continue until the patient is discharged.

Pulse oximetry should be used in all patients receiving sedation. A fall in oxygen saturation below 95% requires correction, ensuring a clear airway, additional oxygen supplementation and possibly reversal of the opiate and midazolam.

ECG monitoring should be used in patients with pre-existing cardiac disease.

Intravenous access   All patients should have an indwelling intravenous cannula *in situ* while sedated.

Discharge   The criteria for discharge are:

- Normal vital signs.
- Steady gait.
- Tolerate oral fluids.
- Adequate analgesia.
- Adequate supervision at home.

The patient should be advised not to drive for 24 hours and that motor skills and judgement may be affected for 24 hours.

Children   The use of intravenous sedatives in children is contraindicated because of the narrow therapeutic margin of these drugs. Oral sedatives may be indicated and promethazine and trimeprazine have traditionally been used although they are often ineffective. Recent reports suggest that oral midazolam may be effective.

Further reading

Royal College of Surgeons of England. *Guidelines for Sedation by Non-Anaesthetists.* London: RCOS, 1993.

Taiwo B, Flowers M, Zoltie N. Reducing children's fear when undergoing painful procedures. *Archives of Emergency Medicine*, 1992; **9**: 306–9.

Related topics of interest

Anaesthesia – general (p. 14)
Anaesthesia – local and regional (p. 17)

SEPTIC ARTHRITIS – ACUTE

The acute infection of a joint may occur as a result of direct penetration from wound, injections or surgery, blood-borne spread from distant sites or septicaemia on local spread from osteomyelitis.

Pathology	Infection usually arises in the synovial membrane, spreading to synovial fluid. There is an inflammatory reaction resulting in erosion of the articular cartilage, which if undiagnosed or untreated can lead to destruction of articular cartilage and bone. The most common causative organism is *Staphylococcus aureus*, although other organisms such as streptococci and gonococci are occasionally implicated. *Haemophilus influenzae* is the most common causative organism in children aged 2 months to 4 years.
Clinical features	*1. Children.* It is most common in the first year of life, the source of infection usually being from the skin or upper respiratory tract. In this age group consider septic arthritis in the differential diagnosis of any child with sepsis of unknown origin as specific signs are not usually obvious. The older child usually presents with acute severe pain in a single joint. The joint is tender and swollen and local movement causes exquisite pain. The child often appears ill with tachycardia and fever. It is important to search for a primary source of infection.
	2. Adults. The signs and symptoms are similar to those in children except that pain and restriction of joint movement may be minimal, especially in the elderly. It is more common in rheumatoid patients.
Investigations	• *Aspiration.* Must be done under full aseptic conditions. Send fluid for microscopy, Gram stain, crystals, culture and sensitivity. Negative microscopy and Gram stain do not exclude septic arthritis, particularly if there is a very short history. • *Radiography.* Usually normal initially, although effusion and joint swelling may be visible. Bone destruction and loss of joint space occur late. • *Ultrasound.* Confirms effusion and can be used to guide needle aspiration, especially in the hip.

- *Blood tests.* FBC, packed volume/ESR, U&E, C-reactive protein (CRP) and blood cultures.

Differential diagnosis
- Osteomyelitis.
- Traumatic effusion or haemarthrosis.
- Acute exacerbation of osteoarthritis.
- Irritable joint in the child.
- Gout and pseudogout.
- Rheumatic fever.

Consider predisposing conditions such as immunosuppression, chronic debilitating disease, e.g. renal failure, diabetes and rheumatoid arthritis.

Treatment
- Admission for intravenous antibiotics and/or surgical drainage. Specific treatment will depend on the suspected causative organism, and advice from a microbiologist should be sought.
- Rest and splintage.
- Analgesia.

Further reading

Shaw DA, Casser JR. Acute septic arthritis in infancy and childhood. *Clinical Orthopaedics and Related Research*, 1990; **257**: 212–25.

Related topics of interest

Febrile convulsion (p. 123)
Limping child (p. 186)

SHOCK

Shock is an abnormality of the circulation leading to inadequate organ perfusion and tissue oxygenation and may be produced by reduction in circulating blood volume, failure of the cardiac pump or inappropriate distribution of the cardiac output. The symptoms and signs of shock are due to poor perfusion of specific organs and tissues. Treatment is aimed at restoring organ perfusion and tissue oxygenation.

Hypovolaemic shock

1. Pathogenesis. A decrease in circulating blood volume may be caused by loss of blood, plasma or serum which may be overt or occult. In the early stages compensatory mechanisms will maintain vital organ functions and therefore symptoms and signs may be subtle. Only when more than 30% of the circulating blood volume has been lost does the classical clinical picture of cold pale skin, altered mental state, tachycardia, hypotension and oliguria become apparent.

2. Treatment consists of intravenous fluid replacement via large-bore intravenous cannulae and specific measures where appropriate to prevent further fluid loss.

3. Research. Recent research using animal models of hypovolaemia secondary to traumatic haemorrhage suggest that aggressive intravenous fluid therapy prior to definitive control of haemorrhage may increase mortality. The relevance of this to clinical practice is as yet unknown.

Cardiogenic shock

1. Pathogenesis. Reduction in cardiac output may be due to reduced preload, reduced myocardial contractility or cardiac outflow obstruction. The commonest cause is massive myocardial infarction with insufficient viable myocardium to maintain adequate cardiac output.

2. Treatment consists of oxygen, preload reduction with opiates and nitrates and, if indicated, thrombolysis. Inotropic agents are useful but require invasive haemodynamic monitoring for optimal therapy. Mortality is high. Cardiac tamponade and tension pneumothorax cause cardiogenic shock by preventing cardiac filling. These conditions are remediable by pericardiocentesis or thoracocentesis.

Septic shock

1. Pathogenesis. The presence in the circulation of bacterial endotoxins such as lipopolysaccharide A produces complement activation and release of vasoactive substances such as kinins and tumour necrosis factor. This results in alterations in the microcirculation with pooling and increased capillary permeability, producing fluid loss from the intravascular space. There is also a fall in peripheral vascular resistance. A compensatory rise in cardiac output occurs, and in the early stages the skin may be warm and the blood pressure maintained with a wide pulse pressure. Later myocardial depression occurs with clinically obvious deterioration in perfusion.

2. Treatment consists in elimination of the source of sepsis and circulatory support with intravenous fluids and inotropes.

Anaphylactic shock

1. Pathogenesis. Exposure to a specific allergen causes release of histamine and other vasoactive amines with peripheral vasodilatation, increased vascular permeability, bronchoconstriction, laryngeal oedema and urticarial skin rashes. Onset is usually rapid.

2. Treatment. Immediate management includes maintenance of airway and oxygenation. Intravenous adrenaline rapidly reverses the life-threatening features of anaphylaxis and is usually given in conjunction with i.v. chlorpheniramine and steroids. Adrenaline may be given intramuscularly in less severe anaphylaxis.

Neurogenic shock

1. Pathogenesis. Interruption of the nerve fibres running to the thoracolumbar sympathetic outflow by spinal cord injury leads to loss of vasomotor tone and arteriolar and venous dilatation. Sympathetic stimulation to the heart may also be lost.

2. Treatment. If hypovolaemia can be excluded, intravenous fluids are administered with CVP monitoring. Vasopressors may rarely be needed. Neurogenic shock is usually transient with return of sympathetic tone in 3–7 days.

Further reading

American College of Surgeons Committee on Trauma. *Advanced Trauma Life Support Course*. Chicago: American College of Surgeons, 1988: 57–88.
Bickell WH, Bruttig SP, Millnamow GA, O'Benar J, Wade CE. The detrimental effects of intravenous crystalloid after aortotomy in swine. *Surgery*, 1991; **110**: 529–36.

Related topics of interest

Anaphylaxis (p. 23)
Intravenous fluids (p. 180)

SHOULDER DISLOCATION

The shoulder (glenohumeral) joint is the most frequently dislocated large joint in the body, principally because of the lack of bony stability which allows the shoulder such a wide range of movement. It is most common in young sporting males and elderly females. Approximately 97% of dislocations occur anteriorly and about 3% posteriorly. Inferior (luxatio erecta) and superior dislocations do occur but are rare.

Anterior dislocation

Anterior dislocation usually follows a fall onto the outstretched hand: the head of the humerus is forced forwards, avulsing the capsule from its glenoid attachment or stripping the glenoid labrum together with a fragment of underlying bone. In the older patient the humeral head may rupture through the front of the capsule.

Clinical features	Pain is severe and all movements are restricted. The normal profile of the shoulder is lost and the humeral head may be palpable anteriorly. Axillary nerve lesions occur in about 4% of cases with loss of sensation over the upper, outer aspect of the shoulder and weakness of the central fibres of deltoid. Injury to the brachial plexus, radial nerve and axillary artery has been reported, therefore a complete neurovascular examination prior to reduction is essential.
Radiographs	Two planes will confirm the diagnosis and exclude associated fracture of the humeral neck. A fracture involving the posterior articular surface of the humeral head (Hill–Sachs lesion) is frequent.
Treatment	Closed reduction under sedation or anaesthesia should be performed as soon as practicably possible.
	1. Kocher's manoeuvre. Gentle abduction, external rotation, adduction and internal rotation of the shoulder. Classically, the procedure is performed without traction, but it is often modified to include it. Reduction may occur at any time during this procedure.
	2. Hippocratic manoeuvre. Principally for use under general anaesthesia. The arm is grasped and pulled caudally, while the operator's foot is placed in the axilla, providing leverage and forcing the head back into the glenoid.

3. Hanging weight method. The patient lies prone with the arm dangling down with a 10 lb weight applied. Reduction may take up to 30 minutes to occur.

4. Milch manoeuvre. Forward flexion and slight abduction of the arm until it is overhead, then continued abduction and countertraction until reduction is achieved.

Whatever method is used, reduction must be confirmed radiologically and the limb examined again for neurovascular deficit. Immobilization is traditionally in a broad arm sling under clothes for 3 weeks, then outside for a further 3 weeks.

Complications

- Neurovascular injury (see above).
- Fracture of the humeral neck or shaft.
- Recurrent dislocation – defined as more than one episode of dislocation. Initial treatment is as above. Elective operative repair of the capsule and glenoid lesion may be considered at a later date.

Posterior dislocation

Posterior dislocation may occur during convulsions or electroconvulsive therapy, following a fall onto the outstretched hand or occasionally as a result of a direct blow to the front of the shoulder.

Clinical features

The history may not be as obvious as for anterior dislocation, and it is important to have a high index of suspicion. Characteristically the arm is held in adduction and internal rotation and all movements are painful.

Radiographs

It is essential to get views which show the relationship of the humeral head to the glenoid articular surface, such as transthoracic shoot-through or axillary view (this is often very difficult to obtain because of the fixed adduction). Anteroposterior views may be misleading and contribute to the frequency with which posterior dislocations are missed, but look for:

- Lightbulb sign. Symmetrical appearance of the humeral head owing to its medial rotation.
- Rim sign. Increased distance between the anterior glenoid rim and humeral articular surface.

Treatment	Closed reduction using traction and external rotation should be performed under sedation or general anaesthesia.
Complications	• Recurrent dislocation. • Fracture of the humeral neck or head (reverse Hill–Sachs lesion). • Neurovascular injury is rare.

Inferior dislocation (luxatio erecta)

This is rare but serious. The arm is locked over the head, typically with the elbow flexed and resting on the head. Radiographs will confirm the position of the head inferior to the glenoid. Closed reduction under sedation or general anaesthesia may be attempted, but button-holing of the humeral head through the capsule sometimes makes this impossible, necessitating operative open reduction.

Complications	• Neurovascular injury. • Rotator cuff tear. • Adhesive capsulitis.

Anterior subluxation

This presents with pain on abduction and external rotation, sometimes associated with a feeling of instability. Diagnosis is confirmed by the apprehension test; with the patient supine and the elbow flexed, abduct the shoulder 90% and externally rotate until the palm of the hand faces upwards. Holding this position the operator's hand is slipped behind the humeral head, which is pushed forwards, causing pain and sometimes subluxation.

Treatment	Treatment is rest in a broad arm sling and orthopaedic referral for consideration of operative repair of the capsule.

Further reading

Kessel L. Injuries of the shoulder. In: Wilson JN, ed. *Watson-Jones Fractures and Joint Injuries.* Edinburgh: Churchill Livingstone, 1982: 513–71.

Related topic of interest

Shoulder problems – non-traumatic (p. 275)

SHOULDER PROBLEMS – NON-TRAUMATIC

The diagnosis and treatment of the painful shoulder requires a full history, complete and thorough physical examination and a knowledge of the anatomy and pathology of the shoulder girdle. Movement principally occurs at the glenohumeral and thoracoscapular articulations but with important contributions from the acromioclavicular and sternoclavicular joints.

History

Pain is the usual presenting symptom. It may arise from any structure of the shoulder girdle and may be referred from the neck, back, heart and diaphragm. Enquire about its nature and predisposing and relieving factors, especially if there is any doubt that the pain does not have a local origin. Stiffness and loss of function are other common presenting symptoms.

Examination

- *Observation*. Look for the typical deformity of anterior shoulder, acromioclavicular or sternoclavicular dislocation, muscle wasting and the position in which the arm is held.
- *Palpate accurately*. Localize the site of maximal tenderness and fully extend the shoulder to palpate supraspinatus under the acromion.
- *Movement*. On abduction initial movement is glenohumeral, thororacoscapular movement contributes until beyond 60° when it accounts for almost all movement.

   Test movement in all planes first actively then passively. Fixed internal rotation suggests a posterior dislocation of the shoulder.

- *Power*. Test all muscle groups including deltoid and note which resisted movements cause pain.

   If shoulder examination is normal then examine the cervical spine. Also consider atypical chest pain as a possible cause.

Rotator cuff syndrome

The rotator cuff comprises subscapularis, supraspinatus, infraspinatus and teres minor. These run under the coracoacromial arch and are separated from it by the subacromial bursa. The principal symptom is pain from inflammation of the tendons, most commonly supraspinatus. It is often worse on elevation of the arm.

Causes:

- Trauma.
- Overuse.
- Osteoarthritis (especially of the acromioclavicular joint).
- Impingement syndrome.
- Inflammatory joint conditions (such as rheumatoid arthritis or gout).

1. Acute tendinitis usually occurs in younger patients after unusual exercise or excessive activity. Pain is maximal between 60° and 120° of abduction (the painful arc). Tenderness is often localized to supraspinatus. It usually settles with rest, NSAIDs, local steroid injections and physiotherapy.

2. Chronic tendinitis usually occurs in older patients. It is often intermittent and follows a subacute episode of tendinitis.

3. Rotator cuff tear may be indistinguishable from tendinitis. Magnetic resonance imaging (MRI) or arthrography will confirm the diagnosis. A complete tear results in inability to abduct the shoulder.

4. Acute calcific tendinitis is caused by hydroxyapatite deposition, usually in the supraspinatus tendon. It presents with a short history of severe pain and limitation of movement. Radiography may show opacity within a specific tendon. It usually settles spontaneously but resolution can be speeded by NSAIDs, local anaesthetic and corticosteroid injections and physiotherapy (and for resistant cases surgical removal of calcific material).

Bicipital tendinitis

This may accompany rotator cuff injury. Pain and tenderness occur in the bicipital groove; treat with local steroid injection or NSAIDs. Bicipital tendon rupture occasionally follows as a complication.

Frozen shoulder

This term is often inaccurately used to describe the painful stiff shoulder. It is in fact a discrete entity, the cause of which is unknown but which may complicate trauma, cerebrovascular accident or myocardial infarction. There is inflammation and adhesive fibrosis of the rotator cuff and the underlying joint capsule. Presenting symptoms are pain and lack of movement in all directions. It usually resolves spontaneously over 1–2 years, but local steroid injections, physiotherapy and manipulation under anaesthesia may speed up the process.

Others
- Unrecognized shoulder injury, especially posterior dislocation of the shoulder.
- Arthritis of the glenohumeral, acromioclavicular or sternoclavicular joints, including rheumatoid, septic arthritis and osteoarthrosis.
- Disuse stiffness.
- Reflex sympathetic dystrophy.
- Referred pain, especially from the cervical spine.
- Polymyalgia rheumatica (causes stiffness rather than pain and is bilateral, often with sudden onset)
- Proximal myopathy.
- Referred pain from diaphragm or neck.

Further reading

Cyriax J. *Textbook of Orthopaedic Medicine,* Vol. I. London: Balliere Tindall, 1982.

Related topics of interest

Chest pain (p. 66)
Myocardial infarction (p. 216)
Shoulder – dislocation (p. 272)

SPINE AND SPINAL CORD TRAUMA

The annual incidence of spinal cord injury within the UK is about 10–15 per million of the population. The cervical spine (48%) is the commonest site of injury in patients admitted to a spinal injuries unit, followed by the thoracic spine (41%) and the lumbar spine (11%).

The commonest causes of spinal injury include:

- Road traffic accidents (50%).
- Domestic and industrial accidents (25%).
- Sporting injuries (15%).
- Self-harm and assaults (5%).
- Others (5%).

In the unconscious patient after a fall or road traffic accident, between 5 and 10% of patients sustain a cervical spine injury. A *high index of suspicion* regarding spinal injury is necessary.

An unstable spinal injury must be assumed to be present after trauma. Inadvertent manipulation or inadequate immobilization must not jeopardize the patient's spinal cord. Early consultation with a neurosurgeon and/or orthopaedic surgeon is essential.

Examination

1. General. *Total spinal immobilization* is best achieved with a semirigid collar, securing the head to a spine board and bolster splinting the neck, or with sandbags and tape. The chest, pelvis and lower extremities must also be securely immobilized to protect the thoracic and lumbar spine. Log-rolling with the help of assistants is essential when moving the patient.

Clinical findings suggesting a cervical cord injury in the unconscious patient include:

- Flaccid arreflexia, including a flaccid rectal sphincter.
- Diaphragmatic breathing – abdominal breathing and use of accessory muscles.
- Ability to flex, but not extend, at the elbow.
- Grimaces to pain above, but not below, the clavicle.
- Hypotension with bradycardia, especially without hypovolaemia.
- Priapism.

2. Vertebral assessment. Pain, tenderness, posterior 'step-off' deformity, prominence of spinous processes, pain with movement, oedema, bruising, visible deformity and muscle spasms may help identify and localize the site of injury.

To visualize the entire spine, the patient may be log-rolled, but only to the minimum degree necessary to allow examination.

3. Neurological assessment

(a) *Motor*

- The *corticospinal tract* controls ipsilateral motor power and is tested by voluntary muscle contractions or involuntary response to painful stimulation.

(b) *Sensory*

- The *spinothalamic tract* controls contralateral pain and temperature sensation. It is tested by pinch or pinprick.
- The *posterior columns* control ipsilateral proprioception and are tested by position sense or vibration sense.

(c) *Reflex changes.*

(d) *Autonomic*

- Loss of bladder control.
- Loss of anal tone.
- Priapism.

A *complete spinal cord lesion* reveals no sensory or motor function and indicates a poor recovery. An *incomplete spinal cord lesion* may be followed by recovery. *Sacral sparing* with sensation still present in the anal, perianal and scrotal areas may be the only sign of incomplete injury and must be noted.

4. Neurogenic and spinal shock. Neurogenic shock refers to the hypotension associated with cervical or high thoracic spinal cord injury. It is caused by damage to the descending sympathetic pathways, with loss of vasomotor tone, and loss of sympathetic tone of the heart. The resultant vasodilatation and bradycardia may be improved by increasing venous return, by atropine (to overcome the bradycardia) and occasionally by sympathetic agents.

Spinal shock is the neurological condition that occurs after spinal cord trauma and is characterized by flaccidity and loss of reflexes. After days to weeks the condition either disappears with return to normal or is replaced by spasticity.

5. Other effects

- *Hypoventilation* due to paralysis of the intercostals in cervical and upper thoracic lesions.
- *Diaphragmatic paralysis* due to C3–C5 damage.
- *Masking of other injuries* due to inability to feel pain.

6. Radiography

(a) *Cervical spine.* Lateral cervical spine radiographs should be obtained after life-threatening conditions are corrected. All seven cervical vertebrae and the C7/T1 junction must be visualized. The patient's shoulders are best pulled down to aid visualization. If inadequate, a *swimmer's view* is the preferred method to visualize C7/T1. After completion of the primary survey and resuscitation phases, further cervical spine views are taken. These include an open-mouth odontoid and anteroposterior views. Oblique views are taken if required. Further investigations such as CT, magnetic resonance imaging and screened lateral flexion and extension views may be required.

(b) *Thoracolumbar.* Anteroposterior and lateral thoracic films are obtained if indicated. Anteroposterior, lateral and oblique lumbar films are obtained if indicated.

Treatment

- *Immobilization.*
- *Intravenous fluids.* Treatment of neurogenic shock may require additional fluids. A urinary catheter is inserted to monitor urinary output and prevent bladder distension.
- *Drugs.* The value of steroids is controversial. The results of the Second National Spinal Cord Injury Study showed that high-dose methylprednisolone is of benefit in patients with either complete or incomplete spinal cord damage if given within 8 hours of injury. Complication and mortality rates were not altered.

  The proposed mechanism of methylprednisolone is inhibition of lipid peroxidation, with a secondary effect of improvement in blood flow at the injury site.

  If steroids are to be given, treatment must be started within 8 hours of injury. Infuse 30 mg/kg methylprednisolone as soon as possible over 15 minutes. Wait for 45 minutes. Infuse 5.4 mg/kg/h over 23 hours.

Exclusions include:

• Greater than 8 hours since injury.
• Age under 13 years.
• Pregnancy.
• Major life-threatening morbidity.
• Injury limited to cauda equina or nerve root.
• Abdominal trauma.
• Systemic fungal infection.

Spinal cord injury without any physical or radiological signs (SCIWORA)

SCIWORA occurs almost exclusively in children under the age of 8 years. The child's spinal column, because of ligamentous laxity, wedge-shaped vertebrae and shallow facet joints, allows for greater flexibility. Thus, severe trauma may result in underlying spinal cord damage without fracture or dislocation. SCIWORA tends to occur in the cervical spine, often high up. There should be a high suspicion of a spinal cord lesion in the multiply injured comatose child even after normal spinal films have been obtained. Full spinal immobilization should be maintained until the child is assessed neurologically.

Further reading

American College of Surgeons Committee on Trauma. Spine and spinal cord trauma. In: *Advanced Trauma Life Support Instructor Manual.* Chicago: American College of Surgeons, 1993: 191–218.
Bracken MB *et al.* Methylprednisolone or naloxone treatment after acute spinal cord injury: 1-year follow-up data. Results of the Second National Acute Spinal Cord Injury Study. *Journal of Neurosurgery*, 1992; **72**: 23–31.
Ferguson J, Beattie T. Occult spinal cord injury in traumatised children. *Injury*, 1993; **24**: 83–4.

Related topics of interest

SUDDEN INFANT DEATH SYNDROME

One in 450 infants dies between the ages of 1 week and 1 year. Occasionally, a cause of the sudden death is found, e.g. congenital heart disease, overwhelming infection, inborn errors of metabolism and very occasionally accidental or intentional suffocation. More commonly, a careful post-mortem examination reveals only evidence of minor illness, such as an upper respiratory tract infection. When no cause is found, a diagnosis of *sudden infant death syndrome (SIDS)* is made, and it is the commonest cause of death in this age group.

Following a cot death, parents feel a profound sense of loss, guilt and depression. For young parents, this is often the first experience of death in their family. The risk to a twin or other sibling needs consideration, and the paediatrician will counsel the family and consider the use of an apnoea alarm.

Aetiology

Many theories have been put forward for a single aetiology, but it is more probably a mixture of factors. The current hypotheses include:

- Abnormality of respiratory control.
- An abnormal response to respiratory infection.
- Hyperthermia, exacerbated by excessive warm bedding during a mild illness.
- Some association with the prone sleeping position.

Risk factors include:

- Winter months.
- Male sex.
- Premature infants.
- Twins.
- Previous apnoea attack(s).
- Unmarried, smoking, young mothers.

Initial resuscitation

Children who are found suddenly and unexpectedly dead are usually brought to the accident and emergency department. All such children should be admitted to the resuscitation room and, unless rigor mortis or post-mortem lividity is present, resuscitation should be initiated. A paediatric cardiac arrest team should be in attendance.

Roles of medical staff

- To confirm the death of the infant and gather preliminary information on the cause of death (history and examination).
- To offer practical advice and support to parents.
- To inform other agencies involved.
- To ensure that the appropriate approval is obtained

for the moving of the dead baby.

- To act as advocate for the parents, if they are unable to communicate clearly.

Checklist for medical staff

- Call senior paediatric and senior anaesthetic staff prior to the arrival of the baby.
- Take the baby to the resuscitation room for assessment.
- Take the parents to a quiet room where they can stay as long as necessary.
- Examine the baby and conduct resuscitation according to European Resusciation Council guidelines.
- Confirm death.
- Sympathetically interview the parents about their baby's health. Use the baby's first name when talking to the parents. Use the present tense before death is certified.
- Record details of history, examination and resuscitation of the child.
- Ensure that all investigation procedures are carried out in accordance with the local protocol.
- After death is confirmed, remove drips, endotracheal tube, etc.
- Clothe and wrap the baby and take him/her to the paents to see and hold as long as they desire.
- Explain to the parents what you think is the cause of death.
- Explain to the parents that the police and coroner have a duty to investigate all sudden and unexpected deaths, and that they will have to make a statement to the police, who may want to examine the baby's room and bedding.
- Offer support and practical advice about the post-mortem examination, funeral arrangements, registration of death, etc. It is important that this information is given in written form.
- Ensure that a suitable person is looking after dependent relatives or other children at home.
- Ask whether the parents would like to see a chaplain/minister, or have their baby blessed.
- If the mother is breast feeding, offer advice on suppression of lactation/expression of milk.
- Take the photograph of the baby for parents. Offer a lock of hair or a hand/foot print, if facilities are available.
- Arrange transport to the mortuary.
- Ensure that the parents have safe transport home.

- Give the parents copies of the 'Information for Parents' leaflet and local support contact telephone number(s).
- Explain that a paediatrician or general practitioner will contact them in the next few days with the preliminary results of the post-mortem.
- Inform the consultant paediatrician.
- Inform the general practitioner.
- Inform the community child health department or equivalent to cancel surveillance and immunization appointments.
- Inform the medical records department and cancel out-patient appointments.
- Inform the paediatric social work department (if offering support in this situation).
- Inform the coroner of the death.

Further reading

Brooks JG. Unraveling the mysteries of sudden infant death syndrome. *Current Opinion in Pediatrics*, 1993; **5**: 266–72.
Finlay FO, Rudd PT. Current concepts of the aetiology of SIDS. *British Journal of Hospital Medicine*, 1993; **49**: 727–32.

Related topic of interest

Child abuse (p. 70)

SYNCOPE

Syncope is sudden, brief loss of consciousness due to transient impairment of cerebral circulation, from whatever cause, usually occurring in the absence of organic brain or cerebrovascular disease.

Typically the onset is sudden or develops over a few seconds. Associated symptoms include blurred vision, dizziness, cold extremities and sweating. If aware of the symptoms the patient may take evasive action and sit or lie down. If, however, venous return remains impaired, muscle twitching and convulsions (*convulsive syncope*) may occur.

Syncope accounts for 1–3% of A & E attendances and 3–6% of hospital attendances. In 30–50% of cases no cause is found despite extensive investigation. Subsequent case fatality is low, but morbidity remains high, with about half having one or more episodes.

Causes

The causes of syncope include:

1. Inappropriate vasodilatation

- *Vasovagal syncope* is the name given by Sir Thomas Lewis to common fainting and results from vagal slowing of the heart and decreased vasomotor tone. It is usually triggered by pain, or emotion.
- *Carotid sinus syncope.* The hypersensitive carotid sinus baroceptors cause vagal stimulation in response to either neck movement or mild pressure which may lead to cardiac arrest.
- *Micturition syncope.*
- *Orthostatic hypotension* may occur with sympathetic degeneration associated with *diabetic neuropathy, Parkinson's disease, Addison's disease* and *Shy–Drager syndrome.* A degree of postural hypotension occurs with advancing age and is exacerbated by *drugs* (e.g. hypotensives, diuretics, phenothiazines and benzodiazepines).

2. Hypovolaemia. It is vital to exclude acute blood loss as a cause of syncope. Sources of haemorrhage to be considered include the gastrointestinal tract, ruptured ectopic pregnancy, a leaking aortic aneurysm or aortic dissection.

3. Cardiac syncope

- *Arrhythmias* such as bradycardias associated with heart block (Stokes–Adams attacks) or sick sinus syndrome and tachycardias may cause syncope.
- *Myocardial ischaemia* or myocardial infarct may present with syncope.

4. Obstruction to ventricular emptying. Causes such as aortic stenosis and hypertrophic cardiomyopathy may be responsible.

5. Reduced ventricular filling occurs in cough syncope (seen in the patient with chronic chest disease with raised intrathoracic pressure during a violent coughing bout), atrial myxoma and pulmonary embolism.

Differential diagnosis includes:

- Epilepsy.
- Hypoglycaemia.
- Transient ischaemic attack.
- Labyrinthine disorder.

History and examination These are the most important factors in determining the cause of syncope. In the younger patient with a history suggestive of a simple faint no further investigation is warranted. In the older patient the diagnosis should be made with caution as cardiac causes are more likely. In the elderly drugs are also commonly the cause.

- The *lying and standing blood pressure* should be taken. Postural hypotension is shown by a significant fall in blood pressure or rise in pulse rate as the patient moves from lying to sitting ($\geq$ 10 mmHg or $\geq$ 20 beats/min) or standing ($\geq$ 15 mmHg or $\geq$ 30 beats/min).
- In all cases, except the simple faint an *ECG* is mandatory. This may reveal myocardial ischaemia, infarction, pulmonary embolism or arrhythymia. Alternatively, an underlying conduction defect such as short PR interval (pre-excitation syndromes) or a long QT interval (familial syndromes) may be found.

During ECG monitoring carotid sinus massage may reveal carotid sinus hypersensitivity. This is best done with the patient lying at 45°, then gently massage in the region of the carotid bifurcation for 5 seconds, on one side only, and with resuscitation facilities available.

- *Full blood count* to exclude anaemia or blood loss.
- *Serum electrolytes* may indicate dehydration or Addison's disease.
- *Chest radiography* might show evidence of cardiac disease or pulmonary embolism.
- *Further investigations.* A useful test is a *24-hour*

continuous ambulatory electrocardiograph since in patients with cardiac syncope sudden death occurs within 1 year in approximately 20%.

Further reading

Gilliatt RW. Syncope. In: Weatherall DJ, Ledingham JGG, Warrell DA, eds. *The Oxford Textbook of Medicine*, 2nd edn. Oxford: Oxford University Press, 1987; 21.51–21.53.

Related topics of interest

TETANUS

Tetanus is characterized by muscular rigidity and spasms and is induced by the exotoxin, *tetanospasmin*, released by the bacterium that grows anaerobically at the site of injury. Between 1985 and 1991 there were 104 cases of tetanus in England and Wales. The highest risk group is elderly women.

Clostridium tetani is a motile, Gram-positive, spore-forming bacillus that thrives within the bowel of herbivores and humans. Tetanus spores are found in contaminated soil. The organism is non-invasive, and spores of *C. tetani* are introduced into a wound, such as a puncture wound, burn, ulcer, umbilical stump or even an unnoticed trivial wound.

The incubation period (4–21 days) is followed by a prodrome of fever, malaise and headache followed by non-specific stiffness and dysphagia. The patient classically develops *trismus* (inability to close the mouth), *risus sardonicus* (grin-like position of hypertonic facial muscles) and *opisothotonus* (arched body, with hyperextended neck). *Spasms* may initially be induced by movement or noise but later are spontaneous.

Prognosis
- With full ITU support mortality is 11%.
- The main causes of death are *respiratory failure, pneumonia, septicaemia, cardiovascular instability* and *pulmonary embolism.*
- Other complications include *autonomic dysfunction* and *fractures/dislocations* (secondary to muscle spasms).

Treatment

1. Specific
- Wound debridement.
- Intravenous human tetanus immunoglobulin (150 iu/kg at multiple sites).
- Intravenous benzylpenicillin.

2. General
- Drug treatment alone with diazepam, phenobarbitone or chlorpromazine.
- Total paralysis regime.

3. Vaccination. An attack of tetanus does not provide immunity and thus vaccination is required.

Prevention

Tetanus vaccine

Immunization is provided by *active immunization* and protects by stimulating the production of an antitoxin that provides immunity against the effects of the toxin. *Tetanus toxoid* is prepared by treating a cell-free preparation of the toxin with formaldehyde. When used as a vaccine it is usually adsorbed onto an adjuvant, either aluminium phosphate or aluminium hydroxide. The *dose* is 0.5 ml given by intramuscular or deep subcutaneous injection.

The *immunization schedule* of infants includes primary immunization, which consists of three doses starting at 2 months with an interval of 1 month between each dose, followed by a booster dose given prior to school entry and for those aged 15–19 years or before leaving school.

Treatment of a tetanus-prone wound

The following are tetanus-prone wounds:

(a) Any wound or burn sustained more than 6 hours before surgical treatment of the wound or burn.

(b) Any wound or burn at any interval after injury that shows one or more of the following characteristics.

- A significant degree of devitalized tissue.
- Puncture.
- Contamination with soil or manure likely to harbour tetanus organisms.
- Clinical evidence of sepsis.

Thorough surgical toilet of all wounds is essential. The aim is to remove all contaminants that could contain tetanus spores and all dead or badly damaged tissue that could provide an anaerobic environment.

Adverse reactions

- *Local reactions*, such as pain, redness and swelling at the injection site commonly occur and persist for several days. They are more common if booster injections are given too frequently.
- *General reactions* include headache, lethargy, malaise, myalgia and pyrexia.
- *Acute anaphylaxis* and *urticaria* occasionally occur.
- *Peripheral neuropathy* and *persistent nodules* at the injection site have been reported, but are rare.
- Tetanus vaccine should not be given to an individual suffering from an *acute febrile illness* except in the presence of a tetanus-prone wound.
- Immunization should not proceed in individuals who have had a *severe reaction* to a previous dose.
- *HIV-positive patients* should be immunized in the

absence of contraindications.
- *Pregnancy* is not a contraindication.

Specific anti-tetanus immunoglogulin

Anti-tetanus immunoglobulin is prepared from the blood of donors who are negative for hepatitis B virus and antibody to HIV. The *dose* is 250 IU, or 500 IU if more than 24 hours have elapsed since injury, if there is a risk of heavy contamination or following burns.

Patients with *impaired immunity* who suffer a tetanus-prone wound may require anti-tetanus immunoglobulin.

Specific anti-tetanus prophylaxis

Immunization status	Type of wound	
	Clean	Tetanus prone
Last of three-dose course, or reinforcing dose within last 10 years	Nil	Nil (a dose of adsorbed vaccine may be given if the risk of infection is considered to be especially high, e.g. contamination with stable manure)
Last of three-dose course or reinforcing dose more than 10 years previously	A reinforcing dose of adsorbed vaccine	A reinforcing dose of adsorbed vaccine plus a dose of human tetanus immunoglobulin
Not immunized or immunization status not known with certainty	A full three-dose course of adsorbed vaccine	A full three-dose course of vaccine, plus a dose of tetanus immunoglobulin in a different site

Further reading

Department of Health and Social Security, Welsh Office and Scottish Home and Health Department. *Immunisation against Infectious Disease*. London: HMSO. 1992.
Adams EB. Tetanus. In: Weatherall DJ, Ledingham JGG, Warrell DA, eds. *Oxford Textbook of Medicine*, 2nd edn. Oxford: Oxford University Press, 1987; 5.265–5.270.

Related topics of interest

Anaphylaxis (p. 23)
Wound management (p. 307)

THORACIC TRAUMA

Chest injuries cause 25% of trauma deaths. *Hypoxia* is the main complication of chest injury and may result from reduced blood volume, failure to ventilate the lungs, a ventilation–perfusion mismatch or mechanical obstruction to the lung or chest wall. Occult *haemorrhage*, which may be massive, may occur within the thoracic cavity.

The treatment of chest injuries follows the ABCs, and specific treatment includes needle thoracocentesis, tube thoracostomy and controlled ventilation. Only 10% of blunt chest injuries require definitive surgery, and 15–30% of penetrating chest injuries require open thoracotomy.

Life-threatening injuries detectable in the primary survey

1. Airway obstruction

2. Tension pneumothorax. Air accumulates progressively under pressure within the pleural space, collapses the lung compressing the mediastinum and thus compromises venous return and cardiac output. Patients with a pneumothorax undergoing positive-pressure ventilation are particularly at risk of developing a tension pneumothorax. Radiographic confirmation is unnecessary.

Signs of hypoxia and shock will be present. Specific findings include:

- Ipsilateral decreased air entry and hyperresonance.
- Tracheal deviation away from the side of the pneumothorax.
- Cardiovascular collapse with distended neck veins.
- Cyanosis (late).

Treatment

- Immediate needle thoracocentesis (to relieve the tension).
- Followed by intercostal chest drain insertion.

3. Open pneumothorax ('sucking wound'). Penetrating trauma associated with a pneumothorax requires occlusive dressing to seal the wound, with one side left loose to allow air to escape.

Treatment

- A chest tube is sited as soon as possible.
- Definitive surgery is usually necessary.

4. Massive haemothorax is defined as more than 1500 ml of blood in the thoracic cavity. Hypoxia and hypovolaemia coexist. Ipsilateral absent breath sounds and dullness to percussion in association with shock are the physical findings.

Treatment

• Rapid volume resuscitation.
• Chest tube insertion.

If 1500 ml is evacuated immediately, or if there is continued blood loss of 200 ml/h then consider thoracotomy.

5. Flail chest. Paradoxical movement of the flail segment occurs, which may be masked by splinting, secondary to muscle spasm. Hypoventilation, hypoxia, pulmonary shunting (due to associated pulmonary contusion) and reduced cardiac output occurs. Arterial blood gases need to be monitored in HDU/ITU.

Treatment: High-flow oxygen, analgesia (including thoracic epidural), and consider ventilation.

6. Cardiac tamponade. This is commonly due to penetrating trauma. Beck's triad of hypotension, distended neck veins and muffled heart sounds is rarely seen. Other signs include tachycardia, pulsus paradoxus and electrical alternans (on the ECG). Cardiac tamponade is a cause of electromechanical dissociation.

A high index of clinical suspicion is required. *Echocardiography* will provide rapid confirmation of fluid within the pericardium.

Treatment

• *Pericardiocentesis* with ECG monitoring using the subxyphoid approach will temporarily decompress the tamponade.

7. A & E thoracotomy. Open thoracotomy, cross-clamping of the descending thoracic aorta, pericardiotomy and open chest massage with intravascular volume replacement is most beneficial in patients with exsanguinating penetrating injuries and those with blunt injury who have arrived pulseless within the previous 10 minutes.

Potentially life-threatening injuries detectable in the secondary survey

A further detailed chest examination is undertaken, an erect *chest radiograph* if possible, *arterial blood gases,* and an *ECG.*

1. Pulmonary contusion. This is commonly seen after chest trauma and manifests as hypoxia, which worsens with time. Maintain oxygenation and monitor respiratory function. If the patient is unable to maintain adequate ventilation then intubation and mechanical ventilation is necessary. It is often associated with a flail chest.

2. Myocardial contusion is underdiagnosed after blunt trauma. ECG and echocardiography should be performed and myocardial enzyme changes should be sought. Arrhythmias may be found.

3. Aortic rupture. Complete rupture is a cause of early death. A partial tear tends to occur at the level of the ligamentum arteriosum, and initial survival is dependent on a contained haematoma or a false aneurysm. Radiographic features which suggest an aortic rupture include:

- Widened mediastinum.
- Fractures of first and second ribs.
- Deviation of trachea.
- Pleural cap.
- Deviation of the oesophagus to the right.

Angiography, trans-oesophageal echocardiography or CT may further image the lesion. Early surgery is warranted.

4. Traumatic diaphragmatic rupture is more common on the left side and is often missed. A chest radiograph may reveal an elevated hemidiaphragm, or gastric contents in the chest, confirmed by the nasogastric tube in the thoracic cavity or peritoneal lavage fluid exiting from a chest tube or by contrast studies. If missed a diaphragmatic hernia will remain. Blunt trauma is associated with large tears, penetrating trauma with small tears. Treatment is surgical repair.

5. Larynx, trachea, or bronchus disruption is frequently fatal. Rigid bronchoscopy is the definitive investigation.

6. *Oesophageal trauma* is usually as a result of penetrating trauma. Surgical repair is essential, otherwise mediastinitis will result.

7. *Subcutaneous emphysema* may result from airway injury, lung injury or blast injury.

8. *Traumatic asphyxia* is associated with facial and upper chest plethora with petechial haemorrhages and may result in cerebral oedema.

9. *Simple pneumothorax* requires treatment with a chest drain. The lung must be decompressed prior to positive-pressure ventilation or air travel otherwise there is risk of developing a tension pneumothorax.

10. *Haemothorax* is due to haemorrhage from a lung laceration or intercostal or internal mammary vessel. It requires drainage via a large-bore chest drain and will usually require no further intervention. If more than 1500 ml of blood is drained or if there is persistent drainage of more than 200 ml per hour for 4 hours then surgical intervention may prove necessary.

11. *Rib fractures*

- *Upper rib* (1–3) fractures are associated with a 50% mortality and necessitate surgical consultation as there is a high risk of associated injury.
- *Middle rib* (4–9) fractures are most likely to result in haemothorax and or pneumothorax.
- *Lower rib* (10–12) fractures carry a high risk of hepatic and splenic injury.

Treatment consists of pain relief (intercostal block, epidural anaesthesia or systemic analgesia) to allow adequate ventilation and prevention of complications, e.g. atelectasis and pneumonia.

Further reading

American College of Surgeons Committee on Trauma. Thoracic trauma. In: *Advanced Trauma Life Support Instructor Manual*. Chicago: American College of Surgeons, 1993: 111–40.

Robertson C, and Redmond AD. Thoracic trauma. In: *The Management of Major Trauma*. Oxford: Oxford University Press, 1991: 63–78.

Related topics of interest

TRAUMA SCORING AND INJURY SCALING

Reliable, validated methods to measure the severity of injury allow physicians to:

- Quantify the extent of the damage.
- Aid triage.
- Predict outcome.
- Audit care for quality assurance and research.

Scoring methods measure anatomical and or physiological parameters.

Physiological scoring

Glasgow Coma Scale

The *Glasgow Coma Scale* (GCS) is a widely accepted measure of assessing the severity of brain damage after head injury. It correlates well with the *Glasgow Outcome Scale*, and forms part of the *revised trauma score*. The GCS has been widely accepted as a reliable scale yet inexperienced or untrained users still make errors when using it. Its use in children under 4 years of age requires modification.

Eye opening

Spontaneous	4
To speech stimulus	3
To pain stimulus	2
None	1

Best motor response

Obeys	6
Localizes	5
Withdraws	4
Abnormal flexion *	3
Extensor response	2
No response	1

Best verbal response

Orientated	5
Confused conversations	4
Inappropriate words	3
Incomprehensible sounds	2
No response	1

Glasgow coma score (total)	3–15

*Abnormal elbow and wrist posturing without extension of the elbow.

The Children's Coma Scale (<4 years)	*Eyes*	
	Open spontaneously	4
	React to speech	3
	React to pain	2
	No response	1

Best motor response

Spontaneous or obeys verbal command	6
Localizes pain	5
Withdraws to pain	4
Abnormal flexion to pain (decorticate)	3
Abnormal extension to pain (decerebrate)	2
No response	1

Best verbal response

Smiles, orientated to sounds, follows objects, interacts	5

Crying	*Interacts*	
Consolable	Inappropriate	4
Inconsistently consolable	Moaning	3
Inconsolable	Irritable	2
No response	No response	1

Trauma score

The *trauma score (TS)* is based on five parameters:

(a) Glasgow Coma Scale.
(b) Respiratory rate.
(c) Respiratory expansion.
(d) Systolic blood pressure.
(e) Capillary refill.

The variables are assigned weighted points that are summed to give the TS. This has a range from 1 (worse) to 16 (normal). The TS is used as a triage tool and accurately predicts the outcome from severe injuries. Patients with a TS of less than or equal to 12 are recommended for transfer to a trauma centre as this level carries an average mortality of 10%. A TS of 3 or less is valuable in identifying patients for whom prolonged resuscitation is futile.

Revised trauma score

The *revised trauma score* includes GCS, systolic blood pressure and respiratory rate. Two versions exist:

(a) *Triage revised trauma score (T-RTS)*. Useful for the rapid identification of severely injured patients on arrival to hospital.

(b) *Revised trauma score (RTS)*. The RTS is a weight-ed sum of coded variable values and yields a more accurate outcome prediction for patients with seri-ous head injuries than the TS.

	Coded value	× *weight*	= *score*
Respiratory rate (breaths/min):			
10–29	4		
>29	3		
6–9	2	0.2908 ×	———
1–5	1		
0	0		
Systolic blood pressure (mmHg):			
>89	4		
76–89	3		
50–75	2	0.7326 ×	———
1–49	1		
0	0		
Glasgow Coma Scale:			
13–15	4		
9–12	3		
6–8	2	0.9368 ×	———
4–5	1		
3	0		

Total=revised trauma score: ———

Anatomical scoring

This information is available from clinical signs, investigations, operative findings and, in fatalities, the post-mortem examination.

Abbreviated injury scale (AIS)

The abbreviated injury scale (AIS) was developed and published in 1971 and undergoes regular revision. Every injury is assigned a code based on its anatomical site, nature and severity. Injuries are grouped by body region.

AIS code	Description
1	Minor
2	Moderate
3	Serious (non-life threatening)
4	Severe (life-threatening, survival probable)
5	Critical (survival uncertain)
6	Unsurvivable (with current treatment)

The AIS enables ranking of injury severity and correlates with patient outcome, but a major disadvantage is that because it codes individual injuries it cannot be adjusted for multiple injuries.

Injury severity score (ISS)

The AIS can be used to derive the injury severity score (ISS). The ISS provides a valid numerical measure of the overall severity of injury in patients with multiple injuries and correlates with mortality, morbidity and other measures such as length of hospital stay. The ISS has been validated for use with blunt and penetrating injuries in adults and also for use in children over the age of 12 years. Every injury is given an AIS code and classified into one of the six body regions.

Body regions used in ISS

- Head and neck.
- Face.
- Chest.
- Abdominal/pelvic contents.
- Extremities/pelvic girdle.
- External, i.e. skin and burns.

The ISS is calculated by summation of the squares of the highest AIS codes in each of the three most severely injured body regions. The maximum ISS is 75 [(5×5) + (5×5) + (5×5)]. Any injury coded AIS = 6 automatically converts the ISS to 75.

The ISS correlates closely with mortality and is the 'gold standard' for anatomical coding of injury severity. An ISS of 16 or more signifies major trauma with an average predicted mortality of more than 10%.

The effect of age on the outcome of injury has been incorporated into the ISS by Bull using probit analysis to derive LD_{50} values for different age groups.

Trauma score injury severity score (TRISS) methodology

Trauma audit using TRISS has been undertaken prospectively in the UK to show that specialized units can improve outcome. The TRISS method estimates *the probability of patient survival based on regression equation* and takes into account:

- Patient age.
- The severity of anatomical injury as measured by the ISS.
- The physiological status of the patient on admission based on the revised trauma score.
- The type of injury (blunt or penetrating)

1. Preliminary method. Unexpected deaths or survivors can be identified by plotting the RTS and ISS for patients on a *preliminary chart*. The P_s 50 *isobar* represents the 50% probability of survival of the baseline normal population. Patients are represented by a symbol depicting outcome: L for live, D for dead.

Unexpected survivors with a P_s less than 50% (L symbols above the isobar) and *unexpected deaths* with a P_s greater than 50% (D symbols below the isobar) are identified for further study.

2. Definitive method. This compares outcome and the patient mix regarding severity of injury in different hospitals with the major trauma outcome study (MTOS) 'norm' data.

The *Z statistic* is a measure that can be used to test whether the observed number of survivors in a specific trauma population is significantly different from what would be expected based on the MTOS norms. Values greater than +1.96 or less than −1.96 indicate a significant difference ($P < 0.05$) from predicted, with greater or fewer survivors respectively.

The *W statistic* provides perspective on the clinical relevance of the Z score. A positive W value is a measure of the number of survivors more than expected from the norm predictions per 100 patients analysed.

The *M statistic* evaluates the match of injury severity between the study group and the MTOS baseline group. Values range from 0 to 1, and the closer to 1 the better the match of injury severity.

Further reading

Spence MT, Redmond AD, Edwards JD. Trauma audit – the use of TRISS. *Health Trends*, 1988; **20**: 94–7.

Yates DW, Woodford M, Hollis S. Preliminary analysis of the care of injured patients in 33 British hospitals: first report of the United Kingdom major trauma outcome study. *British Medical Journal*, 1992; **305**: 737–40.

Related topics of interest

UROLOGICAL CONDITIONS – ACUTE

Loin pain

Exclude referred pain from testes or ovary and ruptured aorta in older patients.

Ureteric colic usually occurs in patients aged between 20 and 60 years. Ninety per cent of stones are radio-opaque and nearly all have associated microscopic haematuria. Eighty per cent of stones less than 0.5 cm diameter will be passed spontaneously.

Investigations

- Dipstick urinalysis.
- *KUB radiography.* Look for stones along the line of the ureter, typically held up at the iliac bifurcation, the pelviureteric junction and the vesico-uretic junction.
- *Intravenous urography (IVU)* is best performed under controlled conditions with radiological supervision. Consider in A & E only if the diagnosis is in doubt or if it will alter management.

Treatment. Diclofenac suppositories 100 mg. If the pain settles, discharge the patient with a supply of suppositories and an urgent IVU and urological referral arranged. Admit if the patient is pyrexial, the pain is not relieved or there is doubt about the diagnosis.

Haematuria

1. *Painful haematuria* is most likely to be due to urinary tract infection but is occasionally due to bladder calculi or a foreign body.

2. *Painless haematuria.*

(a) *Initial stream.* Likely to arise from the prostate, prostatic bed or bladder neck. Differentiate from haemospermia. Examine the external meatus for viral warts, balinitis and carcinoma of the penis.

(b) *Whole stream.* A common presentation of carcinoma of the bladder, less commonly of tumours or stones in the upper tracts. Examine specifically for renal masses and exclude clot retention of urine. Perform a full blood count, U & E and KUB. If haematuria is mild advise high fluid intake and discharge the patient with an urgent IVU and urological appointment. Admit the patient if investigations are abnormal, if there is continuous bleeding or a danger of clot retention. Secondary haemorrhage occurs 2–3 weeks post trans-urethral resection of the prostate or bladder. These patients should be admitted.

(c) *Terminal stream.* This usually originates from the bladder and should be investigated and treated as described above.

All children with haematuria should be admitted, as should all patients who have traumatic haematuria however mild as there may well be pre-existing renal abnormalities. As a general rule all patients with haematuria warrant further investigation with IVU and cystoscopy.

Acute retention of urine   *1. Females.* In women acute urine retention is rare. Examine for faecal impaction and pelvic mass. Consider neurogenic causes, hysteria and urethral carcinoma. Females do not get urethral strictures. Gynaecological referral may be appropriate.

2. Children. Acute urine retention in children is most commonly due to pin-hole phimosis. The prepuce should be pulled away from the glans, not retracted, when visualizing the urethral meatus. Balanitis xerotica obliterans may cause skin to overgrow the meatus. Children must not be catheterized under local anaesthetic.

3. Males. Acute retention by definition is painful. If pain is absent the patient may be suffering from chronic retention and should only be catheterized if uraemic or septic. Catheterization is probably best performed by the admitting specialty as reactive haematuria or post-obstructive diuresis and renal failure may occur. Exclude a spinal cause for acute retention and establish that it is not one facet of a more important problem such as chronic renal failure. If the patient is under 45 years retention is likely to be due to urethral stricture. In those over 45 years prostatic obstruction is usually the cause. Examine with specific reference to bladder size, consistency and symmetry of the prostate. Prostatic size is difficult to gauge prior to catheterization. When catheterizing use an entire tube of lignocaine gel and allowing a *minimum* of 5 minutes for it to work. Use an F16 catheter with 10 ml in the balloon.

If catheterization is unsuccessful or causes bleeding, stop and refer to urologists. Do not use a catheter introducer or bougies or remove a successfully inserted catheter.

Urinary tract infection (UTI)

UTIs commonly present with frequency, dysuria and occasionally fever, chills, strangury, haematuria and loin pain. There is a strong association with sexual activity in women, who are 'allowed' up to three infections a year. Children and males are not 'allowed' any UTIs. They should be referred for further investigation to exclude underlying pathology. All patients should have urinanalysis and mid-stream urine taken prior to treatment. In unusual cases or adults with systemic symptoms perform KUB (which occasionally demonstrates foreign bodies or calculus in bladder). Admit patients if they are systemically unwell or diabetic.

Acute testicular pain

Acute testicular pain is due to torsion of the testis until proven otherwise. Note that a history longer than 12 hours is associated with testicular infarction, after which initial pain may subside. The condition most commonly occurs between the ages of 11 and 16, however it can occur well into adult life. Examine specifically for an extremely tender, swollen, high-riding testicle and occasionally a palpable twisted cord. Examine the abdomen to exclude pelvic pathology including appendicitis and acute hernia. Doppler ultrasound testicular examination may give equivocal findings. Treatment is surgical and if there is doubt then surgical exploration is mandatory.

Other causes of testicular pain include:

- *Twisted hydatid of Morgagni.*
- *Acute epididymitis.* Examination reveals extremely tender, sausage-like swelling of the epididymus. The testis itself is non-tender. Late cases may be associated with gross reddening and oedema of the scrotum, possibly with reactive hydrocele. Investigate with ultrasound and MSU and treat with a 2-week course of doxycycline (the causative organism is often *Chlamydia*) and urgent urological referral. If there is doubt about the diagnosis and in severe cases refer for admission.
- *Testicular tumour.* Pain is an uncommon presenting symptom but a pathological testis is more susceptible to relatively minor trauma and therefore pain.

- *Referred pain from upper tract.*
- *Idiopathic scrotal oedema.* Usually painless.

Priapism

Priapism is persistent erection (usually painful). If it lasts longer than 12 hours it may be associated with intracorporeal thrombosis with subsequent fibrosis and impotence. The most common cause in the UK is intracorporeal injection of papaverine. Other causes include leukaemia, sickle cell disease and spinal cord trauma. Treatment is decompression by aspiration, as priapism may be due to closure of the emissary veins and this procedure allows these to open, thereby breaking the vicious circle and allowing the erection to subside.

Further reading

Stewart C, ed. Genito-urinary emergencies. In: *Emergency Medicine Clinics of North America*. Philadelphia: W.B. Saunders, 1988: 6(3).

Related topics of interest

Genitourinary trauma (p. 132)
Gynaecology (p. 136)

WOUND MANAGEMENT

Wounds account for 25–30% of the total accident and emergency workload, with an estimated 3 million being treated in England and Wales annually. They also account for over 400 deaths annually in England and Wales. Initial management must focus on rapid assessment and treatment of life-threatening complications. *Control of haemorrhage* is achieved by *direct pressure* and elevation of the limb.

Wound assessment

Full assessment is essential and the following is a guide:

1. History

- Mechanism of injury.
- Timing of injury.
- Environment.
- Past medical history.
- Drug and allergies.
- Tetanus status.

2. Examination. After attention to the ABCs in those cases that warrant it, after consideration of complications (e.g. head injury after a scalp laceration) and finally after a search for medical causes of falls which caused the injury, the wound is examined for:

- Measurement.
- Description of wound (e.g. incision, laceration and depth).
- Exclusion of foreign bodies.
- Associated injuries to blood vessels, nerves, tendons, bone and vital organs.

3. Documentation is aided by the use of diagrams and accurate description of wounds.

4. Further investigation

- *Radiographs* are required for exclusion of fractures and radio-opaque foreign bodies. If there is the possibility of a radio-opaque foreign body in the wound then radiographs must be taken. This will include metal, glass, and painted wood as most glass is radio-opaque and some paint is radio-opaque. Radiographs are also indicated for deep wounds of the knee (for signs of joint penetration) and for penetrating chest and abdominal wounds.

- Non radio-opaque foreign bodies such as plastic and wood may be visualized by *ultrasound, CT scan* or magnetic resonance imaging.
- *Bacteriology* is rarely indicated.
- *Blood investigations* will be warranted in patients on anticoagulants or with a bleeding disorder.

Surgical technique

Allow for optimal operating conditions using good light, good equipment, an assistant, adequate anaesthesia and senior advice if necessary. *Poor surgical technique* that neglects adequate wound toilet, debridement and wound exploration to remove contaminants will increase the complication rate.

Thorough wound cleaning using an aseptic technique and debridement is essential. Ingrained gravel dirt may require a scrubbing brush to prevent tattooing. *Excise necrotic tissue. Irrigate the wound.*

Deep lacerations in areas with complex anatomy (e.g. wrist and hand) need to be explored using regional or general anaesthesia under sterile conditions in a surgical theatre with a bloodless field.

Wound closure

- *Primary suture* is appropriate for most wounds 6–8 hours after injury if they are minimally contaminated and with minimal tissue loss or devitalization.
- *Delayed primary suture* is considered for the heavily contaminated wound. Initially clean, irrigate and debride, then dress the wound. Review after 4–5 days and, if the wound is clean and not infected, then the skin can be closed.
- Some wounds require *excision and grafting.*
- Puncture wounds, small cosmetically unimportant animal bites and abscess cavities are often better left to heal by *secondary intention.* They are not sutured but are allowed to heal gradually by granulation and eventual re-epithelialization. Later skin grafting may be needed.

Wound classification

Tidy	Untidy
Clean incised	Ragged edge
Uncontaminated	Contaminated
Under 6 hours	Over 12 hours
Low-energy trauma	High-energy trauma
	Crushed tissue
	Burns

Infection

Factors predisposing to infection include:

- Delay in primary wound cleaning.
- Heavy contamination.
- Puncture wound.
- Human and animal bites.
- Wound with necrotic tissue.

General factors include:

- Nutritional status (vitamin C and zinc deficiency)
- Age – the elderly heal less well.
- Diabetes mellitus.
- Peripheral ischaemia.
- Steroid therapy.
- Immunosuppression.
- Severe anaemia.
- Severe alcoholism.

Bites

Bites are a common complaint. Eighty per cent of mammal bites are caused by dogs, and a further 10% by cats. Most bites should be left open and considered for delayed primary suturing. Some wounds may undergo primary closure but require meticulous cleaning by an experienced surgeon. Tetanus prophylaxis and antibiotics are required.

1. Human bites. Human saliva contains a mixed bacterial flora, including anaerobes, which predispose the wound to infection. Wounds should be debrided, irrigated and left open. There is also the potential risk from hepatitis B virus and HIV which require appropriate management.

Antibiotic prophylaxis is necessary, with co-amoxoclavinic acid the drug of choice. Tetanus prophylaxis should be given as necessary.

2. Cat bites. Again there is high risk of infection, especially with *Pasteurella multocida*, which may involve tendons or joints. Bites and scratch wounds are best left open after thorough cleaning, irrigation and debridement. Prophylactic antibiotics are recommended.

3. Clenched fist wounds occurring at the metacarpophalyngeal joints are at risk from intra-articular infection, capsular and tendon injury.

Pressure injection wounds
High-pressure paint or grease guns may appear benign but through a pinhole the paints or petroleums can pierce the skin and, under the pressure created, spread through the tissue planes and tendon sheaths. They require extensive exploration by an in-patient team and even then have a complication rate of digital amputation of 50%.

Further reading

Wardrope J, Smith JAR. *The Management of Wounds and Burns. Oxford Handbooks in Emergency Medicine*. Oxford: Oxford University Press, 1992.

Related topics of interest

WRIST INJURY

Injuries to the distal radius and ulna and carpus usually follow a fall onto the out-stretched hand.

Colles' fracture

Described in 1914 by Abraham Colles, this occurs most commonly in elderly osteoporotic women.

Clinical features	There is swelling and tenderness around the wrist, often with a typical dinner fork deformity.
Pathology	There is a fracture of the distal radius associated with dislocation of the distal radioulnar joint and sometimes avulsion of the ulnar styloid process.
Treatment	Reduction of the fracture should be performed under anaesthesia or sedation, followed by immobilization in a below-elbow backslab with the wrist slightly flexed and ulna deviated. Plaster can be completed at 24–48 hours once the swelling has subsided.
Complications	• Non-union. • Malunion. • Stiffness. • Carpal tunnel syndrome. • Extensor pollicis longus rupture. • Sudeck's atrophy. • Shoulder–hand syndrome.

Smith's fracture

The lower radius is fractured with volar displacement of the distal fragment associated with dislocation of the radioulnar joint.

Treatment	This is an unstable fracture and requires manipulation and immobilization in an above-elbow plaster with the forearm fully supinated and the wrist extended. If closed reduction fails or the fracture slips, then open reduction and internal fixation with a buttress plate may be required.

Barton's fracture

This is an intra-articular fracture of the distal radius associated with subluxation of the distal radioulnar and wrist joints. The fracture is unstable and often requires open reduction or internal fixation with a buttress plate.

Radial styloid fracture

This is an intra-articular fracture that will require manipulation if displaced. Closed reduction can usually be achieved but very occasional reduction and internal fixation is required.

Carpal dislocation

This can easily be missed by the inexperienced. There are a wide variety of dislocations and fracture–dislocation combinations. Perilunate and lunate dislocations occur through the mid-carpus, usually resulting from a forced dorsiflexion injury.

1. Lunate dislocation. There is volar displacement of the lunate into the carpal tunnel, which may become compressed. These injuries are often associated with fractures of the other carpal bones, especially the scaphoid.

2. Perilunar dislocation. The lunate retains its normal relationship with the radius but all the bones around it and distal to it are dislocated dorsally.

3. Trans-scaphoid perilunar dislocation. This is similar to perilunar dislocation, but it is associated with a scaphoid fracture, the proximal pole of which retains its relation with the lunate while the distal fragment is dislocated dorsally with the remainder of the carpus.

Wrist sprain

True wrist sprain probably does occur, but the symptoms should settle quickly with rest. Persistent disability, pain, weak grip and loss of function may indicate more serious soft-tissue injury. Occasionally diastasis of the distal radioulnar joint may occur.

Carpal instability   It is now recognized that major ligamentous injury to the carpus can occur such that, although the bones do not dislocate, the relationship between them is altered. The most common result is dorsal tilt of the lunate (less commonly volar tilt). Occasionally the ligaments between scaphoid and lunate are completely disrupted, resulting in a gap between them. This may be seen radiologically as the 'Terry Thomas' sign (a famous film actor with a gap in his front teeth). It is important to recognize that these major ligament injuries do occur as they can easily be missed and the symptoms of continuing pain, weakness and loss of function attributed to hypochondriasis. Standard anteroposterior and lateral radiographs may be normal but an anteroposterior radiograph taken with the fist tightly clenched may demonstrate carpal instability. Alternatively radiographic screening may be used.

Treatment   The best treatment is still being debated, however these complex injuries should be managed by experienced hand surgeons. Ligamentous reconstructions are not thought to be very successful. Some patients may require arthrodesis.

Further reading

Fisk GR. Injuries of the wrist. In: Wilson JN, ed. *Watson-Jones Fractures and Joint Injuries*. Edinburgh: Churchill Livingstone, 1982: 716–26.

INDEX

ALSO AVAILABLE FROM BIOS SCIENTIFIC PUBLISHERS LTD

Resuscitation: Key Data

M.J.A. Parr & T.M. Craft
respectively Bristol Royal Infirmary; and Royal United Hospital, Bath, UK

This pocket reference guide is an invaluable collection of essential data and treatment guidelines for the resuscitation of newborn, neonatal, paediatric and adult patients. Information is presented in a clear format which allows instant access to key data in an emergency situation.

Based on the latest recommendations from the European Resuscitation Council, the American College of Surgeons and other bodies, together with information derived from BCLS, ACLS, ATLS and PALS training courses. Treatment protocols for a broad range of conditions including trauma, burns, cardiac arrhythmias and drug overdose are clearly presented as flowcharts and decision trees. Tabulated information includes Apgar and Glasgow coma scoring, the constituents of intravenous fluids, antiarrhthmic drug doses and normal values for some of the more common investigations.

"This book is definitely not one for gathering dust on the bookshelf, but would be more at home in the white coat pocket where I have no doubt it will become well thumbed." - *J. Br. Assoc. Immediate Care*

"Don't just keep it in your pocket. read it, use it and keep using it." - *Colin Robertson, Chairman of the UK Resuscitation Council*

Contents

Part 1 Adult resuscitation: Basic life support; Advanced life support; Cardiac; Trauma; Burns; Anaphylaxis; Acute severe asthma; Hypothermia; Drug overdose. Part 2 Paediatric resuscitation: Basic life support; Advanced life support; Newborn; Infant and child; Trauma; Burns. Part 3 Normal physiological values: Biochemistry; Haematology; Coagulation; Blood gases; Conversion factors.

Of interest to:
All doctors, nurses, paramedics and practitioners trained in resuscitation.

Paperback; 96 pages;   1-872748-53-8; 1994

Key Topics in Anaesthesia

T.M. Craft & P.M. Upton
respectively Bristol Royal Infirmary, UK; and Radcliffe Infirmary, Oxford, UK

Contains essential information on 100 major subjects pertinent to modern clinical practice in anaesthesia. The uniform, systematic structure of the text is designed to encourage a problem-based approach to clinical scenarios. An ideal revision aid for trainee anaesthetists and a useful reference source for qualified anaesthetists.

"I think this book is a winner. What about those to whom it is aimed? I have not yet found a member of our junior staff who, prior to taking the test [FRCA part III], has not already purchased a copy. May I also recommend it to their teachers?" - *Today's Anaesthetist*

Contents

Each topic includes (wherever the subject allows): introduction; essential problems; anaesthetic management - assessment and premedication, conduct of anaesthesia, and postoperative care; further reading; and related topics of interest.

Of interest to:

Trainee anaesthetists (e.g. FRCA, European Academy of Anaesthesiology examination candidates); qualified anaesthetists, anaesthetic assistants, nurse anaethetists and surgeons.

Paperback; 312 pages; 1-872748-90-2; 1992

Key Topics in Obstetrics and Gynaecology

R.J. Slade, E. Laird & G. Beynon
respectively University Hospital of Wales, Cardiff, UK; Northampton General Hospital, UK; and Queen Elizabeth II Hospital, Gateshead, UK

A compact, easy-to-read text for trainee obstetricians and gynaecologists. This book provides information on 100 major topics regarded as essential knowledge to pass the MRCOG examination. Wherever possible, the information is presented in a uniform, systematic format to encourage a problem-based approach to clinical scenarios. Each key topic can be read at an individual sitting. The book is an ideal revision aid for postgraduate examinations and an invaluable reference source for qualified doctors wishing to update their knowledge of specific topics between cases.

".. a useful guide to preparation for examinations from final MB to the MRCOG." - *Brit.J.Obstetrics & Gynaecology*

Of interest to:
Trainee obstetricians and gynaecologists (e.g. Part II MRCOG examination candidates); Practitioners (e.g. DRCOG examination candidates); Medical students.

Paperback; 296 pages; 1-872748-07-4; 1993

ORDERING DETAILS

Main address for orders

BIOS Scientific Publishers Ltd
St Thomas House, Becket Street,
Oxford OX1 1SJ, UK
Tel: +44 865 726826
Fax: +44 865 246823

Australia and New Zealand
DA Information Services
648 Whitehorse Road, Mitcham, Victoria 3132, Australia
Tel: (03) 873 4411
Fax: (03) 873 5679

India
Viva Books Private Ltd
4346/4C Ansari Road, New Delhi 110 002, India
Tel: 11 3283121
Fax: 11 3267224

Singapore and South East Asia
(Brunei, Hong Kong, Indonesia, Korea, Malaysia, the Philippines,
Singapore, Taiwan, and Thailand)
Toppan Company (S) PTE Ltd
38 Liu Fang Road, Jurong, Singapore 2262
Tel: (265) 6666
Fax: (261) 7875

USA and Canada
Books International Inc
PO Box 605, Herndon, VA 22070, USA
Tel: (703) 435 7064
Fax: (703) 689 0660

Payment can be made by cheque or credit card (Visa/Mastercard, quoting number and expiry date). Alternatively, a *pro forma* invoice can be sent.

Prepaid orders must include £2.50/US$5.00 to cover postage and packing for one item and £1.25/US$2.50 for each additional item.